The Life and Times of Claude Rains

by

Carmella Felice

Bloomington, IN  Milton Keynes, UK

AuthorHouse™
1663 Liberty Drive, Suite 200
Bloomington, IN 47403
www.authorhouse.com
Phone: 1-800-839-8640

AuthorHouse™ UK Ltd.
500 Avebury Boulevard
Central Milton Keynes, MK9 2BE
www.authorhouse.co.uk
Phone: 08001974150

© 2006 Carmella Felice. All rights reserved.

No part of this book may be reproduced, stored in a retrieval system, or transmitted by any means without the written permission of the author.

First published by AuthorHouse 11/20/2006

ISBN: 978-1-4259-5301-0 (sc)

Printed in the United States of America
Bloomington, Indiana

This book is printed on acid-free paper.

TABLE OF CONTENTS

PREFACE	vii	
CHAPTER 1	WILLIE GETS A VOICE.	1
CHAPTER 2	CLAUDE RAINS, ACTOR!	17
CHAPTER 3	OFF TO THE GREAT WAR!	39
CHAPTER 4	CAN I, START AGAIN?	49
CHAPTER 5	RAINS SAILS FOR THE UNITED STATES OF AMERICA.	69
CHAPTER 6	WORK, WORK, AND MORE WORK!	85
CHAPTER 7	A MOVIE STAR AT LAST!	91
CHAPTER 8	WARNER BROTHERS, HERE I COME!	109
CHAPTER 9	WAR AGAIN, AS HE BUY'S THE FARM!	117
CHAPTER 10	FILMING CASABLANCA	133
CHAPTER 11	$1,000,000, AND GREAT BIG BUZZ BOMBS!	143
CHAPTER 12	BOY.... AM I LUCKY!	159
CHAPTER 13	BIG STARS IN TROUBLE, OH MY!	183
CHAPTER 14	AT HOME ON THE FARM, BUT NOT FOR LONG	189
CHAPTER 15	BACK TO THE STAGE.. YOU SAY!	203

CHAPTER 16   LONESOME AGAIN 217

CHAPTER 17   A NEW LIFE...227

CHAPTER 18   ALL THINGS ONCE ARE THINGS
              FOREVER 239

SOME ARTICLES WRITTEN ABOUT CLAUDE RAINS 247

RADIO SHOWS 255

MOTION PICTURES 263

TELEVISION PLAYS 269

PREFACE

Readers of this novel might ask "Why should this author choose to write about "The Life and Times of Claude Rains?".

Well, shortly after retiring from Civil Service with the City of New York, my heart started to give me some trouble. My doctor gave me some medication, but the thought of dying kept me up at nights.

One night as I lay awake watching the rain hitting my bed room window, I noticed a form taking shape on the black shinny surface of the glass. At first I couldn't make out the face, I thought it might be my grandmother coming to see me from the after life as she had done when I almost died at the age of ten.

Suddenly the face cleared and took form. It was my favorite actor Claude Rains as I saw him in many films, when I was younger. In my head, came the words "No one remembers me!" I was too scared to move as I watched the apparition glow brighter

"Tell my daughter I love her very much!" came the next message a few seconds later, then the apparition faded very quickly.

Curiousity sent me to the public library thinking I would find a few books on Mr. Rains. None could be found which seemed so unfair to his life and work. After a month a friend told me about the Lincoln Center Library, where I could find newspaper clippings, photos and references to books his name was mentioned. To my surprise I found where Jennifer (Jessica) Rains had gone to College. I wrote to The Dean of the School hoping he would forward my letter to Miss Rains.

Jessica Rains (stage name) was very kind to write me back thanking me for her father's message. But the words "No one remembers me!" rang in my mind, so I decided to write his life story. Thank You Mr. Rains for your great body of work and your great love for America.

William Claude Raines, at the tender age of ten, decided to leave school, and go to work, to help out his poverty stricken parents. As luck would have it, he became a "call-boy", at "His Majesty's Theatre", under the tutorship of the great actor, Sir Herbert Beerbohm Tree.

At the theatre, he was taught to be a carpenter, electrician, master mechanic property man, treasurer, stage-manager, teacher, and director. Seven years later, Claude asked his mentor, if he could be an actor in one of his plays Sir Tree answered, "No, because you don't have the good looks to be an actor!".

Five years later, Rains proved his mentor wrong by becoming London's most likable, flamboyant actor. Standing a mere five feet, eight inches, he moved his audiences with the wave of his hand. He had piercing brown eyes and expressive eyebrows that revealed his emotions. He had a full head of brown hair, with an unruly lock of hair that fell over his right eyebrow, adding to his boyish face

In 1915, he served in World War 1, where he was gassed at Vimy Ridge, France losing eighty percent of his vision in his right eye. The Chlorine gas also left him susceptable to colds and stomach problems.

In 1927, he came to America for a second time, to zfind his fortune. He liked New York City, with all of it's sights, smells, and theatre world. Although he was married at the time, he liked to watch the beautiful women, as they paraded down fifth Avenue in their furs.

Mr. Rains made the hammiest screen test in the history of the Motion picture industry, but when a friend saw it, he was hired at Universal to make "The Invisible Man" because of his melodious honey-sweet, clear voice. He attributed the sound of his voice, The effects of his wounds in the Great War.

He rose in the ranks of great stars, at the Warner Brother's Studio, in the 1930's, and 40's. He liked good conversation, piano music, a workable script and a good cigar.

He was called upon to give many interviews during his tenure as a star. While he was working on the set of "The Unsuspected" he was asked to give his "views" on acting. The following are his own words on the matter:

"Ask yourself, have I any talent? If you think you have, then observe, observe, observe your fellow man. To be interested only in yourself is short sighted. Forget about yourself, and get interested in people. Watch their reactions, and learn why they work properly, they keep your body from doing all the foolish things you see in most amateurs when they masticate the scenery. Antics are not a substitute for acting. The greatest problem an actor has to learn not what to do, but what not to do.

Especially in pictures, this is true. The actor is vulnerable before the camera. He is in danger every minute. Once he starts this, it's the surest way to oblivion!

Let's get something straight! Instinct is one thing, and talent is another. You acquire talent, but instinct is God-given! The actor is an indefinable something that gives us the ability to interpret what we see in life. It is combined with energy and enthusiasm, for delineating people who walk off the streets into our souls! Talent is the tool with which we chisel at instinct to sculpt the perfect character. This, through blood, sweat and tears, is what keeps us from being hams.

I once saw Lawrence Irving, son of the great actor, Sir Henry Irving, do a performance of Don John in "Much Ado about Nothing", which was the foulest thing I ever saw. But.... He died, in my opinion, the greatest actor on the English stage. He had instinct... it took years to develop the talent!

Of course, there are times when some of us are supposed to have obtained a degree of success, fail to use our talent properly. The critic, John Mason Brown, brought this quite forcibly, but diplomatically, to my attention once after one of my Broadway performances, when he wrote; "Only such a good actor, could give such a bad performance!"

Claude Rains, the teacher, always gave of himself to help his country, or a fellow actor, having trouble perfecting a character, if he was asked to do so. He loved his family, and devoted himself to his daughter, Jennifer. So as a fan who loved his work on the screen, I write this book of the life and times of William Claude Rains.

CHAPTER 1

WILLIE GETS A VOICE.

"Nothing, nothing, nothing!" was the cry of the people, who lived in the "East End" of London England. In the 1990's, the section called "Camberwell" was the melting pot of the city, were Chinese, Jewish, Indians, and a small Russian community resided. They had all come to England, to find a better future for their families. But the "East End" was a blotch on the face of the great city, because it was so near the thriving center of the British Empire.

Camberwell-men did not have starched collars, nor gold watches to look upon, but wore old clothes to go to their meager jobs. The women didn't have leisure dresses with long feathered hats. They were lucky to have two dresses to their names. As for the children, they had even less for which to live, than did their parents because of recent wars, a depression had caused great poverty through out the beautiful countryside, which was lined with two hundred year-old houses.

Frederick Rains was a "jack of all trades", who was presently working as an organ builder. In 1889, the family lived in a two story cottage, which was almost three hundred years old. For extra money Frederick took in a boarder on the second floor, while he and his family occupied the first floor flat. The rotten wooden floor had large cracks in it, that allowed mice and other vermon to escape into the house. The dirty wallpaper once might have been an elegant pattern covering the walls, but time had destroyed it. A large oak table with six chairs circled it in the middle of the room, while a faded sofa hugged one wall quietly. A fireplace owned another wall, where a gas heater was placed inside to heat the house in the winter time. In the kitchen was a small black-belly stove with a bin to it's side, which contained some coal. A few old landscape pictures hung from a couple of walls, but it didn't brighten up the home any! In the small bedrooms, beds made from hay, lined a couple of the walls. The Rains family was living hand to mouth when William Claude Rains was born on November 10th, 1889, in his parent's bed. His mother Emily, had given birth to twelve children in her life time, nine of which died from malnutrition! When Emily gave birth to William, he had an older sister who had survived, her other babies. Young Willie didn't speak until he was almost three years old. The Doctor called it a "Lazy Tongue"! "Willie will speak, when he finds something interesting to say"!" said his doctor. When food was scarce, the Rains's would send their children to their grandparent's cottage in Kent, where the elderly couple had a half-acre, on which to grow a vegetable garden "You will never starve as long as we have a little land to grow vegetables on" his grandmother would tell him.

One day while playing at his home with his sister, who was a sickly child, Willie saw that his sister couldn't catch her breath. She started coughing uncontrollably, so he ran to get his mother in the kitchen. "Mum, mum, come!" He yelled. It startled his mother for a moment, for it was the first time, he had spoken, so she knew something was wrong. Rushing to her daughter's side, she picked up the child and started to pound on her back, trying to dislodge anything stuck in her windpipe. Willie started crying, thinking his mother was punishing his sister. But finally, the girl caught her breath as Emily gave a sigh of relief.

When he began to talk, little Willie was not taught proper English because of his defect. His Cockney accent grew worse as he mingled with the street urchins. He could not pronounce the letter "R" because he would say them like "W"'s. So a word like "Work", would become, "Wowk".

Everyone in the 1900's would help his neighbors in time of desperate straights. The Churches Chapels and Synagogues also helped the poor. Places of worship were filled with the followers of God, as they were told that, "Their sufferings were heard by God!" On hot nights, all nationalities gathered in front of their homes, to talk about the government and why they weren't doing anything to make things better. Children played on slippery cobble stones, where garbage was thrown. Some of the older children would go into the sewers to search for shillings, silver spoons or small valuables on their way to the ocean.

Because of the constant exposure to bacteria, these children developed an immunity to some diseases of the day. These children were called "Toshers" by the locals. Children had no time to play, only help the family to survive, regardless of their health. At an early age, most of them went to work at other jobs like making brushes or stuffing mattresses with hay. They also went to work at the nearby docks, loading and unloading the ships. They were only paid about a dollar a day, but it helped feed the family. Children grew up quickly in the "East End" and little Willie was no exception.

The family liked Sunday mornings, with all the parades through the streets by the religious people who would carry religious statues. Passing each home they sang as they went by each home. It kept their spirits up in a time of great sadness. Frederick, Willie's father now had a steady job, which brought in a few more shillings, while Emily tended to her boarders. Jews and Indians had opened up small businesses towards 1899 and Willie would work for the green grocer, for a few apples a day, at the age of seven. Then his father enlisted him in school, which changed his son's life. Willie's speech was awful, so the other children taunted him to no end. After three years of it, he started to play hookey constantly.

At the beginning of the 1900's there was class segregation. The school system wasn't set up to help children with Willie's speech problems. In the model schools the teachers could have corrected his speech, but the family didn't have the money to send him to those schools. So he played hookey and went to work selling newspapers at ten years of age. He was very small for his age, mostly because he didn't have the proper nourishment, like milk in his young life.

One day, Willie's headmaster humiliated and ostracized him for his speech problems and playing hookey. Willie vowed never to go back to school. He told his best friend to tell the headmaster that he had gone to Kent to be with his grandparents and would be doing his schooling there.

He was out of school for six weeks, when he made a friend of a young red-headed boy, who used to buy a paper everyday. One day, the red-headed came by dressed in a long white robe, lined with a red underdress. Willie asked his friend, "hat's ya d'ess up fo?"

Carmella Felice

"I'm going to choir practice." smiled the young man with a space between his teeth.

"'hat's chio'w p' p'actice?" Willie asked confused.

"I sing with twenty other boys at the Palm Street Church" answered the boy proudly.

"Can I be in the chio 'w??" Willie asked sheepishly.

"I don't know. You would have to ask the minister. But we did lose a boy, because his voice changed." This interested Willie immensely. He thought, "Maybe I can get me a new voice!" So he asked in his cockney accent,

"Maybe I can take his place? I would like a new voice, too!"

"Oh that doesn't happen until you're fourteen or fifteen!" laughed the choir boy.

"Willie smiled and said. "I can 'ait it out!"

So the choir-boy, whose name was John took Willie to the church to meet the pastor of the church. The pastor asked him to sing a few Christmas songs, then looked a little impressed with Willie's range. After accepting him the pastor told Willie to go into the cloak room and find himself a robe that fits. Willie ran to the small room and grabbed a robe, and put it on. The pastor smiled and said, "I think your mother will have to take it up a bit!"

A few days later, Queen Victoria died, and all businesses, schools, and daily activity stopped to mourn the loss of their beloved Queen. The family decided to pay their respect to the monarch. Willie's father ushered his family onto a horse drawn bus to go see the parade. It was the first time Willie had seen such a wonderful looking buildings.

When they reached the parade route, Willie pushed to the front of the lines to see the magnificent soldiers on their horses, and remembered his mother's stories of Kings and Queens.

"Can I be a soldie'?" came his first question to his father.

"Not with that mouth on you, laddie!" came a reproach from his father.

But his mother told him he could be what ever he wanted to be, just as King Edward VII passed in his carriage, behind his mother's coffin.

The Life and Times of Claude Rains

After that day, Willie knew there was something better in life than just living in poverty. He was determined to get his piece of that bright world he had just seen that day.

One day at choir practice, the minister said that they would be going to the Haymarket, to do a bit of singing. Willie thought the Haymarket was a park in London. The minister gave all the children a paper that would release them to go to the Haymarket. Willie was still playing hooky, so he signed the paper with his father's name. That Saturday, the children all met at a bus stop near the church. He gave his release to his minister, and climbed aboard the horse drawn bus. A group of parents were going along to keep track of the children, on the trip.

Willie heard the nine o'clock bell ringing at St. Mary's Bow Church as he settled down in his chair. Soon he was passing Covent Gardens, and some other wonderful looking buildings. Within the hour, they had reached their destination, the Haymarket Theatre. Willie's mouth dropped when he saw the theatre. He thought he was going to the park to sing, not a theatre. He sighed with delight at the thought of going past the doors of the theatre. A sign in front of the the theatre read "Sweet Neil of Old Drury". The stage manager had hired a few choirs from within the inner city to sing to the audience before the play began. He also needed a few urchins to be in a street scene. Willie was glad the minister had told him not to eat after they sang, because his stomach was turning as his turn came up to be on stage. As the choir took it's place, He could see all the faces of the people, who had come to see the show.

The music began, and Willie sang in his little low voice. When they had finished their songs, an applause came from the audience that was deafening. Willie loved every minute of the experience. He had caught the stage-bug and he wanted more of it. The stage manager paid the minister eight pounds for his choir, and each boy recieved ten pence and a sandwich. Now Willie knew that he had to get more of this new world of acting. He asked his minister how he could make his wish come true.

"It just so happens the manager needs some boys to play street urchins, in the first scene, would you like to do that?"

"Yes!" yelled Willie. So on August 13th, 1900, at the age of ten, Willie became an actor for one day.

Carmella Felice

That night he returned home to his father, who was very upset at little Willie.

It seemed Frederick had gotten a letter from Willie's headmaster asking when the child was going to return to school, His father had learned he had played hooky for six weeks. Fred picked up his son and placed him over his knees, giving him a few painful hits on the child's backside.

"Where have you been spending your time?" asked his father

"Crying with all his might.. he said, "I can't stand school!"

Everyone laughs at me! I knew you needed money father, so I went to work selling newspapers. Willie took out of his pocket almost a pound, and gave it to his father, "I just wanted to help the family.. I can't stand school, I have more money under my bed... I'll go and get it," Willie said, running to his bedroom. Returning, he gave his father another pound. "Please father, take me out of school! The more he cried, the more he saw that his father was feeling sorry for him.

Willie's parents felt sorry for him as they looked at the money their little son had earned for the family. Willie continued to act and cry pulling at his parent's heart strings, until he knew he had them just like the audience at the Haymarket Theatre. His passionate pleas brought tears to his mother's eyes, while his father felt ashamed of how he had treated his son.

"Please father, don't make me go back to school... I want to work for the family!

In the 1900's the English Government allowed the children of poverty stricken families to leave school, at an early age, with their parents consent. Officials did not think children of the poor, needed an education, especially those kids who lived in the "East End" of London.

Frederick weighed the problem of education against needed funds to sustain the family. He decided Willie should go to work. His mother did not object to her husband's decision, because she knew how school was affecting her child. But Emily hoped one day he would grow into a learnt man.

Willie made a lot of friends and tips working at the green grocer and the news stand. His places of work were only a few blocks from his house, so he used his saved carfare to visit the theatres of London.

Because he wanted to earn more money in the theatre. His passion to become an actor pushed him into taking chances.

Every week he'd turn his little salary over to his father. Emily was a frail woman as was her daughter. So Willie helped with the house chores too.

He finally went back to his minister, who had contacts in the theatre world. He asked for a letter of character. His minister knew of a job opening at the " Haymarket Theatre" he told Willie it's sweeping up the theatre during the day. Willie didn't care, because it was his starting point.

After working at the Haymarket for a few weeks, Willie heard of an acting job, at the newly renamed, "His Majesty's Theatre". As he sat waiting to see the owner of the theatre, a large man stood over him and asked. "What's ya her for?"

"An acting job, siw, I have lettews fow a Mw. Twee!" Willie said with confidence.

"An actor, are ya?" the man laughed. just as Willie was about to give the jolly man a piece of his mind, a loud bellowing voice came from the top of the staircase, where some of the workers were cleaning the mirrors on the walls.

"What does that boy want?" Tree huffed.

"He says," hidden laugh…he's an actor, Mr. Tree."

"Is he now? Well send him up here!" yelled the tall man with black beard. Slowly, Willie walked up the stairs that curved around to the second floor. As he reached the top of the landing, Willie handed the man all of his papers releasing him from school, and a letter of reference from his minister. "Come! Tree said as he wrapped his black robe about him. Swinging open the tall wooden doors to his office flat, he threw his letter onto his long desk. Pouring himself a brandy he looked back at the child before him. "Tiny.. aren't you? But an actor you're not. I have a call-boy's job... if you want it.... it pays a pound a week.

"I don't know what a call-boy is. Mw. Twee! I would like to be an actor! Willie smiled, "Are you married, Mr. Rains?!" Tree asked.

"No Siw... I'm only ten!" Willie answered, watching the large man walk into another room, where portraits lined his walls with Mr. Tree as the center figure in each picture.

"Like them?" Tree said pointing to his likeness on all the walls,

Carmella Felice

"Pwetty! Willie smiled. He had seen more portraits in the hallway, but he didn't know what they represented, until Tree explained.

"These are scenes from my plays. I'm Richard ll, in this one. Tree pointed to the one over a large bed.

"That's what I want to be! An Actor." Willie smiled.

"You have a very bad cockney accent boy! How do you think the public will take to that?" Sadly Willie lowered his head in shame about the way he spoke.

"Listen here son," Tree said "a call boy is well respected. All you have to do is call the actors on stage when it's their time to speak their lines. In the mean time maybe we can correct your speech."

"Believe me siw, I've been twying to cowwect it."

"Well you'll have to, if you work for me. I pay a pound a week for the call boy's job. If you do any errands for me, that is extra pay... now what do you call yourself?"

"Willie Wains siw!" came the cockney accent.

"No, no, no... What is your full name?"

"Willie Claude Wains! the boy winced.

"Claude... that's it... you say that very well and that's what I will call you. Claude Rains. Say it, Claude Rains. And Willie repeated, Claude Rains!"

"Good! You start tomorrow.. in a couple of days, we will have opening night and the King will be here. He has giving me a lot of heartache about our usher's uniforms. The King wanted us to change the color because the uniform looked too much like his own court guards' uniforms. So everything has to be perfect, understand?"

"Oh yes... but?" Claude winced.

"What Claude.. what is it?"

"Do I get a uniform?" he asked, almost in a whisper.

"Of course you do. Now go downstairs and tell Homer to fix you up with a uniform.

"Claude smiled and hurried away to begin his new career. That afternoon, a woman who worked for Tree fitted him with his own uniform as Homer explained what a call-boy's duties were. "We are in what we call a transitional period in this theatre. You know the Queen died!"

Claude shook his head that he knew that. "Well this theatre was called "Her Majesty's Theatre" while she lived. Now we have permission to change the name to "His Majesty's Theatre. So we have a lot of work changing signs and uniforms for our ushers. The King has been quite a trial to Mr. Tree.. expense wise. So it will be your job to get the actors on stage in time. Now, a lot of our actors might drink quite a bit, especially on Friday, which is pay day. You will have to, at time go into pubs to get them out, before they get drunk...... understand?

Claude agreed to everything the stage manager wanted, so he could keep his job at the theatre. But he knew he was too small to yank large actors from pubs! But he so loved his uniform that he was willing to try anything once.

When Claude was out of uniform, he worked moving scenery about the stage, unloading props from horse-driven carts. Then he would sit down with the men to have his lunch. He was taught about the lighting, the parts of the stage, plus how to make scenery. Opening night had gone well with the King and Tree was pleased with the play. But Tree still wasn't satisfied with Claude's speech. So one day, he called the young boy to his office. Claude thought he was going to be let go for something he had done. But Herbert Tree wanted to talk to Claude about Learning to speak properly.

The actor gave Claude books on elocution. He told the young boy he wanted him to study the books and return in a week's time, to see how he had progressed." Claude took the books home with him and practiced trilling his tongue, so that he could pronounce his "R"s properly. In a weeks time, he was back in Tree's office showing off his accomplishments. His parents couldn't believe the change in their boy. Tree gave the boy the "Classics", to read, which the boy memorized in a couple of days. When production was on stage, Claude would ever throw a "line" to the drunken actor.

After a couple of months at the theatre, Claude became a little naughty. Herbert Tree had a habit of emptying his pockets onto his desk. On this particular day, his boss emptied his pockets and left the room. Claude saw his chance to make a few extra pences, and and he took a shiny new coin. When Tree returned to the room, he went over to the desk and looked at his change.

"Claude, how much money do you have on you?"

"I don't know sir?"

"Well... could you see? Put all your money on the desk, please!" Tree huffed. Claude emptied his pockets in front of his boss and out came the shiny silver coin he had taken.

Tree picked it up and examined it saying, "I've suspected your actions for some time. So I made a mark on one of my coins.. a "T"! Lo and behold, it was in your pocket. How do you explain that?" Tree sighed. Knowing he was caught, Rains didn't say anything. "I want you to come along and see me Sunday morning at my house in the city. Here is my address." Tree said, handing Rains a card. Claude was desperate on the bus going home. He didn't tell his parents that Tree might be sending him to prison for stealing. He suffered all week until Sunday came, and he found himself on Tree's doorstep. Ringing the doorbell a maid opened the door, with Mrs.. Tree and six children behind her. Claude didn't realize that Herbert was such a family man. "Maybe that's why he spent so much time at the theatre" Claude thought.

Mrs. Tree was very pretty and pleasant as she showed the youngster into the library where his boss was seated in a large brown leather sofa. Tree rose from his arm-chair, and walked over to the blazing fireplace. He took a cigar from a box on the mantleplace. Biting off the end of the cigar, he lit it with a long flaming straw. Puffing, he said, "Sit Claude.. I've come to a decision about your foul action! I think you might make a fine actor one day. The thing that is going to prevent it is your speech. For your punishment, you are to take lessons at Miss Beatrice." From the highly polished side table, he picked up a check and said calmy. "Take this check to her, on the address on this card. She will teach you to talk proper King's English. She is a kind lady, and I don't want to hear you have been disrespectful towards your new teacher." Oh, no sir!" Claude said sighing with relief that he wasn't going to prison for stealing Tree's money. "Is that all I have to do, Mr.. Tree?" Claude said with relief, as he held his head down.

"Yes... and I will give you some acting lessons. I want you to learn how hard an actor works for his money. Then one day when you make your fortune, maybe you will give a break to a young fellow who has stolen from you!"

"I don't think I will be as kind, as you are, sir! But I will always try."

The Life and Times of Claude Rains

"I have many children Claude, but none as bright as you are. I hate to see you go wrong, with such a keen memory."

Suddenly Tree's maid opened the door and wheeled in a silver tea cart with cookies and milk, in a silver cup. Claude would have been in a lot of trouble if Tree was another kind of man and Claude knew it." After working for Tree for about a year, Claude was given acting lessons, with other teenagers like himself at "His Majesty's Theatre.

Beatrice had taught Rains well, being careful not to injure the boy's great ego. She forced him to repeat over and over his vowels. First alone... then in sentences. Claude began to speak very clearly by his second year with Mrs. Beatrice. Every night after work, he would ride the big red bus back home, reading Richard II.

He had become very fond of Herbert Tree. He was the father figure that Claude had always wanted in his life. While dressing Mr.. Tree one night in his dressing room, just before a performance, Rains asked. "Mr.. Tree, when will I be given a chance to act in one of your productions?"

"When you can recite with feeling, Richard II, in all it's glory!" Tree snapped.

"I can do that now sir." Claude said, helping the actor on with his robe.

"Not the way I want you to! But you are learning, so I will give you a reward. I can't make it to the opening of the Stage Society's play tonight. Why don't you take your family to see the production tonight? You can have my box. I will leave word at the box office that you will be using my box tonight. I think they're putting on Richard II!"

"Oh no sir, they're staging the 'Power of Darkness' by Tolsty." Rains corrected.

"Tolsty! Tree huffed. Are you sure?"

"Yes sir... I read it in the London Times." Rains said softly.

"Well... any ways... you go... take the family, if you want. I will leave word at the theatre about the box. Tolstoy? Well I 'll be."

Rains left the theatre early to get washed, dressed and asked his parents if they wanted to go with him to see the play" To his surprise, they wanted to go, at his mother's insistance. After seeing the play, his father said, "Next time Mr. Tree has free tickets, tell him to keep them. That play was too much like my life to entertain me."

Carmella Felice

Claude tried to explain that Tolstoy, wrote about the ills of the world, but Fred didn't really care, because he had bigger woes than Tolstoy's play.

Claude was upset because he and his father didn't agree with his evaluation of the play. The next day he went back to work as usual, when Homer told Claude that the boss wanted to see him. He ran up up the long flight of stairs to Tree's Dome office.

Knocking on the door, he heard the familiar voice bid him to enter. "Well Claude.... how was the play?"

"Very interesting, but my father didn't care for it!"

"Seems that George Bernard Shaw agrees with your father. Listen to what he had to say about the play:

"Tolstoy opened to mixed emotions. But to me it was a horror! the Cockney accent used in the play was disgraceful! With phrases like, "S"elp me... Culd"ya" used in the play during the course of the night "Baah! Tree exclaimed. See how Shaw shows his displeasure at the making fun of a fragment of our society? They can't fight back! But some of the players were really good. I like Miss Dolores Drummond playing the role of a peasant. true to the way it's done in the novel. She was graceful in her utterances and gestures. Miss Etalia Conti, for whom the main story rested on, did quite well, I thought." Claude smiled.

"Oh Oh... dear boy... you have an eye for the ladies I see." Tree laughed. Tree knew that the shy boy he met at ten was now a grown man, and soon he would leave the nest.

In 1909 Herbert Tree was knighted by the King of England, to everyone's delight, except that of George Bernard Shaw. Claude had always seen the two men battling over lines in Shaw's plays. Tree was always in trouble with the "National Census", over Shaw's use of words. Tree wanted Shaw to refine his words in a scene or two, but Shaw wouldn't budge. As assistant manager, Claude would be on the stage listening to the two men go at each other, cursing for hours.

This is where Rains first met George Bernard Shaw, who in his life time would prove to be most beneficial to his pocketbook in future years. He became a big fan of the playwright, from the very first play he read of his. He wanted to play a role in one of his plays, but Herbert always denied him a part. Claude had educated himself, learning to be an electrician, a carpenter, a make-up expert, plus a good actor, he thought. But every time the teenager would ask the great actor for a chance to act, Tree would say. "You're not ready yet!" But the statement that really got on his nerves was "you don't have the face to be an actor!"

By 1910, Claude was unhappy with his job at "His Majesty's Theatre." He heard that the Haymarket Theatre was looking for some young actors. Claude went over a couple of blocks to the old theatre and asked the manager for a job. They agreed to give him acting jobs, if he would be an assistant manager at the Haymarket. Rains agreed to a two year contract, then went back to work to break the news to his boss. Sir Tree looked like he took it well, but deep down he was heart broken that Claude had seen fit to leave, after all he had done for the boy.

Rains still saw his friends, from the Majesty Theatre every now and then. They could come over to his theatre to see the new stars or have dinner with Claude. On One such night, a friend came over to talk, mostly about Sir Tree. He told Rains of a young man who had written to the actor, asking that the play begin at seven-thirty, instead of eight at night. He informed Tree that he lived outside of the city limits and eleven o'clock was the last train he could catch. Tree wrote back that would be impossible to agree to. So on Saturday night, the young man hads showed up at six o'clock, asking to talk to Sir Tree, and to his surprise the actor agreed to talk to Mr. Pearson.

"I showed Mr. Pearson to the great man's dressing room." I'm always happy to talk to a fan." Tree said "So I showed him to Tree's room" said the friend. Tree was combing his beard when I walked in with the very small youngster. "Hello... I'm Hesketh Pearson!"

"Oh yes... you wrote me about changing the start of my play to seven-thirty."

"Yes that's correct... I didn't think you would remember."

"Sorry my boy, but the theatre has rules about the timing."

"I'm sorry that you didn't see fit to take my suggestion. That is why I am here a little early to talk to you. I live hours away from London, so it is a hardship for me to get home after a play."

"Sorry, but the outlanders have to cope with our schedule. We have to try to have the train schedule moved to 12 P.M, but they have rules too."

Young Mr. Pearson didn't like Tree's answer and continued. "You really should have pity on the theatre-goer who lives outside of London."

"Precedent cuss! Rains laughed at his friend's account of Tree's encounter with Pearson. Then said Claude's friend, Mr. Pearson asked the actor. "I would like to be one of your students, Mr.... Tree. I have studied a little in my town, and wish to further my studies with you."

"Brash young man to say the least!" Claude huffed, drinking his glass of milk.

"That's when Tree started on him." said the friend. Can you speak German?"

"No sir... does one have to know German to be an actor?"

"Yes... if one is a German actor in Germany... yes it would help." smiled Tree putting on his make-up.

"But I would be acting in England not Germany!" said the confused fellow. "Do you know any languages at all, sir?"

"No... I don't know any at all."

"What a pity, because one should always swear in the foreign language at rehearsals. It helps break up the tensions... you know?" Tree smiled. Rains laughed again when he heard the tale recalled.

"Is there any necessity to swear at all?" asked Pearson. Tree stood up and faced the youngster saying, "Not a necessity, young man.. but a great relief!"

"Are you fond of your wife?" Tree Smiled.

"I don't have a wife, Mr... Tree." answered the confused man.

"Well then... are you at least fond of her?" came another question.

"How the dickens can I be fond of a wife if I don't have one?" shouted Pearson in disgust. Claude shook his head as he heard the tale, saying "He's got him now!"

"Then Tree asked..."Do you read much?"

"It depends upon what you call reading much" replied Pearson.

"I mean the perusal of a vast quandry of words, printed on paper and bound-up into books!" Tree's mouth flared up into a wicked smile.

"Of course I knew what you meant... but to what class of reading do you mean?" asked Pearson.

"Oh, oh... he's coming back for some more punishment" winced Claude.

"Yes Claude... But Tree said dryly, "Novels... facts. figures, bookeeping?"

"Aaah... Claude yelled. "He does miss me, keeping his books! Trying to find a replacement... is he?"

"Of that I have no doubt. Claude, I know I can't do all he wants of me! Including bookkeeping."

"After you do it for a while, you can get the hang of it, John."

"If only he had given you a chance to act!" John shook his head.

"I think we all regret that. But what of Mr. Pearson?"

"Tree told him to be aware of encyclopedias... because a little knowledge is a dangerous thing, but it ruins one's digestion!" Rains smiled as his friend completed his story, of the weekly events at his Majesty's Theatre.

"Well at least Tree was polite! He's always been polite... I can remember a couple of mistakes I made as a small boy working for him."

"Like what?" John asked.

"Oh... as you know, for a long while, his memory has been a problem for him. When I was eleven, the stage manager had a bright idea, so that Tree could complete his lines on stage. He ordered giant cardboard cards made. and wrote Tree's lines on them. Then he placed me in the orchestra pit, with these giant cards, that were bigger than I was. One night Herbert forgot his lines, and slowly walked over to where I was in the pit. As he neared the footlights he shook his head at me, stared and shrugged his shoulders! Then he walked to the prompt corner, to recieve his line.

"What's the line?" he said, not moving his lips. Stanley Bell, standing there, said.

"Boss... Claude has your lines all written down for you on the cards, down in the pit!"

"I know... I know... But he's holding them upside down."

CHAPTER 2

CLAUDE RAINS, ACTOR!

The Edwardian Era had blasted off with gaiety, capable of intrapping the lowliest of the King's subjects. King Edward was a patron of the arts who encouraged his people to see plays, visit garden-parks and take their children to the free museums to learn about England's history. The city's water fountains were architecturally perfect for young lovers to sit and talk under an umbrella of water. Claude had a new love too....

The Model T. Ford. It had evaded the shinny wet cobble stones, of old London town.

The noisy vehicles frightened the horses with it's loud backfires from it's tremendous motors. The horse and carriage still had its charm over the new invention, but Rains was caught up in the "Bohemian" atmosphere of his city, as his career began at the Haymark Theatre.

He had grown into a boyishly handsome man, with sharp features, piercing brown eyes, expressive eyebrows and brown hair with an unruly curl that insisted on covering his right eyebrow. He stood five feet, eight inches and weighted about one hundred and fifty pounds.

In his mind, Claude still wanted to be a great actor like Sir Tree. He joined the "National Theatre Group" in order to be an actor, signing a three year contract with some reservation about the pay scales, but confident that in a company of forty-two actors and twenty-one actresses, a role could be found for his talents.

All new actors were first tried out in small roles, because they lacked experience.

He wondered if the actresses were at the theatre to learn or to find themselves husbands with a good future. The girls seem to like him well enough, when he was the assistant stage-manager, but as soon as he completed for attention on the stage, they became very tempermental!

His speech problems as a child had left its scars, as he shyed away from the opposite sex. Many of the women were well educated, unlike himself, who was self taught.

Now as an actor it came in handy, as writers like Lord Dunsany thought Rains came from good breeding because of his speech. Even though his voice and manner reflected the air of nobility, deep down, he felt inadequate. He dressed very dapper, with silk scarfs and a hankerchiefs in tow. His shoes were always at a high polish and he carried himself with a noble walk.

Then one lucky day, a ray of sunshine popped into his life. His boss handed him a script for a new Lord Dunsany play called, "The Gods of the Mountain" His boss, Charles LaTrobe, told Claude that Lord Dunsany wanted him to play one of the beggars in the play. Lord Dunsany had gained the support of the public with his books.

Now they wanted him to put his work on the stage , with Rains playing "Slay" in the new play, at the Haymarket Theatre where he had first gotten the acting bug. Rains was a fan of Dunsany, after years of reading his books. The names and places and people, appearing in his stories were worthy of study, because of their complexities.

Each one of his stories were aptly suggestive, as if generations of men had been at work shaping them. Rains rejoiced in his new role and with such, a celebrated author offering him his friendship.

In the story, one sees the atmosphere of fatality, only found in Greek dramas.

The characters of Lord Dunsany speak as simply as those of the man on the street, sharply and to the point. There can be no mistaking of the lines. So it was fairly simple for Claude, to learn the role of "Slag" the beggar, for he felt he had been a beggar all his life. He rehearsed his lines with the other players, but all the time building his character up to what he thought he should be like. He learned from his director where to stand on stage, but he brought the beggar to life. The first time the Director called on him to read his lines, he almost fainted, but held steady, as he spoke the lines clearly, He was determined to make the little part his as he spoke his lines.

"My master was three times knocked down and injured by carriages there," He said, (pointing to a spot in the road). He was killed and seven times beaten and robbed... and every time he was generously compensated. He had nine diseases... many of them mortal!

He knew all of his lines, now all that was left was to be measured for beggar's rags. The first time he put on the costume, he felt like a harlequin who had been run down by a Model T. Ford.

"These are rags". he yelled.

"There're supposed to be!" the director yelled back.

"Well can you drap them shapely on my shoulders somewhat better?"

"Why?... you'll still be a beggar!" Laughed the director.

Most melodramas had at least three scenes in each act. A full set, followed by a "front scene". It was played well over the footlights, in front of a "cloth" or a pair of "Flats". The "Flats" were mostly used when an interior was necessary and were pushed on from the side, meeting in the center. The interior wings were pushed forward to complete the picture. Claude had to worry about these sets, as well as his role in the play. Edward John Moreton Drax Plunkett was the real name of Lord Dunsany. He was the eighteenth member of his family to bear the title. He loved the outdoors and tried to get Claude to go fox-hunting with him. But Claude was to busy with his job to enjoy Lord Dunsany's invitation. Claude still thought of himself a commoner, and didn't want to play on Dunsany's good graces. Dunsany had an air of dignity that came from having a formal education. Rains felt that Dunsany's education went far beyond his. But he liked the way Lord Dunsany carried himself, so he tried hard to copy his stands and walk.

He held his head high and cocked to the side, in a rich looking manner.

There was another ray of sunshine in his life, which Claude had been waiting all of his life for, His father had finally found a profession he liked he had become an actor, too, as well as a director of silent pictures.

Now at least he could keep most of his earning's for himself, as long as his father was doing well directing.

La Trobe drove Claude hard at work, but the little stage manager-actor performed well at any task that his boss set before him. The income of all theatre players regularly attached to a theatre, for different terms of employment, differed. Some were given three year contracts to prove their worth to the "National Theatre". Claude was a subordinate and probationary actor, on a fixed, yearly salary. As any other actor would have. The English theatres weren't run like the ones on the continents, where a repretory company was kept on salary, with a guarantee of a certain number of performances a year. In this way, an actor could survive, in hopes of becoming a star one day.

The chief advantage to the "National Theatre" was a fee system, which had actors starting at a set fee for a number of years, until his popularity increased. Then their earnings could not be diminished, with the fee system in place. But management of any theatre could adjust the earnings of a performer to his practical usefulness to the company, more readily than by actual teration of their salaries. So Rains, as assistant stage manager, was allowed to keep both jobs, with the permission of management.

The role of "Slag" was a simple one, but performing in front of an audience wasn't. Lord Dunsany, the playwright, was on stage every day with the director, who found fault with everything. Claude was one of the seven beggars in the scene, which took place by the Great Wall in the city of "Kongros". Herbert Trench, the director, was sometimes a soft-spoken man who didn't want to go up against Lord Dunsany's suggestions. but Claude knew the director was depressed, by the way he bossed him around the stage.

The play was a success and ran for three months, at the Haymarket. This put both director and playwright in good cheer. Seeing that Rains could handle acting and directing his workers, the Haymarket's management offered Claude a new job in Australia!

Claudes loyalty and dilligence had finally placed his feet on the right path. He accepted the job of actor-manager, for two plays called, "The Blue Bird" and "You Can Never Tell". He would direct-manage "The Blue Bird" and act in "You Can Never Tell."

The first play was to open on April 3rd, 1912 in Sydney. He was very excited as he bid his family goodbye on a ship bound for Australia. It was in mid-February that the company sailed, along with all the sets, in the bowels of the ship, it took almost twelve days to reach the large continent, as the ship made it's way down the North Atlantic, then into the South Pacific, and into the Indian Ocean. The warmer waters of the South Pacific felt good on his face as the island came into view. Sydney's port was bustling with trade, as they entered the blue-green waters of the large port. The ocean salt water flowed briskly against the white sandy beaches of Sydney. While it was Winter in London, on the sandy beaches of Australia, it was a windy sixty degrees. Some of the cast who had been seasick for most of the trip, couldn't wait to get off the ship. Customs didn't take long, because the Stage Society of Sydney, had sent an official to help rush the company, past the red tape. Then they were guided to a waiting horse-drawn carts that took them to a small boarding house. It was located just a few minutes from the "Criterion Theatre" where the play was to be performed. The rooms came with one meal, so most of the players chose breakfast as their free meal. The cast rested for a day, before going to the theatre to sort out the sets. Rains found some of the scenery damaged, and he set to repairing it.

Norman Page, the producer of the play, was a " hands on" type of a man, as he watched every aspect of the production. Furniture had to be bought in Sydney, for props in the vine-covered woodcutter's cottage. Rains was given extra money to buy any new props, that he needed for the "Blue Bird" set. It gave him great pleasure to search for old pieces of furniture in the small town of Sydney, while seeing the sights.

The important role of "Tyltly", was admirable portrayed by little Gertle Cremer, whose tuneful voice thrilled her audiences. Cremer was twenty years old, playing a twelve year old. Another actor was eighteen, playing a ten year old with a very large wig. Vera Sparell timidly played the other child, dressed in a red riding hood scarlet cloak. Another actor played a clock with eyes that winked. Enan Brooke played that part to perfection. The sets had been built in London, by Rains and his team of carpenters. Then it was carefully packed and loaded onto the ship to Sydney. During the shipping a few pieces of scenery had been damaged so Claude set to work repairing it.

The young actors gave Rains a hard time, wanting to see the sights of Sydney before having to work. Rains gave into their demands, as he set up the lighting fixtures. As he looked around the "Criterion Theatre", it reminded him of some of the province theatres, on the outskirts of London.

Opening night arrived on April 3rd, with Rains in a tense state. He ordered the young actors to take their positions on the stage, as he worked the curtain to the sound of the music. Next, he nervously pulled the lever to light the stage. The play began at 8 p.m., with Claude watching over the actors like a mother hen.

The first act started with a dream sequence. In the dream, the children catch a

"Blue Bird", who has the powers, to cure their sick friend. But when they awake, all they see is their white dove in her cage. As they take out the trained Dove from it's cage, it flew away over the stage another cage backstage, where it could be secured by Claude. As the bird disappears off stage, Tyltly says, "Don't worry.... I will find him again.

The action starts again as other actors dressed in costumes dance onto the stage.

They represent the souls of animals, plus the wind, fire and water spirits. In the last scene, the two children find themselves at the foot of the "Palace of the Night". The band played tones of terror as the two children approach the palace. Mytly said... "Give me your hand little brother, I feel frightened and cold." As Claude lowers the curtain to get ready for the next act. Meanwhile, the patrons go to tea break in the lobby of the theatre. For fifteen minutes, the cast works to set up the next scene that takes place in a graveyard. Claude prepares a long hose planted in the backstage, that will pump out a fog-like mist out onto the stage floor. Then hooks up the hose to a fog machine, just a minute before patrons hear the bell to take their seats for the next act.

The audience sees a a fog-bound graveyard, with the children looking very scared.

The children are holding on to each other, as the spirits of wind, rain, and air dance about them. The an earthquake takes place, as the actors fall to the ground in terror.

As the fog becomes too dense to see the stage, the spirits move all of the tombstones off the stage and replace them with fake flowers. Then the fog is stopped to reveal a wonderful land of flowers, where the graveyard had been. The illusion of a garden created a great stir with the crowd. One of the children asked, "Where are the dead?"

And the other child says, "There are no dead!"....... and the curtain comes down on the final act.

The local gentry cheered the actors for nine curtain calls, which was a good sign that the play was a hit. The locals were thrilled by the graveyard scene and it was the talk of the town. After the play, the actors went to a pub around the corner from the theatre to eat supper and await the morning newspaper review. Claude drank a little too much, as he waited for the news. The other actors played dart games, while Claude was entranced by the game of ping-pong!

Two weeks after "Blue Bird" was set to play a few months, Claude started to rehearse his own role in, "You Can Never Tell". His play was to start on August 24th, after "Blue Birds" run was completed. As the dust rose off the plains of the town, Claude's opening night began. The next day, he recieved a good review from the critics.

One wrote: Mr. Rains, besides being the stage manager, appeared as Bohan K.C., a part demanding a more commanding presence but the self importance of which he performs the part, leads him to achieve or to develop effectively."

Claude didn't like the review, but his bosses thought it was quite good. After the summer passed they packed up the company to perform the two plays in Melbourne, Australia. At the end of the tour, the company returned to England with the producers and managers satisfied with the tour. So much so that they offered Claude another play called, "The Golden Doom", by Lord Dunsany. He would be a spy in this play. His play ran with another play called "An Adventure of Aristide Pujol", by Frederick Harrison. Both productions only ran for forty-five minutes, with a fifteen minute intermission.

While he was on stage working, a group of young ladies flew by him in brightly colored dresses. Lord Dunsany had called for an audition for his play in the local trade papers. All the girls were beautiful, but one stood out among the rest. She was thin with long curly blonde hair, set high on top of her head, which was the fashion of the day.

Her greenish eyes flashed, as did her warm lips. Claude couldn't take his eyes off the girl. One by one the girls took to the stage to read for the part, as he watched from a distance. As one actress was chosen among the rest he saw tears come into his lady's fair eyes. Walking over to the director, he asked, "What is that girl's name?" Isabel Jeans!" Came the reply. As the actress turned to leave, he went over to her and asked.

"Is anything wrong?" You seem very upset."

"I really wanted this job!" she said in a low, sweet voice. "Some times it takes time... it took twelve years for me to get a part." He smiled.

"Are you in this play? Mr.....

"Claude Rains... and your name?"

"Isabel Jeans!" She smiled.

With that began their friendship, which would lead to marriage. Claude seemed to open up to this young lady, something he hadn't done before, with anyone.

Jeans had wanted so much to be part of the "Haymarket Theatre", production company. Jeans made him laugh with her funny squeaky voice. He soon was asking her out to see his family. Emily was happy that her son had finally found a nice girl to settle down with. His father even invited the couple to his studio, to watch him make a silent picture with him, but Claude wasn't interested in this type of life.

By 1912, Frederick Rains had made three more films, two of which he directed.

At Isabel's insistance, Claude took her to see the studios one day, the studio was filled with hundreds of people working on twelve different sets. Yelling and shouting was going on in each section of the floor. Claude found his father directing a movie called, "Who said Rats?" Isabel watched intensely as the actors made all kinds of motions according to their scripts.

Soon after this film was finished, Claude moved out of his father's house and into a small flat in a men's club, near the theatre section. The couple waited a while to get married, because he wanted to save up a little money to get a small cottage of their own. His father had started filming another film called. "Love's Victory Over Crime" and he asked Claude to play the lead, but he turned down his offer.

Rains needed the quiet of the theatre to concentrate on his characters. Claude had heard from a couple of friends that Herbert Tree had gone to America to make a film in Hollywood. Even the clown Charlie Chaplin was caught up in the Hollywood fever.

But he stuck to his guns, refusing to do a silent film. His father had told him that a couple of people were working on a system, so that the movies would have voice in the coming years. Fred worried when that day came there wouldn't be any room for him any more.

The Life and Times of Claude Rains

His son told his father to save his money if he thought that day was coming because he was going to marry Isabel and would need all of his paychecks.

Isabel and Claude were going steady, when he became fast friends with an actor by the name of Grandville Barker. Barker was older than Rains by several years. The two men worked at the "Haymarket Theatre". Barker was a manager-actor, with the same beginnings as Claude. But Grandville had made it big on stage, while Claude was still struggling.

The two men had been friends since 1910, when Barker and Shaw had organized a matinee performance on behalf of the "Funds of the National Shakespeare Memorial Committee". Barker was producing one of Shaw's play called "Dark Lady Of The Sonnets". Shaw had specially written it for the occasion. Shaw had been looking for Grandville for an hour, when through the side door he appeared, where Claude was working. He whispered to Rains.

"Claude old boy" Rains turned to see his friend waving in a drunken manner.

"Claude, where is Bernard? he asked. Walking over to the actor, Claude said, sharply "Mr. Shaw has been looking all over the place for you. You have to go on in an hour."

Claude old fellow... do me a big one.... get me to the basement without him seeing me like this. "Right," Claude smiled and helped Barker down the stairs to the basement, where all the costumes were kept.

"Now dear boy... get my costume and a couple of cups of coffee, fast... will you?"

"Of course... but what about Mr. Shaw?"

"Forget about him for now," He sighed, I'll talk to him later on."

So Rains got him a pot of black coffee, his clothes, and a basin of water to wash up with. You could hear Shaw yelling all over the theatre... "Barker... where are you?"

After 30 minutes, Claude asked how he felt.

"I don't feel anything my boy, that's the cruxes of it." which made Rains laugh.

"How long before curtain time, Claude?"

"Twenty minutes, sir."

"I'll be alright by then... hopefully!" he cried. Hearing Shaw yelling for Barker, Rains asked Granville if he was up to doing the play?

"Of course Claude," Barker said, struggling to his feet. Slowly the two actors walked up the rickety steps, to the stage area. Shaw greeted his leading man, with several choice words. "Been drinking again.... I see!" Claude agonized as Barker tried to stand straight, but fell backwards, into the waiting arms of his fellow actor. "I'm fine...

Mr. Rains on with the play, my lord! "How can you perform in your condition?" Shaw asked.

Suddenly Charles Richett, the costume designer, ran across the stage in a huff.

"Look at what you are doing to my costume! Claude, why is Mr. Barker on the floor? Never mind, I know. Look at my costume, it's all dirty!" Barker looked up and said.

"It's the floor that dusty! Why don't you keep it cleaner!"

Picking at the hem of the cloak Charles moaned, "Now look at what you've done to the hem!" Rising to his feet, Barker said, "Don't worry, ...I'll just throw it over my arm, like this." Rains watched as Barker flung his cloak over his arm. Shaw shook his head in disbelief saying, "God, Barker.. I don't know what to do with you anymore You're incurable!"

Ten minutes later, the cast hit the stage, as Barker got ready for his entrance.

Richett watched as Barker dragged his cloak along the floor. Annoyed, he threw up his hands in disgust. He felt it was a reflection on his work, if the costume wasn't presented properly. Rains was more worried that Barker would fall down on stage. Although Barker came through like a trooper, he didn't give his best performance.

Rains didn't see much of Barker, until two weeks later, when he came to the Haymarket Theatre. He thanked Rains for all his help and showed him a post card from Shaw, about his performance. It read: "Forget to warn you that made an astonishing XIX century satiate by saying. On the contrary! Instead of "Far from it!" Were you in your cups or did you forget? Remember endless naughtiness to a gentleman as lewd as yourself, cannot be fruitful in this industry. Your costume was telling, there has been a great rally of the adoration" Rains laughed at the remarks, in the postcard, saying "Sounds like Mr.. Shaw was in his cups, when he wrote the note."

"G.B. likes to carry on with these in postcards when his people mess up! But you were a true blue friend that night, and I and Mr. Shaw owe you!"

"I don't understand why Mr. Shaw owes me anything"

"Didn't you save his life, when you worked at His Majesty's?"

"I sir?... I don't understand... all I remember was Mr. Shaw, took a fainting spell once at the theatre, a few years back. I ran for a doctor, I recall at Mr.... Tree's request."

"Then you don't know the whole story... Claude shook his head no, as Barker continued. "He had a high fever, from a leg infection. Almost lost the leg! If you hadn't got the doctor to come to the theatre. He would have lost his leg! Shocked, Rains said "Good Lord! I knew nothing of this. "I'm happy my little legs could be of service to Mr. Shaw." Claude sighed.

"Now here is how we are going to repay your kindness. Mr.... Shaw and I have gone into partnership. We are going to produce a few plays in America, and we wish for you to come over with us as assistant-manager-actor. The U.K stands on the brink of war. Nothing is going to stop it! I have friends, high up in the government, and they think it's best to leave England at this time. So what do you say to this deal?"

"I was planning to be married soon." Claude smiled.

"Good, now is the best time Claude. Marry your girl and take her to the United States with you."

"How long will this engagement take?" Claude asked with interest.

About a year, my sources say that Germany is building up a very large army. They are on the brink of a conflict with Poland. It might take about a year." Barker told the would-be actor.

"I'd better tell my family to take some precautions with their savings, and his father's new job." Claude worried.

"Take care of what you have to. But are you in on our deal?" Barker asked.

"Yes, yes. Rains agreed and within a month, the newly married couple was sailing for America. Claude signed up with the "National Registry" before he left, just in case there was a fighting war. He really

Carmella Felice

thought that England and Germany would work out their problems, without the need of war.

Crossing the Atlantic on a ship was very romantic for the honeymoon couple. Beneath blue skies and moonlit nights, they had a wonderful time. Rains had been given the role of "Spintho", in Shaw's play. Barker had told Claude that American bankers had invested six thousand dollars for the sets, with more money promised, if the play went well on Broadway.

The Rains's were excited when they saw the skyline of New York City. Claude felt a freedom he never felt before, as the greenish-colored Statue of Liberty came into view. People were yelling and waving from the decks below, and they also joined in the celebration of reaching their destination.

A week later, Claude was hard at work at the theatre, preparing for the play. In the play, Shaw retells the Christian story of a timid slave who plucks a thorn from an anguished lion's paw. In the Roman arena, that same lion saves his life. The play of course was "Androcles and the Lion". Claude enjoyed his small role, because Shaw told him. "From little acorns, bigger trees grow!" Claude was willing to be an acorn for a while, if it lead him to bigger things. Barker even gave a small part to his wife so that they could be together during the day. New York papers were filled with the impending cries of war in Europe. Claude kept thinking about the "National Registry", and the papers he had signed, if the war was declared. Granville Barker and Shaw were at the theatre for opening night to take their bows.

American backers met Shaw and the Barker's at the pier, with fifty reporters at their heels, to publicize the play. They shook hands with the Mayor of New York City and the photographers. Claude was to pick up his bosses at the pier, but he couldn't get through the volley of reporters, flashing their cameras at all the stars. Finally he caught up with them at customs.

Isabel didn't go to the ship, to meet Shaw and the others, because they had just moved into a new flat on EightyEight Street, and Eighth Avenue. Isabel didn't like the accomodations at the hotel the company was staying at. At the same time, her husband was escorting his bosses to the Wallach Theatre, she was pulling up bright yellow curtains in her new kitchen. Besides Lillah, Granville's wife was the star of the play, and Isabel didn't want to take away any of the star's glory, in the eyes of the reporters.

Granville, being old enough to go to war, had made a deal with his friends in the English Cabinet. Barker was to come to America to make friends with the rich and as many political-types, that might help the English cause, if war was declared. So while the cast rehearsed at the Wallack Theatre, Granville was attending to his government's business, going to all kinds of parties, and meeting with bankers.

Claude and his wife didn't know what Granville's mission was. All they knew was that Claude was working hard to make the show a success, because Shaw and Barker had shown faith in his abilities. A brand new curtain had to be affixed scenery unpacked and rehearsals attended. Isabel was having fun too, in her new role as wife and actress.

"Androcles and the Lion" had a very large cast, with Lillah as the star headache.

She didn't like that Granville was out almost every night, with or without her at his side.

More often than not, without her on his arm. Isabel told her husband she thought they were having marital problems. "I think there's another woman in his life. Claude!"

"Nonsense. He is just a busy man. He has to find some money to keep the play going, if it's not a success." Even Shaw was getting worried about Barker's actions.

A big problem did pop up for Granville, as he went from party to party, trying to raise money for England's war effort. He met a beautiful fair haired debutante, by the name of Miss Helen Huntington. She was very young, tall and she loved Granville. The instant that he saw her dancing, he fell in love with the beauty. Her father was very rich and interested in the plight of the world while Barker was only interested in his daughter.

Granville knew when the news broke in the papers about Helen, his work for his government would be over. When Bernard Shaw arrived for opening night, Lillah went to him crying that Granville was in love with another woman. He calmed her down so that she could perform in the play, but promised to talk to Granville about the affair.

The yelling from Granville's dressing room could be heard back stage by all the cast members, including the Rain's, Shaw and his wife had loved Barker as if he was their own child. Now the child was acting like a fool in the eyes of the great playwright. But Granville didn't want want to give up Helen. Shaw went to lillah and told her not to give up on her husband, and for months, she didn't.

At the end of the performance, Shaw, Granville and Lillah, took their bows as though nothing had happened a few hours before. The production played for three months on Broadway. Then they started a new play called, "Iphigenia in Tauris".

It played in New Haven, Connecticut. Mr. Phillip Merivale was the actor who played the "The Heardsman", in New Haven. But when Shaw saw his performance, he ordered Granville to change the actor, when the play came to Broadway. "put Rains in the role, he knows how to act that part!" Shaw was always looking after Claude's interest, because he liked the young actor. Maybe it was because of his disillusionment with the Barker's affair that made Bernard lose faith in Barker's ability to properly cast his actors.

In his new role, Claude built the character of the "Herdsman" into a strong believable soul. He practiced the timing, his hand movements, the spring in his walk to capture a new look for the character.

Lillah was pressing her husband to return to England, and to break off the affair with Helen. Granville wouldn't do it, so when her contract was up with the company, she went back to England in the middle of a war. She thought her husband would follow her back to England, but he didn't.

Rains was becoming known with his role in "Iphigenia in Tauris" The New York Times had this to say about Claude,

Claude Rains seems to have modified somewhat the sheer physical vigor of his performance as the Herdsman, but it remains as exceedingly effective contribution to the play, so good, in fact, that many must regret that during the long Barker season at the Wallack's Theatre, he did all his work behind the scenes.

By April of 1915, the Mayor of New York City, the Honorable John Purrro Mitchel had seen the two Greek plays and wished Barker to perform the plays at the college of the City of New York. A new stadium had just been completed, and the school needed a good production to set off their new jewel.

This is the letter that the mayor wrote to Granville:

Dear Sir,

I was very much interested in the plan for producing Professor Murray's translations of "Iphigenia" and the "Trojan Woman", under your directorship in the new stadium of the college of New York City which was erected through the generosity of Mr. Adolph Lewisohn.

I am especially interested in the opportunity which it is proposed to afford to the students of the College of New York City and of the higher grades of the public schools to witness these productions of the great Greek dramas. It augurs well for the future of the stadium of the City's own college that it should be opened under such auspices. I attach so much importance to the success of your plans, not only because of their immediate educational value but as an inspiration to make the new stadium of the City College a center for great dramatic production intended to appeal to large audiences, that, with the approval of Mr. Lewisohn, President Mezes and the Board of Trustees of the College of the City of New York. I am appointing a Citizen's Committee to co-operate with the Board of Trustees and faculty of the college.

After recieving the Mayor's letter, Granville put Claude to work, asking him to go to the college and bring him back the layout of the new stadium. Claude was on his way to the stadium, as Granville wrote a reply to the mayor:

Dear Mr.. Mayor: Wallacks Theatre, New York City, April 10th, 1915

We are most grateful-my wife and I for cordial recognition you are good enough to give to the production of these Greek plays, with which it is our privilege to be concerned. New York is indeed fortunate in the generous gift to the City college of its Stadium. And you will understand with what enthusiasm we discover in it an almost perfect pattern of a Greek theatre.

I believe that Greek plays themselves livingly treated are still Living things. The "Trojan Women." surely might have been written for the tragedy of this war today. Nor was their appeal limited to a narrow audience.

By their very nature it cannot be they can only deal with the universal themes and in the simplest manner possible. If we are but familiar with a few old stories, nothing stands between us and them. So we look forward with particular pleasure among our audiences at the dedication performance and the others that will follow not only students and those more immediately interested but the experience what fine listeners are these last.

Many of us feel, too, that upon Greek Drama with its one-time appeal to great throngs of people of all sorts and ages, can be founded a modern drama with just a wide appeal, that in time this beautiful Stadium (apart from its other uses) maybe a place where American poets provide also for the spiritual recreation of their city, taking such themes as our traditions and life and ideals provide, not such a far cry this perhaps as it may seem.

Meanwhile, may we tell you that as it has been our good fortune to be concerned from the beginning in Professor Murray's achievement of making these old masterpieces seem new, so we feel and we know he would feel that the choice of one of these plays to be part of this dedication ceremony is a fine crown to the work. That you see fit, more over to appoint a Citizen's Committe to further our plans does us and our art the greatest honor to make a claim for it in comedy and tragedy alike.

We thank you sincerely and I speak I know all our fellow workers. We will try to make the work we do worthy of the honor you have done it. Faithfully yours, (signed)
Granville Barker."

The whole crew was excited about performing at the stadium, including Claude. A portable stage had to be built, than transported and reassembled at the Stadium. The cast consisted of nine people with Lillah McCarthy as the star. Claude worked with the manager, A. L. Flynn, the stage director, Randolph Hartley and Murdock Pemberton, who was the press representative for the company. Will Hitchins and the Musical Director Elliot Schench, constantly asked Claude how the stage was going to be centered, so they could arrange for a band stand to be built adjacent to the portable stage. Murdock Pemberton wanted to know all kinds of information from Claude.

"How much are the tickets going to cost?"

"Two dollars, one dollar and fifty cents... a dollar and fifty cents!" answered Claude.

"Will the company be recieving a fee for their services?" asked Murdock.

"We don't work for nothing, Mr. Pemberton. Claude snapped back quickly and continued. But you'll have to talk to Mr. Barker about that!"

During all what was going on, Lillah kept saying after these performances, "I am going back to England." Which sent a chill through Rains, because without the star, the show was nothing. But he knew how hurt she was with Granville and didn't blame her for her outbursts. The war between England and Germany was spreading and she wanted to go home to help in the war effort. But Granville kept telling her that the theatres had all been closed, because most of the players had enlisted into the armies. But she insisted she was going home to be with her family. Claude knew she would get her way in the long run, but for now he had a stage to assemble on the grounds of the large Stadium.

He centered the stage, so that it could be seen and heard from all parts of the theatre.

As actors spoke their lines on the stage, Claude ran around the top of the Stadium to see if the actor could be heard on the top rows.

The Mayor had told them that six thousand students would be coming to the ceremony of the dedication, besides the professors who would all be dressed in black cap and gowns. They told Claude that a procession would come from the college and take seats to the side of the stage. After their program was completed, the play would begin.

The first performance would be on May 31st, which Claude understood was the American Holiday of Decoration Day. The performance was slated to begin at 4:30 p.m. Then on Wednesday, June 2nd, and again on Saturday, June 5th, they were going to do "Trojan Women."

Over the open-air Stadium, Claude could see tenement houses, which spoiled the illusion of being in Greece, along with all traffic noises, which Claude thought would be a problem for the actors. Lillah was being her temperamental self, while agreeing it would be her biggest audience to date.

Mr. Donn Barber and Professor Lewis F. Mott, watched Claude and his crew of carpenters as they set the stage, they showed Claude the hidden facets of the stadium.

Thanking the teachers, Claude found a large room off the side of the structure that could be used for a dressing area. He fitted it with mirrors and a couple of make up tables for the actors to prepare themselves. The Giant concrete Stadium with its eighteen rows of concrete steps, climbed on a curve in a semicircle. Its frontage on Amsterdam Avenue was 460 feet. The semi-elliptical colonnade ended in two pavillions, between which extended a Doric Colonnade of 64 columns, each 15 feet high. In the pavillions were located the showers and dressing rooms for the students or in case this time, the actors.

The seating capacity was 6,000 people, with room for 1,500 standers. The material of construction Claude could see was gray concrete.

All supplies were brought in from the theatre, by carpenters Claude had hired for the job. As they place the three sections of the stage together a large chorus and songs that would be used in the play. They were clad in gray and red robes and reminded him of his days in a choir. The day of the play to be presented to the students, Claude watched as two long lines of professors and Members of the board, marched to their chairs.

It was a striking scene for the Rains' to see. The City's flag with its blue, white and orange colors, were seen from the top of the Stadium. The speeches honored Adolph Lewisohn, the man whose money built the Stadium. Except for the trolly-car noises, they could hear the speeches very clearly. After that the actors turn came as "Iphigenia" started.

The play takes place at the Temple of Artemis on the sea coast of Tauris, between the years 412 and 414 A.D. So a special backdrop had to be built to represent the Temple.

At 3 o'clock the doors were opened to a stampeding hoard of students pouring into every seat in the Stadium. Claude was on stage attending to last minute adjustments, that the morning rain had caused. Now the sun was shining brightly, drying up the concret seats. Pulling the backdrop curtain into place, several students sailed paper airplanes onto the stage area. Claude went out to pick up the pieces of paper, which could cause an accident if an actor slipped on it. The students cheered as he did so. He smiled and waived to the students saying, "Please do not sail anything on the stage, because it can cause a serious accident to the players!" They yelled and waved back, as Claude took a low bow in appreciation. By 4 o'clock the stadium was filled to the hilt.

The Mayor of New York and officers of the college had taken their seats in the front of the stage, as the choir began to sing. "Peace, Peace, upon all who dwell by sister rocks that clkash in the swell of the friendless seas!"

Claude enjoyed the part of the herdsman, in the play "Iphigenia", because it was a very meaningful one. The play wasn't really a tragedy, but merely a romance. It begins in a gloomy atmosphere, than rises to a fast and dangerous adventure. It was considered a tragic play because of the characters ' sincerity. Iphigenia especially with her mixed emotions or revenge and for love. Her hatred of the Greeks made her suffer, but her love of her country keeps her going.

Iphigenia was the daughter of Agamennon, who was supposed to have been sacrificed by her father at Aullis. She was saved by Artimus and becomes the high priestess of the Goddess of the land. The Taurians are fierce race of people, who kill all strangers in their land. Her task was to prepare them for death. But one day her brother Orestes a Greek, whom she doesn't know by his face, comes before her to be prepared.

When she finally recognizes him, it is the most fabulous point in the play. She plans his escape, which forms a thrilling story, as they are both too far from Greece to send for help.

Professor Gilbert Murray Regius was professor of Greek laws at Oxford College.

He was the one who translated the works into English, because he loved the stories so much he wanted his students to love them too. But of these plays had been presented on indoor stages in comfort, not like in the new Stadium.

Norman Wilkinson had designed the wooden stage in three stages so it could easily be broken up into pieces to be transported anywhere.

The Trojan Women was performed in Athens, twenty-four centuries ago as a tragedy. It did not have a plot till the professor constructed a story line. There was not a hero, so great men of the times, were presented in a contemptible light. It made these men angry, to the point of resenting the audiences that attended these plays. Some took action against the audiences who went to see the play, by throwing rocks at people in their seats.

In 1915, half the world was at war, small countries were being trampled upon by the German Race. The suffering of the Trojan Women, in the play "hit home for many of the students watching the show. The words in the story were meant to purify the soul of man. The tragedy of was sets the scene, as the God "Poseidon" mourns over the ruins of the city of Troy, as any mother in wartorn England would be doing over the loss of a son. English soldiers were dying everyday, as American students went to school in peacetime.

The actress Chrystale Herne spoke these lines, as her character, "Cassandra"

> "Would ye be wise ye cities:
> Fly from war!:
> Yet if war comes, there is a crown in death:
> For her that strweth well and perisheth:
> Unstained, to die in evil wore the stain:

After the show, the cast was invited to a small reception at the college. The Mayor shook each cast members' hand, including the Rains'. The next day the play was well recieved by the local newspapers. Claude was surprised that a few lines were even written about his performance, because he didn't have a starring role.

Lillah was the only one that was displeased with the whole affair. One reason was the New York Times' review, dated May 30, 1915. The critic wrote this about Lillah's character'." Her performance has dignity and certain heroic quality. And pageantry of woe. It is also true that the inflexibility, the formalish and the intense artificality of her delivery and her playing leaves something most earnestly to be desired in the passages, when the great humanity of the role cries out for utterrance."

After that review, Lillah wanted out of the United States, even if it meant sitting out the war in London. Granville would argue against it, but in the long run, she won out and set sail for England alone.

Claude's father had written Claude, telling him that all the theatres had been closed due to the war. Each theatre now was being used by the government to make training films, or to train new soldiers. Even filming at his studio had been stopped, because all the young men had gone to war, and there wasn't anyone to work the cameras.

He also kept track of Claude's number in the "National Registry" Nearing his call up number, Claude decided to go back to England while they could. He wanted Isabel safe, before he had to go in the army.

On the ship, Claude watched as Lady Liberty passed, Homer Saint Gaudens approached Claude saying, "She's a beauty, that one!"

"Magnificent!.. Claude sighed... just magnificent!"

"Wish I was staying." Homer sighed.

"So do I... but I'll be back one day.. I promise, Dear lady!" Claude promised.

CHAPTER 3

OFF TO THE GREAT WAR!

Granville Barker had promised Claude to speak to his friends in the English government about giving him a position with the Red Cross. Claude felt he couldn't kill anyone and he knew his boss had already been granted a job in the Red Cross. Granville had stayed in New York City, because the English government had assigned him to promote funds for the war effort. Also he didn't want to go back to his wife, but rather to stay with Helen. After the Rains' returned to London, Claude didn't hear from Barker or any government official.

With the theatres all closed for the duration of the war. Claude knew he had to find a job or enlist earlier than he expected to. He would walk from theatre to theatre, but he couldn't find a job. As he was passing the Haymarket Theatre, he spotted a tall man in a Scottish uniform. He looked grand to Claude with yards and yards of plaid cloth wrapped around his waist and one shoulder. A large silver bucket sat on his leather belt, just above the Tartan cloth. The actor in him made him stop the soldier asking, politely.

"Pardon me, but what regiment are you from?"

"Ladies from Hell!" laughed the grand looking man.

"Pardon?"

"That's our nickname, I'm in the London Scottish regiment!" the soldier said proudly.

"Where can I enlist into this regiment of yours?"

"Oh.. are you Scottish? You have to be a Scot, to be in our company.

"Thinking for a second, Claude answered. "Yes I am."

"Good laddie, I'll write down the address for you, but you have to bring the commander a letter from your relatives, that you are Scottish."

Claude's eyebrow rosed as he thought how he could do that. The soldier gave him his commander's name and recruiting address. That afternoon he went to see his father to ask if there was any Scottish blood in the family".

"I think your grandmother has a wee bit in her blood!" his father laughed. So he hurried to take a train to Kent, to ask his grandmother. She couldn't remember, but Claude made up a letter saying she was and had her sign the document. The next day he went to the recruiting office to see the commander. He showed him the letter and that he wanted to join the unit. The Scottish unit had lost so many men, that the commander just added his name to the unit for enlistment.

He trained in the local London parks, because Scotland's borders were all closed due to the war. He put down Isabel as his beneficiary and she would collect two-thirds of his pay while he was alive. The war was getting Isabel down, even though she had taken a small job at a near by hospital cleaning and washing the soldiers who had been wounded.

After three months of training. He was ordered to go to the French front. He said his goodbyes to his family and kissed Isabel, telling her not to worry. Then he was transported to a port, where he boarded a small ship that would cross the English channel.

On board were Canadians, Indians from India, Australians, and even a few Americans who had joined the English army. It was a very dark, damp night, as he pulled his large woolen coat close about his body. He was scared, just like the young boys, who were his buddies. The ship twisted and turned in the choppy waters of the Channel. It made all of the soldiers, a little sea-sick. They huddled together in fear as they neared the French coast line. Claude stayed on deck watching the coastline of France draw nearer.

"Here goes nothing." he thought to himself.

"I've had a good life, I had my dream forefilled about a career. I am married, but I had always hoped for a child to carry on my name. There youngsters haven't had any of these. There 're only babies! Suddenly his commander yelled,

"Let's go Ladies... were docking."

The Life and Times of Claude Rains

Claude could see in the early morning light, small horse drawn carts lining the road side near the coast where he had landed. They all disenbarked the ship, as Red Cross trucks made their way to the ship with wounded soldiers. His unit was ordered into the carts as the rain began to fall again. The roads were muddy, from days of rain. The driver told them they were headed to the front. He sat back in the cart and watched the sun come up over the French farmlands. Barrenness was all they could see for miles around. This Should have been the time for planting, for the French, but they had taken what ever they could, back across the front toward Paris. The overpowering smell of gunpowder and death filled the air, as they saw dead bodies lying along the roadside. One soldier asked,

"Why don't they bury those poor blokes? The answer came back. "Too many of them!"

When they reached the front, the grenadier ordered them off the carts and into a bunker. "Find a bunk." he ordered.

"How about some breakfast?" asked one of the younsters.

"If we have rations, you will get them." said the grenadier. Claude didn't the sound of that, as he found a cot, up against a damp wall of the bunker. "Well isn't this a bloody mess!" yelled one of the men.

Suddenly gunfire could be heard in the distance and they all reached for their rifles instinctively. The grenadier ordered them all out of the bunkers and into the trenches.

"Dig in Ladies, the bombs come next!" He hardly had gotten the words out of his mouth, then the shelling began. Claude hugged the earth with fear, as did the others.

He didn't think he would be facing the earth with fear as did the others. He didn't think he would be facing the battle so soon, but he was! But the grenadier ordered them to stay put, while officers on horses rode back and forth on the English side of the front, yelling out orders.

The shelling lasted for fifteen minutes, but no one was hurt in his company except for one soldier who was hit with a flying stone. This went on for months, as the Allies gained foot by foot of farmland.

The "Germans" wanted the town of "Ypres" and the "Allies" were there to protect that piece of land, with their lives.

In a month's time, the unit had come together as a fighting team. Then Claude was ordered to a detail that dug trenches that would lead passed the front line. Instead of moving on the land, the English would dig tunnels toward the German line, shoring up the earth with planks of timber, as they went. On one ocassion a few men were given passes to go to Paris for a few days, to recover from shellings. Or taxi-drivers from Paris would bring young girls to the French soldiers for some fun and relaxation. They would bring wine, cheeses and fresh bread with them, which was a treat for the soldiers.

Their corporal was very good to his "Ladies", bringing them Brandy sometimes from his trips to Paris. It was July, but the nights were always chilly from all the rain that fell.

When Claude had watched in the mornings, he could hardly see a thing for all the white fog that blanketed the land. Sometimes he thought he heard a sound or two, but it only turned out to be large crows that had survived the shellings.

On quiet nights, he could hear the men singing to keep up their spirits which he had heard in the theatre. They would sing over and over. "Maybel's got a houseboat on the Thames, River Thames, Mabel wears the most expensive gems lovely gems. A Flat you would adore it.. and nothing to pay for it. A thing that smart society condemns..." Rains would join in the serenade, as he looked at Isabel's picture on his wall. She had written him at least once a week, as did his family. She told him that she was writing a play to keep herself from going crazy and that his father had volunteered to be a block watcher.

In case of bombing he was to get his people into shelters, until the all clear was sounded.

The war had made Claude into an insomniac, because of all the shellings. He began to hear ringing in his ears from all the noise and wished for the quiet of the theatre.

Sometimes just as he was falling asleep, his corporal would yell for them to get to the walls of the trenches. He was wet all the time from the damp earth and he hated to be dirty all the time. A few German snipers had infiltrated, "No Man's Land", and were headed towards Claude's line. He hugged the dirt with his rifle ready to fire on the enemy. One of the younger Scots said. "I can't see a bloody thing in the

The Life and Times of Claude Rains

fog "Quiet!" said the corporal. But the youngster was scared and said. "Creegon Featherstone isn't frighten of these huns!"

"That's a bloody marvelous handle, Mate." another soldier whispered. Gunfire flashed to Claude's left as he heard the soldiers down the line charging the German soldiers.

They listened for the results of the battle with great interest. The flashes from the guns could be seen through the fog that was lifting. It was the French soldiers that had been ordered to charge the German line, but had been pushed back by heavy gunfire.

As the all clear sounded from his corporal, he lit a cigarette and puffed on it hard, as one of the younger soldier asked for a drag. They sat in the trenches talking about what they were going to do when they got back home. Most of the men wanted to stay in the service, because it was the only home thay had known. One finally asked what Claude was going to do when he got out of the army. "Guess I'll go back to what I was doing.... I hope!"

"And what's that old man?" asked Featherstone.

"I was an actor-manager... worked for the Haymarket Theatre." Claude said proudly"

"An actor! Can you recite anything from your plays?"

"I think I can remember my lines... would you like to hear them?"

"Yes!" they all said and sat listening to Rains put on a small performance in the trench.

Every one down the line from his group, became very quiet to listen to the actor entertain them. After that, they wouldn't leave poor Rains alone, asking to hear stories or songs from the theatre.

Rains was told by one of the soldiers that had been in the trenches for four months that Claude had missed a big battle on June 9th through the 12th. He told the new group that on the 6th, the 28th Battallion which included the 6th, Battallion and the 2nd Canadian division, had been assaulted by the Germans in their trenches. The English forward trenches were lost, but with the help from the 31st Battalion, they held the line. They needed to reach the high ground south of the Menin Road but because they had lost so many men, General Currie regrouped all his brigades into one force. The General was going to attack, with whatever he had at hand. On June 12th, the barrage lasted ten hours..

back and forth, the shells flew. That night there was a half-hour of shelling in the heavy rain.

The Canadians were sent to attack the German lines, and the Huns were knocked down.

Their trenches had been blasted out of existance. Then the Canadians won the hill. They started to dig their own trenches, which was shaped like a "T". Now the front was one hundred and fifty miles long. The Germans wanted to break through the lines so they can take Paris.

The next few weeks were spent digging new trenches towards the German lines.

Claude had blisters on top of blisters, from all the digging, with no rest and little food to eat. All he wished for was a proper bath and to sleep for a week. But things were heating up along the German lines and all leaves were canceled by the General. The German generals wanted the stalemate to come to an end at all costs, including gassing the allies.

The German soldiers were planting canisters of Clorine gas along "No Man's Land".

The smell of death filled the air which every soldier could inhale at the front. Parts of bodies were being found along a new line of defense. It was a monstrous thing for soldiers to witness. His unit was in France for five months, when rumors of a big battle was being passed down the line. On the damp night of November 17th, the first snow fell on the battlefield. It was like a dream gone bad, as ther blood and bodies were covered in pure white snow.

The Germans wanted the land back that Claude's troops had taken, around the town of Vimy. They wanted control back from the English very badly, so the Germans ordered more troops around Vimy Ridge.

Claude was in France for five months, when the weather started to turn colder. Soldiers were called upon to dig out cave-ins, to rescue trapped men under tons of earth.

Lack of oxygen killed many men in the tunnels before the troops could dig them out.

On June 25th, Rains faced his first big battle, which lasted two days. The Scottish infantry, capured forty-six German prisoners on the third day. French farmers heard about the battle and rushed to the front with buckets of wine. Claude drank too, just to forget the sight of his friends, dead on the battlefield. The boys drank a little too much, and they started to sing.

"We beat them on the Marne. We beat them on the Alsne. We gave them hell at Neuve Chapell and here we go again".

Nearly a quarter of a million shells were fired at the Germans, in just one hour on the 29th. The bombing was so loud, that people in Hemstead Heath North of London heard the bombings. At 7:28 A.M. Claude's unit charged along part of the twenty-five mile front, he carried his rifle, ammunition grenades, rations a water proof cape, four empty sandbags, plus his steel helmet. On his shoulder hung his gas mask, and a pair of goggles just in case they were gassed. He was also told to carry a water bottle, a mess tin, and his trusty shovel. Rains turned to his buddy saying.

"Now, I know, how the knights of old, felt.. fitted into theit tin suits. Running from tree to tree, he could hear, the young Scottish drummer, pounding out a beat on his drum. "Over the top"! yelled his Lieutenant. Suddenly machine guns fired in his direction, and the men fell to the ground. Claude aimed his rifle at the direction of the gunfire and pulled the trigger. After a couple of rounds, his rifle misfired! Clearing the chamber, he reloaded more bullets into the hot chamber. Claude and the others found large holes in the earth made from German shells, and they jumped in. His gun had jammed again, because it was overheated. He sat in the trench, taking his rifle apart, as he was taught to. As he reasembled the unit, he could hear the men yelling for "Medics"

His ears were ringing, and the voices seemed to have a hollow sound to them. A "Medic" jumped into his fox hole, asking,

"Did someone here call for a medic?" One soldier said, "No. the voice came from our right." As the medic jumped onto the field again. Claude wondered if he would make it. Suddenly silence came, as the German Medics went to help their soldiers, in "No-Man's Land". Claude had dug in, as they waited for orders from their commander. A few hours later, the lieutenant reported that they had lost 20,000 men, with 25,000 wounded. Claude thought it was a high price to pay, for seventy yards of earth. That night the men huddled together waiting for the next battle to begin.

They couldn't smoke so Claude, entertained himself, reciting poems he had learned with Sir Tree. Claude didn't realize it, but he was speaking aloud his poem.

"O my children!
My Father, My Mother!
O city, ruined land;
Ashes and smoke wasted;
Wilderness of War;
I live, but live as a slave; forced to a foreign land, torn westward this is death!"

"What's that from, mate? asked one of the soldiers, watching the field.

"A few lines from the play, "Hecuba". It was written in 480 B.C. That was a bloody marvelous war too." Claude said dryly.

"Guess they had their trouble too." said another soldier.

"Greek tragedies"... Claude sighed "...there's a whole slew of them. A man named Eupipides wrote them. He wrote eighty-eight plays in fact. Greek gods play a big part in all of their stories.. like Zeus, the king of gods. The play, "Trojan Women", is a good example of what war does to people!"

"You sound like a blooming teacher, Rains!" coughed another friend.

"I heard about Troy... Isn't that where they build a bloody wooden horse and the soldiers, hide in the belly of the thing!"

"That's the one! Claude said softly, rising one eye.

"Do you know that story, Rains?" asked another man.

"Oh yes.. I know it well, the story of Helen, Ion, and Rhesus". The men wanted to hear it, and Rains told the tale.

For a while, the soldiers forgot about where they were as they listened to Claude.

Snow began to fall toward morning, on "No Man's Land" Suddenly from a post forty feet in front of them, they heard.. "GAS! GAS!" All the men took out their gas masks, and soaked the padding with water, as they waited for orders. Within seconds, their Captain ordered them to fall back to English lines. Claude's hands shook, as he and others ran from the trench. The green cloud of "Chlorine" gas cross "No Man's

Land". Claude couldn't get his goggles on, as he finally dropped them to the ground along with half of his gear hooked onto his belt. He ran as hard as he could, back to friendly lines, but couldn't make it, falling head first into the snow. His lungs burned, and he couldn't catch his breath, as he fell unconscious on the ground. It would take two hours for the "Medics" to find him, still unconscious. He would stay that way, as Medics, washed out his eyes, put him in a Red Cross truck and finally shipped him over to England, with the other survivors of the great battle.

In England, he was taken to the nearest hospital, where his family was notified of his condition. His doctors told Isabel and the family that his lungs, throat and eyes had been burned by the gas. One eye was very bad and the doctors didn't give much chance for it to have sight returned to it. The doctor reported. "If our new invention the Mark tank, hadn't pushed back the Germans, many soldiers would be dead."

Claude was unconscious for a week and when he slowly came back to the living, he couldn't see out his right eye, couldn't speak and his lungs still hurt. Isabel couldn't stand the thought of him being blind but she tried to be strong about it. It took him two months before he tried to talk, then he couldn't recognize his own voice. It was lower, harsh and he felt like half a man. He was decorated for valor and given a wartime commission. When his voice returned to him, he was asked by his captain, if he wanted to go to Officers Trainning School. Claude agreed and for the next few years went to school to become an officer. He figured only the service wanted him with one good eye, He felt he couldn't go back to the stage with the handicap. It made his life a misery. He couldn't sleep at night. Soon his actions got on Isabel's nerves, so they decided to a parting of the waves.

By 1918, Rains had finished his training, with the rank of Lieutenant. But he still had nightmares about the war. He would stay up all night just watching the sky. By February of 1919, he was promoted to Captain. With the war at an end. England wanted to rebuild the Australian Army, So Claude volunteered to go back to that beautiful country, and try to forget the war. The thought of the Canadian soldiers, who had held the line, while all the other troops were called back to English protected lines gave him a chill, every time he thought about it.

Carmella Felice

The theatres had opened up by the beginning of 1919, Claude felt the need to walk past the theatre again before he left for Australia. He knew his blindness would stop him from being an actor, but he wanted to smell the air of the theatres, once more, As he passed the Lyceum Theatre, he saw an old pal of his coming out the front doors. He yelled to him and the two hugged in the streets, happy to see each had survived the war. His friend talked him into the theatre to read for the role of Mears, in "Uncle Ned." Claude insisted his voice had changed and he didn't think he could carry his voice to the back of the theatre. But his friend insisted even more, "That voice is wonderful!" So he read for the part and the director hired him on the spot. Then he had to go back to his Commander and pull the transfer and put in for a discharge. His Commander said he could have his papers in a couple of months but in the meantime, he could have a leave from the army to perform in the play.

Rains took a flat at the "Eventic Club" on Ryder Street in Saint James South West. He felt blessed to be alive and acting again. What the directors didn't know about his blindness, wouldn't bother them. He would have to live with the condition. He didn't want anyone feeling sorry for him. By the time another play called "Reparation" opened on September 28th, 1919, he had been legally separated from the Army retaining the title of Captain. He opened to a packed house and even Sir Herbert Tree came to see the play. It was a Russian musical, filled with gay Gypsy songs, written by Norman O'Neil and Alfred Kalisch. It gave the audience the feeling of gaiety, which they needed so much after the World War. The English people wanted to laugh again and the actors were ready and willing to fill the bill.

That night Sir Tree came back stage to see his old pupil, to tell him how wonderful his voice was. That was the greatest compliment that Claude could hear from his old teacher.

CHAPTER 4

CAN I, START AGAIN?

In 1920, Rains was out of the service, working as a stage manager at the St. James Theatre. He had a place an invisible shield around himself because of his shyness. He created a persona of a dashing and charming man, just like he would have made-up a role in play. His real hurts were buried deep inside his mind. His poor eyesight in his right eye, didn't help his ego any. But the way he carried himself made people think, he was in control at all times. It worked so well, he was offered the role of "Casca", in Shakespere's "Julius Caesar".

Within a month's time of starting the play, he met a young actress, by the name of Marie Foster Hemingway. She was a promising young actress, who had a small part in one of his plays. He was thirty-one years old and she was twenty-seven. She had an overly protective father, Harry Hemingway, a man of independant means. Harry didn't like the idea of his daughter being an actress, or even dating an actor. But the beautiful young girl, with long silky brown hair, and oval brown eyes, fell inlove with Claude the first time she saw him. She stood two inches shorter than he, which was to his liking, and she seemed to be a good luck charm for his career.

Now a full time actor, traveling around the countryside of England, he couldn't keep his manager's job. The cut in pay wasn't much, but he still didn't like to have idle time on his hands. After a wonderful year on the stage, he married Marie on December 14th, 1920. Both Fathers and Marie's mother, Emma, accompanied the couple to the General Register Office, to sign the papers of their marriage.

A few months later, the London Times reported, that George Bernard Shaw, had purchased two buildings on Gower Street where he was going to build an acting school. Shaw had gotten a bunch of investors together, to start the Royal Academy of Dramatic Arts. Shaw was looking for a couple of good teachers to apply for teaching positions. After talking it over with Marie, they decided it was worth the tryout for one of the teaching positions.

As he approached the still under construction site, he felt it was the right thing to do to supplement his salary now that he was married again. Except for the two long concrete statues on either side of the doorway, it seemed like any other building on the street.

He had called for an appointment to see the Principle J. H. Barnes. It was wintertime and Claude had on his tweed overcoat, hat and silk scarf, wrapped tightly around his neck as he entered the office of the Principle Barnes. To his surprise, G. B. Shaw was seated in a chair in Barne's office.

"Mr. Rains.. This is a real pleasure to meet you, I've heard so much about you from Mr.. Shaw."

"How long has it been Mr. Rains?..1915.. the American tour?

"Shaw said smiling.

"Yes Sir, ..the American tour. Claude said removing his overcoat and taken a seat.

The three men stared at each other for a couple of seconds, before Shaw asked "What have you been doing with yourself of late? "I've just finished Louis Venevil's "Daniel at the St. James Theatre."

"Oh yes, C. Aubrey Smith is in this one!" Barnes injected.

"And your role.. Mr.. Rains?" Shaw asked.

"Daniel Renault. would you like to see a recent London Times critics report of my role?" Claude said taking a small piece of paper out of his jacket's pocket. He unfolded and gave it to Barnes, who read it out loud. "Rains was a brilliant success as a corpse-like invalid. He made a haunting thing of it-an utter wreck, but a picturesque, romantic wreck, a choice curio shattered the irretrievable ruin on something comely and precious.

"That's quite a mouthful of compliments." Shaw said pulling on his beard.

"I'm opening in March with Guy Bolton's "Polly with a Past". Rains smiled.

"That's wonderful.... you have come far since 1915, my boy! I understand you were in the service, during the war. You were gassed?"

"That's correct.... changed my voice as you can hear, Mr. Shaw."

"For the better.... my boy. Have you seen Mr. Barker, since your return?"

Claude winced and said, No".

"I haven't spoken to the "cad", since he divorced his wonderful wife".

"I haven't seen him neither. I think he's still in America". Shaw changed the subject which was depressing to him. "So you want to teach here?

"Yes. I quit my managers' job, so I could pay full attention to my acting career. I'm married and I could use the extra money."

"That's no problem, Mr Rains." Shaw said quickly.... you have a rich theatre background with Mr. Tree. And I'm sure Mr. Barnes agrees you will be an asset to my school.

So Rains was given a one year contract to teach an acting course at R. A. D. A.

His classes were given between the hours of 9 A.M to Noon. When he wasn't in a play he could put in more hours with the school. His old teacher Tree was quoted in the newspapers as saying this about Shaw's school: "The better part of the art of acting cannot be directly taught, but certain of its constituent elements can and ought to be!".

When the school was opened, Rains was given a classroom on the first floor. He had all the females hovering over him because he was a handsome prominent stage actor. This made for aguments with his new wife, who visited the school. Then there was the penny-pinching that Marie had to put up with from her husband? Her father had given Marie everything she wanted, which Claude couldn't match! Soon it got on both their nerves and after a year of marriage, the two decided to divorce.

"Polly with a Past" and "Legion Of Honor" were his next success. These were followed by a good part in "William Shakespeare" in the role of "Kit Marlowe", at the Globe Theatre. Hundreds of years before the "New Globe Theatre" was built, Shakespere used to have his plays at the "Old Globe Theatre". In the 1700's, an actor had to have a license to perform in the theatre, along the countrysides of Old England. The taxes were high for actors, because the King didn't want commoners to be entertained.

That was reserved for the rich in castles. Shakespere was the people's playwright who put on plays within the city's limits.

Claude's new play was about William Shakespeare's love-life. Shakesphere was married to Anne Hathway but was in love with another woman who he called the "Dark Lady of the Sonnets". Miss Moyna Margill, an Irish actress, played Shakespere's wife.

His girl friend was portrayed by Mary Care. Rains held the audiences spelled bounded by his role of "Kit Marlowe," Shakespeare's best friend. When the playright tells his girlfriend he wouldn't divorce his wife, she takes up with Kit. Will becomes very jealous of his girlfriend's affair! One night, he follows her to where she is meeting Kit. Will breaks into their room, and finds Kit on the bed with his love. Kit draws his dagger to protect himself from the enraged Will Shakespeare. As they fight for the dagger, Will throws Kit to the floor, where he falls, on the knife.. dead! In real life Shakespeare never killed Kit, but for drama, Dane played it that way.

The script by Clemence Dane was intriguing to London's theatre-goers. To watch Shakespeare's life unfold before their very eyes, was enchanting. In every performance, Rains steals the last scene, as he lies dying at the hands of Shakespeare. The production had a long run at the Shafesburg Theatre. The London Times decribed the play as a "Mighty pretty entertainment, making free with great names. It makes a claim to be historically true, but it suggested the experiences which went to the developement of Shakespeare's genius. Rains's silky voice made women cry for him, when he dies in the last scene!"

A couple of weeks into the play a deadly outbreak of influenza gripped London. The R.A.D.A. closed it's doors, so the flu wouldn't spread to the students.

At the height of the "sickness", he was still working as "Kit". One night in a heavy downpour, only fifty people showed up at the theatre.

As Clemence Dane peered out the hole in the stage curtain, he knew the show had to go on, for the brave souls who had braved the storm with influenza.

Short men tend to have quarrelsome or biligerent qualities, that's why they make excellent fanatics like "Napoleon"! Rains brought this enthusiam for life into his portrayal of "Kit". This slight notch in his personality lead Claude to a near-riot that night.

As "Kit", he had the romantic lead. Weighing only 120 pounds he was to pick up the leading lady in a fit of passion and carry her to a nearby couch.

Claude braced himself to lift the portly 150 pounds of lovely lady. He staggered under her weight. A smart-alec in the theatre groaned "Oh No"; he's going to drop her!"

Rains tried again to lift the girl but failed as the crowd, in the balcony moaned "That's the boy, lift'er up!"

Sweat poured out from every pore as he came at the actress for another go at it. From the theatre goer's came a yell. "Pick her up!"

Claude turned to the crowd and said in a loud roar! "Come on down and lift her up yourself!

Then he rolled up his sleeves... The expression on his face was violent. So much so, it frightened the crowd into silence.

The actress got to her feet as Claude walked slowly towards her, but now she was showing her irish temper staring him down! As he reached her she smacked our hero across the face and walked off "Stage Right"!

When the last curtain came down, Clemence had decided he didn't want the people to go home unhappy, so he took his bow and announced, "If you wish to stay awhile our artists will sign your programs.

Claude was besides himself at Clemence's announcements. He didn't know if the leading lady would ever speak to him after the proceedings on the stage. His face was still burning from the slap when Dane came over to him.

Please Claude, he pleaded, don't mess this up for me. I'll have Miss Margill on my side of the stage. You go over to stage left with Mary Rorke, Phillip Merivale and Arthur.

Claude agreed for the sake of the play having a long run.

As he took to his side of the stage's staircase, he noticed a few women carrying flowers.

Suddenly a tiny young woman came up the aisle towards him. She had blonde hair that was turned up in curls on the top of her head. Her green eyes twinkled like two shining marbles. Giving him a big smile, she said softly.

I thought you were a brute tonight! But I am still your fan. Her voice was like a shy little whisper to his ears

thank you Miss?

"Beatrix Thompson" she replied handing him her program book. He couldn't take his eyes off the pretty woman. As he handed the program, back to Beatrix, she said.

"I'm hoping to be an actress someday. I was thinking about going to the new acting school!".

"I'll teach there... I hope to see you there, if you are serious about acting.

"I am... I cried when you died in the play.... you were brillant in that scene".

"So they say. he laughed.

"You were very good in that scene!" came a voice behind Beatrix, who was getting impatient at being kept so long.

"See.. I'm not alone in my opinion of myself." Claude laughed. He watched the girl walk up the aisle, as he took the next person's program to sign.

A few months later, he was about to start a new season at R.A.D.A. He had put on his best tweed jacket, with a pair of grey pants, and shinned his black shoes to a high gleam. His boss had told him he would have a few more students, with the start of the new term. His class had been increased to eighteen men, and six women. Arriving early in his classroom, he moved the chairs into a semicircle in front of his desk. The room had large windows, that let in the bright sunlight. Soon his students marched into his room. One of the students was Beatrix Thompson.

"Miss Beatrix Thomson I believe?" He smiled.

"You have a good memory, Mr.. Rains." she smiled.

"I didn't think I'd be seeing you so soon."

"I was attending the university, but they didn't have a good course in acting. So I auditioned here."

"You must have impressed the board, if they gave you a seat in my classroom. He said dryly.

"I guess it was significant enough to rate a chair, in this school." she smiled. "I should say so, The founders of this institution are very particular about their students. Each pupil will play a major role in creating a name for this place especially in Mr. Shaw's mind.

"Then I guess it was my writing ability that impressed the great playwright!" she smiled.

"Well.. well.. you can write too!. I might need that talent when we have our plays at the school's theatre."

"Any time, Mr. Rains." Beatrix smiled and took a seat in his classroom. This new term would bring a new problem child to his class, by the name of Mrs. Molly Thompkins.

She was an American heiress, that had befriended G.B. Shaw. Molly wanted to be an actress, so Shaw enlisted her in his school, without an audition. He than told Barnes, to put her in Rains' class, because Claude had patience, to handle the wildcat. But Shaw really didn't know Claude, because the actor took an instant dislike to Molly.

The dark haired, dark-eyed heiress thought she knew everything. Claude had a bad habit in that if he didn't like you, he didn't pay you any attention. No eye contact and very little to say to the woman. Molly was selfish, spoiled and she started trouble at the drop of a pin. She hated Claude, because she wasn't the center of his universe. Rains had a bigger ego than Molly's and they clashed almost every day about her acting ability.

Mr. Lawrence Thompkins was just as bad as his wife. He was preoccupied with designing a "Shavian Theatre" on whose Romaneque facade, he planned to carve in stone the story of Shaw's creative evolution. The Thompkins' had decided that Shaw was a religion, a prophet, a social philosophy all wrapped up in one shiny package! Passing Molly through the doors of the school just added to their love for Shaw. When G. B. was in town, the trio would take in a play, than have dinner at the Thompkins' lavish flat.

There she would tell insulting stories about Rains and Principle Barnes, saying, "They used their positions of trust to capture some poor actress into their lires," which was far from the truth and Shaw knew it. The stories magnified at the school until Claude heard about them from one of his students. He went to his boss wanting to quit his job. "But Barnes talked him out of it saying, "If you leave, it will only

Carmella Felice

reinforce the lies" So Claude withdrew his resignation. In December he was chosen by the board to direct a Christmas play. It was a three act story, acted by all of his students. He told his pupils to make their own costumes for the contemporary play. His pupils worked hard, painting sets, rehearsing lines and selling tickets. Two hundred tickets were sold to relatives and friends and the money would go to the school's schloastic fund.

Nervously Rains paced the stage floor, preparing the lighting, by the foot lights. Beatrix was in the play just a short while, than she took over in the cafeteria, serving tea and cookies. Lord Dunsany, a ticket holder, came backstage before the performance to wish Rains "Good Luck ". He talked to Claude for a while about going to his estate. "Meath, in Ireland, for some fishing and hunting". Rains agreed that he needed a vacation so he agreed to go to his estate for a few days. The latest pulp magazine phenomenon had asked, "Who was the best new writer in England? Lord Dunsany, Blackwood or Machen?" For Rains it would be Dunsany. He loved to read his supernatural tales of horror and ghosts. While working on the playwright, he had seen Dunsany flip through a bible to find his stories. Dunsany had lived through two wars and felt that life was a gamble, filled with second chances. So did Rains.

At 7 p.m., the music started playing, as the last of the guests, took their seats. As the play progressed, everyone performed very well. When the last curtain dropped, a large applause flooded the small theatre. Then the crowd retired to the school's cafeteria where Beatrix was serving tea and coffee. Dressed first, Molly almost ran to be seated with Shaw, Barnes and Lord Dunsany, Rains was the last to enter the large room.

Spotting Molly seated with Shaw, he walked in the opposite direction, where Beatrix was serving at the counter.

"What'll be?" Beatrix asked in an Irish accent.

"Coffee me dea!" He replied in like.

Staring at Shaw's table, he lit a cigarette. Beatrix handed him a cup filled with coffee saying. "Looks like "Ducks" over there is pushing for an acting position with Lord Dunsany."

"Now. now, Miss Thomson.. we must not fault Molly so long as she doesn't fancy coming over here.. I am happy."

"She is a pompous, persistent, primative..." Beatrix's tongue twisted with "P's".

Claude laughed for a while, than said. "I say you do have your "P's" down pat, my girl."

"Wish I was." whispered Beatrix.

"What's that Miss Thomson.... It's so noisy in here?"

"Nothing sir. She said shyly. "Then Lord Dunsany headed towards the counter saying,

"Rains old fellar.. why is it, I always find you in the company of beautiful woman?

"My charm sir?" Rains smiled.

"You are a cad! turning to Beatrix he asked for another cup of tea. He continued to talk to Claude as Beatrix poured the tea into a new cup.

"Is she one of your students?" he asked Claude.

"Yes, she was in the first act. She is one of our best at the school." Beatrix heard her teacher compliment her and a tear came to her eye.

"Here you are Lord Dunsany," Beatrix said giving him his tea.

"How would you like to audition for my new play?

Beatrix couldn't say a word but Claude answered for her.

"You bet she would!"

"Good! Here is my card. How about Friday afternoon at three?" Beatrix just stared at Lord Dunsany, as Rains answered again for his student.

"Yes she'll be there!"

"Now listen here Claude, you can't take her test for her too!"

"Yes, yes I'm sorry sir, yes, thank you very much." she finally replied happily.

The next day before classes, Barnes told Claude. "That Mrs. Thompkins, didn't stop trying to to get our guests, to hire her. She knows I make these decisions by seniority!" Rains thought "I have to tell him about Beatrix." So he said,

"Lord Dunsany asked Miss Thomson to test for him Friday."

"That is wonderful; she was my next choice to give a "part" to. Barnes was happy with Beatrix getting the role, but Molly did cause a fuss, when she heard about the offer. Now, she really had it in for Rains and Barnes as she lied about how Beatrix obtained the part. "If she wasn't Rains girlfriend, I would have gotten the role!"

Claude went to Barnes again about Molly's lies so he called the woman into his office saying, "Do you have proof of those accusations you are making of Mr. Rains?

"No"! She huffed.

"Then as they say in your country, a person is innocent until proven guilty. So please hold your tongue in these matters!" For a while, Molly held her tongue, but she started writing letters to Shaw, condemning the men. Shaw wrote back "Molly you are being too melodramatic!".

Shaw had suggested to Molly that she study "Phonetics" because he didn't think her American accent would be excepted by the English people. He told her to go see a friend of his at the London University. His name was Professor Jones and he had helped many other students from the school with their speech problems. After two weeks of studying under the professor, she quit, saying she didn't have the time to spare. A month later Professor Jones wrote to Barnes asking where Mrs. Thompkins had gotten to, He called Molly to his office and asked her "Why haven't you been attending your "Phonetics" class at the university? I have a child to take care of, when I'm not at this school. I can't take anymore time away from my child, because someone says I can't talk well enough to their liking. Besides the professor has a Welch accent and he's trying to teach me diction lessons."

Shaw found out about her not going to her classes and wrote her a letter saying:

"Molly Thompkins, Molly Thompkins! They lay all your sins on my shoulders and when you behave like, "Sarah of Red Gutch", instead of the distinguished Mrs. Lawrence Thompkins, with a patient University College English accent. They come to me and ask me desperately. "What they are to do with you?". The letter went on asking Molly to behave herself. Molly knew her mentor's patience was wearing thin. But it didn't stop Molly from spreading lies about Rains. She claimed favoritism in Claude's class, which infuriated the actor. Again he went to Barnes, asking to be set free from his contract, because of Mrs.. Thompkins. But Barnes told him to stay. That he couldn't run away from the problem, but had to face it!" Rains calmed down and returned to his class the next day. Shaw called Barnes, to see what the problem was with Rains. He told the author, it's not Rains' fault that the woman dislikes him. He's just charismatic and he is a wonderful teacher. Molly must stop her lies!"

Shaw wrote to Molly again, "Sarah of Red Gutch. If you must make rows with Mr.. Barnes and Mr.. Rains, for Heavens sake, make them as rowdy as possible, give them some tragic acting. Call them names, especially their Christian names. Accuse them of impossible crimes and then fall weeping convulsively upon their chests. Do anything rather than oddly polite, and insolent. But if I tell you to do these things there is a horrible danger of you literally trying to do them, and I don't think you can act well enough yet to make a success of it. But if you deliberately tell Mr.. Rains' principal in his presence that his preference for more amiable students has a corrupt motive, which is the very worst thing you can suggest of a teacher." Mrs.. Thompkins knew she couldn't count on Shaw's protection any longer. She wanted to leave Gower Street School, but in her own way. It was almost the end of the term and Molly knew that Barnes would pick a few senior students to play in "Summer Stock". She found out a position had opened up with the Plymouth Repretory Theatre. Before Barnes had a chance to send one of his seniors up for an interview, Molly got on a train for the country. She met with with Michael King, who was head of production.

She was signed to a three month contract without an audition because she mentioned Shaw too. With Molly gone for a week, Claude's class was a happier place, but he wondered where she had gotten to. One day, Barnes called him into his office. The principal was redfaced and flabbergasted, saying.... "Do you know what that woman did?" What woman, Mr. Barnes?" Claude asked.

"Mrs. Thompkins.. that's who!" he yelled at the top of his voice.

"What.... what, did she do? Rains winced.

"She went over to my friend Michael King and told him I had sent her for a job!"

Claude giggled saying, "What did he say?"

"He wanted to know why I sent him an actress that couldn't act!"

"Well, look at it this way. Claude laughed... she is out of our hair!" Which made Barnes look at the situation in a new light.

Molly lasted out her three month contract, then never acted again. After her husband finished his work for Shaw, the couple and their son

Carmella Felice

returned to America, never to be heard from again. But Shaw a true friend that he was, wrote to the Thompkins for twenty years after their visit to England. Molly wrote letters to Shaw, but upon her death, all the letters were destroyed.

The next term found Rains teaching a new group of hopefuls, included in the class was lovely Beatrix. After a couple of months, Claude was asked to direct another play called, "The Rumour", which he had performed at the Globe Theatre.

It became a habit with Rains, to have breakfast in the cafeteria of the school. "Henney" a good natured cook, who worked for the R.A.D.A. was Henney was a heavyset woman with grey hair, and steel black eyes. She loved Mr. Rains, who would give her free tickets to all his plays. Henney knew that Beatrix was in love with Claude, but he was disappointed by romance and marriage. So he kept his distance as a teacher. His students knew his habit of having breakfast at the school, where lovestruck girls like Bea would eyeball Claude.

Beatrix's heart pounded as she sat in her corner table, watching her mentor reading his newspaper, as "Henney" the cafeteria's cook, walked over to the handsome teacher.

"Hi Ducks"! came the familiar greeting from Henney... Want a toasted muffin this morning? It's very fresh, very tasty! And you need some meat on those bones of yours." Rains smiled from ear to ear as he put down his paper, saying, "That sounds good to me! Thank you.. and a cup of coffee."

"Now that's the spirit, duckie. Now you can go back to reading your paper and I'll bring you over a tray."

The jolly lady wiped her hands on a towel and set up a tray for her favorite teacher. A few minutes later, she delivered the tray to his table, as Beatrix rose to go to class. She looked over toward him, as he took a bite out of the muffin, with an interest. Continuing her conversation with Rains, Henney asked, "My Paulie enjoyed your last play. When are you having another one?"

"I'm working on that now. I just have to figure out which student plays what part?"

"What about the big boy?"

"Who? Oh you mean John Gielgud. He's going to be a fine actor, if I can get his feet to move properly on stage!" he said, taking a bite out of his muffin.

"Why don't you drill him? My Paulie said he had two left feet, until the army taught him how to march."

"That's a very good idea, Henney. That might work." Claude said, taking a sip of his coffee.

Twenty minutes later, he was in his classroom, surrounded by his students. Gielgud looked uncomfortable, seated in one of the narrow wooden chairs. Beatrix was seated at her desk, reading a book. Rains had some booklets from the National Theatre, showing how the "Fee System" worked in England.

With vitality and enthusiasm, he started to read the first page in the booklet. When he had read a couple of pages he began his lesson.

"The "Fee System", has been with us for a very long time. Every player has to cope, with this system, if they are to act in a theatre."

"It's not a fair system.. is it Mr. Rains?" came a question from one of the students.

"I speak for myself, when I say I don't like it but this is the way the theatre is run."

"Do we have to join it?" came another question.

"Yes.. Mr. Shaw wants the "National Theatre", to have first claim on some of you students who win schlorships. They will get three month contracts, in a local theatre.

Now you must learn how this system works. You will probably start at the lowest salary which is twenty-two pounds a performance. Do not settle for anything else! You have to be extremely good to survive as an actor. Artists like Sir Herbert Beerbaum Tree, Lillah McCarthy and Miss Terry have achieved the highest pay scale to date. I'll give an example of this world you want to enter. Miss Terry who was paid forty-five pounds a performance, had to buy her own wardrobe which cost her eighty-five pounds, which didn't include the cleaning bills. Some bills exceeded her pay check. The actor is left in a doldrum, as some of those bills pour in for wig cleaning. shoe-shinning and sometimes food." Standing he walked around the room, as he continued his speech. "For example a good actress can command nine hundred pounds for three weeks of work. That is nine performances a week, at the age of thirty.

That same actress would know that at the age of fifty, she would only earn one-third of that figure. So at the first sign of her salary going down by fifty pounds, the actress would leave the theatre.

"Now you take me" he smiled. "After working, for three years, I have tenure. I have established a good reputation.. I hope." he said boldly.. as the class laughed. "I have tenure enough to decline a role which I haven't to date. I cannot be dismissed from the theatre unless.... er.... unless their is a very good reason to do so. The National Theatre, doesn't want their repertory companies to became stale, so they try to keep everyone on their toes. I can now join two repretory companies, because of my tenure. I have the priviledges of a pension. So as long as the roles keep coming, the higher your paid will raise.

"Now producers and directors wanted to stay on good terms with each other, so they allow some players the freedom of taking roles, outside of their corporation. I have had the good fortune in the past few years, to be able to work for a couple of theatres. Now the R.A.D.A. would prefer to have their pupils first go to a college or the University of London to obtain literary instruction first. But I taught myself by reading all the books I could get my hands on. It is impractical to go to the University at the same time you are attending this school. After the Great War, there was a demand for players, because most actors had been killed in battles. If you have to learn your craft from the ground up. then do so," he completed his talk.

"Do you think this is a good system, Mr. Rains?"

"No... but we have to live with it as long as no one objects to it."

"Do you think an actress can become a star under this system?" Beatrix asked loudly

"Yes.. if the popularity is there for the actress."

"Claude said walking around the room with his hands in his jacket pockets.

As his lecture came to an end, he gave them a reading lesson. At the end of the reading, he advised his pupils that they had been chosen to put on the school's play and he had picked the play, "Reparation". Tomorrow we will talk about all the parts and who will act them. Rains built all the scenery, with the help of his pupils. He talked the shy Gielgud into playing the role of "Fedya", to his "Ainey" role. At rehearsals he notice John was having trouble moving his feet on stage.

He thought about Henney's suggestion, about marching Gielgud so that he could control his legs. John said he would try it, and allowed Rains to march him around the stage for fifteen minutes a day. Soon, John was in control of his movements on stage.

Claude's students made their own costumes, from odds and ends they found around their homes. Gypsy dresses were called for in the story, old hats and colorful shirts mostly borrowed from their parent's closets. He asked Beatrix to do some re-writing for him, because she had a flare for keeping things simple. Not that Rains wanted to change the writings of "Tolstoy", but rather to keep the flow in the wordings, which made it simpler to memorize.

It was a cold night in December when the play was presented to an audience. Nervously Rains paced the stage, peering out pass the curtain ocassionally. As he looked through the part in the curtain a few minutes before curtain time, He noticed a familiar face seated in the front row, Claude gasped, just as John passed in back of him. Rains turned and gasped! "My God"!

"What's the matter?" John asked.

"Do you know who is out front, sitting in the first row? Claude asked wildly.

"Who sir? May I look?" John asked as he parted the curtain slightly.

"See that older woman in the front row, dressed in the red silk dress?"

"Yes sir. It's my grandmother.... she bought a few tickets" John smiled replacing the curtain. Rains was stunned by his words.. "Your grandmother is Miss Kate Terry?"

"Yes, you see Mr.. Rains, the family wasn't too keen on my love for the theatre. But I've been staging my own plays, ever since my father bought me a toy stage."

I use to put on stories with my little puppets, to entertain the family!"

"I was wondering where you had inherited your flare for acting!" Claude said raising one eyebrow.

"I wanted to do this on my own sir, that's why I didn't tell anyone at the school about my grandmother." Claude shook his head in disbelief saying, "I've been marching Terry's grandson like a soldier in my regiment!.. Well let's go then, and show your grandmother what you have learned here."

Rains gave the signal for the house lights to be lowered, as the musicians started to play, "Hail to the King". At the end of the play, a healthy roar applauded the youngsters. Family members were delighted with their children's abilities as the cast take their bow. A cheer went up, that sent a chill down Claude's back.

After cleaning up their make-up, teacher and students made their way to the cafeteria where John introduced his uncle and grandmother to Rains. Kissing Miss Terry's hand, with all the pomp and ceremony of a Knight embracing his Queen. Claude smiled at the great actress. The retired actress said softly, "I've heard very good things about you from Johnny."

"He's one of our best teachers, Miss Terry!" Shaw said, smiling at Rains. John kissed his grandmother on the cheek and asked, "How did you like the play?. It was better than those puppet shows you put on for me when you were ten!" She laughed as Claude said proudly. "He's my best student!"

"Oh I can see you are a real charmer too Mr. Rains. I thought your performance was quite thrilling. It reminded me of another great actor Herbert Tree. Do you know him?"

"He was my teacher when I worked at His Majesty's Theatre. There I saw you perform many times with him." Claude smiled proudly. Well, I'll be.... yes, I remember you well. You had a sweet cockney accent!"

"Yes I did. It's sweet of you to remember me!"

"My, my, you have changed for the better! How is Herbert?" she asked.

"He came to the school a way back to speak to my students. He is fine!"

"I never forgot you Miss Terry. You will always be a favorite with me." Claude replied softly. "See grandmother, you are the youngest person I know!" John said quickly.

"He's a good boy, Mr. Rains, and a good actor, that I can see. I'm glad he has you for a friend!"

"He has an inbred talent for acting. It's his feet I worry about! I had him marching for weeks, just so he could make his turns easily on stage." Claude laughed.

"That's clever of you. John had a touch of rickets as a child. I'm surprised he grew so tall! He didn't get that from me." Terry laughed.

Suddenly, from across the large room, a heavy-set man, with salt and pepper hair, rushed over to the table yelling. "John old man... I didn't think you had it in you. You were wonderful tonight!"

"Nigel, I didn't think you made the show!" John said, hugging the man.

"I wouldn't miss it for the world John.... and Miss Terry, you are looking lovely as ever.

The man said kissing the actress on the cheek. "Mr. Nigel Playfair, this is my teacher Mr. Rains.". Playfair said aggressively." I realy enjoyed both of your performances. I got here a little late, and stood in the back of the theatre, intrigued by all the performances. Especially yours Mr. Rains.... In fact I'm starting a new production called, "The Insect Play".

"The insect Play! Nigel, that title takes the cake!" Miss Terry laughed.

"Miss Terry, please don't mention cake around insects", Nigel grinned from ear to ear, as his friends laughed.

"What's the play about, Nigel?" John wanted to know.

"It's about insects that have human problems, just like you and me. Like the beetle is a drunk, in the storyline, I was thinking you could play the butterfly, because you were so graceful in the play tonight!"

"Butterfly!... what is the theatre coming to!" Miss Terry huffed at the suggestion that her grandson play the butterfly.

"That's a flighty part, John" Rains injected, which made the other laugh.

"And I want you for a couple of roles, Mr. Rains, including playing the Beetle.

"A Beetle? How does one play a beetle?"

"The same way he plays a butterfly!" John injected.

"This sounds very interesting, Claude. I would love to see that!" Shaw said dryly.

Rains eyebrow lifted with Shaw's remark, as he said. "It sounds like fun. If you want to do it John? I'm in!"

"That's wonderful. Now I need a few more of your students to play the other parts." Nigel said.

"I have a few students that might suit your needs. In fact, they were in the play tonight. Charles Laughton and Elsa Lanchester. They are sitting over there in the corner." Barnes pointed, to the couple.

"Oh yes.... I enjoyed Miss Lanchester, very much." Nigel smiled, as he watched the couple.

"Laughton is one of my pupils too. He is a fantastic actor, but a little hard to direct! Tell him to create a character and he gets straight to it. But tell him his character has faults and he thinks you are underminding him." Rains said quickly.

"Yes, Dorothy Green thinks he will be a fine actor one day. We were impressed by his credits. After the war, he returned to his parent's hotel where he worked for a while, before he joined the "Scarborough" players. Barnes said softly.

"His parent's are well off then?" Nigel asked.

"I don't know about that. But thay have owned the Victorian Hotel in Scarborough for a long while." Barnes informed the producer.

"I've been to that Little Inn, several times, when I worked in summer stock," injected Miss Terry.

"He has two brothers, Tom and Frank, who now run ther hotel. He played "Sir William Gower" in Trelowey of the Wells. He recieved very good reviews by the Scarborough Press. But he is a very nervous man. I think the war caused that condition, of which I am well aware of! But he is a fine actor!". Rains injected quickly.

"If you say so, Mr. Rains. I'll take him, too! May I meet the both of them now?" Playfair asked.

"I'll go fetch them, Nigel." John said as he rushed off to talk to his classmates. The group watched as John told the pair to come over to his table as Elsa jumped up almost two feet, when John told her, while Charles just sat, drinking his tea, cool and collective. Elsa pushed him out of his seat, almost spilling his tea all over him and pulled him over to Shaw's table.

"Here they are, sir! Miss Lanchester and Mr. Laughton, my friends."

Nigel interrupted with, "And I am Nigel Playfair and I would like to hire the both of you for my new play." Elsa was ecstatic to meet, Miss Terry and Playfair then she kissed every one at the table, including Mr. Shaw.

The Life and Times of Claude Rains

"Good! Now that we agree, we will set up some contracts with Mr. Barnes, to play at the "Old Vic". Elsa's flaming red hair, flew in the air with excitement. Her high pitched voice sounded throughout the large cafeteria.

The next day Rain's class, found out about their classmates good fortune and begged for roles, in the "Insect Play". Nigel agreed to have some of the class to be stand ins, to gain experience. The whole group started rehearsals, a couple of weeks later, while Claude still held classes at R.A.D.A. John couldn't get the hang of playing the butterfly.

Dressed in white silk Leotards, he had to contend with two narrow sticks attached to his arms, where his wings were attached. Elsa also had her troubles, starting her career as a ladybug! While John kept tripping over his wings, Elsa's wings gave her trouble too!

The director was a very handsome man, six feet tall, with black hair and eyes, by the name of James Whale. Jimmy had collaborated with Playfair before, as an actor in one of his productions. Now he had to direct, half of Claude Rains's class. He did it with fun and humor, that endeared him, even to Charles Laughton, Rains and Whale, became fast friends, because they both liked the beautiful, brilliant, dress designer, Doris Zinheisen. She had designed all of the sets and the clothing the actors were to wear. Jimmy had won the girl's heart, to Claude's great disappointment. Rains would joke with her. "Are you sure, Jimmy is the man for you?"

The romance between Jimmy and Doris became the talk of the production company Rains could see that Doris loved Jimmy very much. Why shouldn't she? He was charming soft-spoken, mild mannered, and was very humorous. But a few weeks later, as the play was about to close. Doris came to Rains crying. "What is the matter? Doris" Claude asked.

James broke up with me! Doris cried

"Why"? he asked shocked.

"He told me he was kidding himself, that he could be happy with me, because he had pondered his life style, coming to the conclusion he was a homosexual. Doris left the company a couple of days later bewildered. Rains could see that Jimmy was upset by her departure, but he wouldn't talk to anyone about it.

Carmella Felice

Playfair decided the night before opening, night to hold a cast party in his new home. He had bought a small white cottage with a thatched roof, off the Brompton Road. Nigel had just rebuilt the inside of the small house to his liking. The house warming was to show it off to his fellow actors. As Claude passed into the square hall, with tesselated pavement, which lead to a short wooden staircase with white panelled walls to make the hallway look bigger than it was. "Very English"! Rains said in a low voice as he prevailed the structure. Playfair had set an ornate table, filled with flowers and exotic foods. Two chandeliers hung in the dining area, which Claude thought came from a theatre. They talked about their roles, while eating small ham sandwiches. At one point Nigel and Whale argued about the first act, but Jimmy won, leaving the scene intact.

John complained about his costume, which consisted of a white flannel jumper black pumps, white shirt and green laurel wreath, with a golden battledore and shettlecock. "I can't move properly!" he kept telling Jimmy. So Jimmy showed John how he should be more graceful as he moved in his butterfly costume. Charles hadn't come to the party, but Elsa was being her chatterbox self, as she giggled every few minutes at what Nigel was saying looking at this crowd of players, Rains didn't have much confidence that the play would last long.

Circumstances being what they were, the play only lasted six weeks. But everyone had persisted for six weeks, before it closed. Playfair wasn't one to hold a grudge, for the lack of success with the "Insect Play". He enjoyed the players company, that he hired them to do another play called "Robert E. Lee." this play lasted three months, which was a good run in those days. Meanwhile Elsa had taken a fancy to the heavyset Laughton. Rains could see Elsa was very much in love with Charles, as they married after they graduated from the Royal Academy.

CHAPTER 5

RAINS SAILS FOR THE UNITED STATES OF AMERICA.

After his role in "Robert E. Lee", roles came more readily to Rains. He had recieved positive reviews by the critics. Nigel had pushed many of Claude's students into the lime-light, increasing their chances to get roles with other companies. Other students like Frank Martin, Gerald Jerome and Basil Cunard, didn't have much luck in "Robert E. Lee," but Gielgud's career was affirmed.

Rains' next role was, "Vale Derek" in the Earl of Trenton, he met a few professional actors, who were very funny characters. Arthur Treacher was a tall six-footer, who made the whole cast laugh all the time, along with a jolly Edmund Gwenn and high spirited Gordon Harker. Harker's long sad face was enough to make anyone laugh. He learned comic acting from the trio, who kept him in stitches all the time.

The Broadway stage was calling for English actors to cross the Atlantic, to fill a gap in talent on the American stage. Arthur treacher told his co-stars, that he was going to America to find his fortune. Isabel Jeans Claude's ex-wife was also in the play and was picked by an American agent to go to New York, after her contract was up. Alfred Lunt was producing wonderful plays on Broadway and he was calling English players to come join his company.

"Lunt, has nothing, compared to me!" Treacher said one day.

"Love yourself.. do you Arthur?" Isabel said affectionately.

"He's going to take me with him." laughed jolly Edmond Gwenn.

"I wish I had the money to start my own production company on Broadway. I can't take this "Fee System" with all it's rules about money." Arthur yelled.

"And what of the American actors? Arthur. Do you think they will like an invasion of English actors, flooding the American market?" Claude asked politely.

"Arthur shot back. Who cares!!

"Granted! But what about the Barrymores?" Rains asked.

"So long as you join the actor's Equity Association. No one can stop you from finding an acting job on Broadway". reputed Arthur.

"They do want us Claude." Isabel said calmly.

"Damn right they do. If all they have are the Barrymores!" Arthur laughed.

"I understand Lynn Fontane, is thinking of doing a revival of "Pygmalion". I would love to be in that one". Isabel sighed.

"Aaah there's a fine lassie. Edmund sighed.

"Do you think they could use a good comic in that one." sighed Harker.

"Sorry to break this daydreaming up. But I do have the better chance of getting a position with Lynn. I did give Lynn her first acting job."

"He did." Isabel agreed.

"Well tell us Claude.. How you performed this miracle? Rains bit off the top of his cigar lit it, and began to tell his story. "I was assistant-manager at "His Majesty's Theatre" when Herbert was holding an audition, for a few small roles, in his new play. They were all wonderful looking girls, but one stuck my fancy. She had brought a letter from Miss Terry, recommending her for a position, at the theatre. Tree auditioned twenty girls for one role. He pulled me over to center-stage, to ask me, which one I liked? I told him, Miss Terry's letter was good enough for me and she was a beautiful woman. So he picked her to get the role"

"Does she know you picked her?" Arthur asked excitedly. "Yes".. Tree told her.

And we became friends." Claude smiled, While Isabel snapped. "I'll bet"

"Claude made her remark pass but Arthur told Rains, that he should go to America and ask Lynn Fontane, to repay the favor with a job.

"Oh I doubt she would remember me." Claude smiled.

"Oh I wouldn't say that!" Isabel said piercingly. Arthur huffed.... "I wish I had given Miss Fontane her first job. I would love to be in your shoes, dear boy!"

"Maybe you're right... When I see one on my students like Charles Laughton shooting up like a star, while I have worked all my life to get this far... maybe I will go back to Broadway one day!"

"Rains said, taking another puff from his cigar.

In Europe, new acting techniques were being used, which soon spread to America and England. The acting styles of Tree, Irving, Forbes and Robertson were out of style.

Tree had taught Claude to use every part of his body when he was on stage. Now the calmer approach was being used. The loud voice that could be heard in the back of the stage was out dated. Play-goers want realism, not boorish yelling and screaming. The old days of skriking gestures were ebbing away quickly. Even Beatrix, who he had befriended after she graduated from R.A.D.A., had become a fan of the new ways of carefree acting.

In 1925, Rains had been in six shows in the West End theatres but top billing had alluded him. His pay scale had remained at the same level as it had been the year before.

Elsa and Charles Laughton had become big stars on the London stage.

But Claude still felt sorry for Elsa, because Charles could be very stubborn at times.

The Rain's liked Elsa very much, even though she could be outrageously funny at times, in her mannerisms and speech, Claude called her a natural actress, who could take on any thing. She was the complete opposite of her husband. As outgoing as Elsa was, that's how withdrawn Charles was! The war had changed Laughton for the worst, where it had given Claude the knowledge and stability to run his life. Charles was raised in a middle class environment, in contrast to Claude's life of poverty. Sometimes he couldn't believe what nonsense Elsa had to put up from her husband.

Claude encouraged Beatrix to audition for the new Margaret Kennedy-Basil Dean Production of, "The Constant Nymph," Claude had helped his wife study for the test, for the part of "Theresa Sanger".

Carmella Felice

When auditions started. Claude was right there to cheer her on. "Dean", the producer, quickly picked her for the role. Now with two plays under her belt, she felt confident she was meant to be an actress. The only hitch was the play was going to New York City. Claude told her not to worry! "take the part!" he urged.

Rains, was under contract so he couldn't go to America, until he finished his play. But he promised his wife as soon as he completed the play, he would be on the first ship to Broadway. In the meantime she could find a little flat for the both of them. Within a month's time, Claude gave up their apartment in London and sailed for America.

Claude was flabbergasted at all the work Beatrix had put into the new apartment. Even though the rooming house wasn't situated in the best part of town it was in walking distance of the Selwyn Theatre, where his wife was starring. It was a two room cold flat with a small kitchen and a large bathtub attached to the sink. Beatrix had bought a new bed, a wooden table with chairs, a small sofa and end tables with lots of books lying on them. Cheerful curtains hung from each window, which made the rooms look airy. He could hear automobiles passing his place all day long.

Thirty-eight street and eighth avenue was a very active street, which entertained him, from his third floor apartment. He had been trying to find an acting job for weeks with no success. Finally he went to work as a French waiter in one of the fashionable restaurant, within the area. He treated his waiter's job as another acting job, along with a French accent to complete the illusion.

Beatrix felt wretched that her once famous actor in London, was downgraded to take a waiter's job for a few dollars a week. She wrote a letter to her father Benjamin Thomson, asking for advice about the problem. He wrote back, "Maybe you should take things into your own hands!" So she devised a plan to do just that.

Claude's self-esteem was very low, when his beautiful wife walked into his place of business, accompanied by the two men on her arms. She looked wonderful in her tea colored wide brim hat, with large light pink ribbons wrapped around the top. Her long moss colored dress blended with an embroidered white blouse. A Scottish Broach he had given her was pinned to her dress? The pin stood out with its three white flowers on a red background. Finally he saw that her gloves and shoes matched her hat. She hadn't told him that she was coming to lunch, let alone with two men.

The restaurant was fairly crowded at One o' clock in the afternoon, so heads turned as she was shown to one of his tables. Some people had recognized her from her picture in the papers, so they smiled as she sat down. The head waiter signaled Claude to attend the table, so in his best French accent, he greeted the trio.

' Monsieurs, Madam. I am your waiter Claude, how may I serve you?

"Would you like to see the menu? Or will you have a drink first?"

"I'll take a Scotch and Water, no water." said a tall man dressed in a gray tweed three piece suit. He was starting to lose his brown hair and he kept brushing his hair over the bald spot, with his right hand.

"That sounds good. Get me one too! said the shorter heavyset man with a full head of salt and pepper hair. He also was dressed in a gray suit.

"And you Madam?"

"Please don't call me that, waiter".

Beatrix will take a Brandy, waiter!" replied the taller gentleman. Claude smiled as he turned to prepare their drinks. He watched the three from his vantage point at the bar.

At one point when the two men weren't looking, she winked at her husband. Wondering what she was up to, he returned with a silver tray, with three glasses on it.

"Monsieurs, your drinks! He said placing the glasses in front of each person in order. "Would you like to order now?" he grinned showing a silver capped tooth, in the back of his mouth. Beatrix took a sip of her brandy, than made a face, saying.

"What is this?" A brandy madam!" Claude answered.

"Waiter, don't you understand English? I don't want you to call me that!" Claude jumped back, with her show of anger, as the two men looked up at Claude, as to say... Please don't make a fuss!" Changing the subject, one of the men ordered a steak rare with a baked potato with sour cream. The other man thought that it was a good idea and ordered it too. Claude smiled again and asked Beatrix.

"And what will you have?"

"A Caesar salad and take this so-called brandy back. It tastes awful!"

"Why are you going off on the waiter Beatrix? He is only trying to do his job!" Basil snapped!

"Basil.. are you taking his part? Well! Bea huffed!"

"Beatrix you were fine before we came into this place would you rather go some where else?" asked her producer.

"No.... I'm fine.. but I would like to have good service."

"Well, let us just have a quiet lunch and go back to the theatre where you can take out your frustrationsout, on your role!"

"You're right of course. I am a little tired after rehearsals this morning."

"That's right.. O.K.. waiter, that's our order." Dean said as he waved the waiter off, so that the conflict would stop at the table.

"Speaking about the play, I understand, Larry is leaving at the end of the week?"

"Yes, he is Beatrix. It's a small part. I'm sure we can replace him quckly."

"I'm so use to him being there. The waiter's role is an important one."

"Well, he was offered a larger role in another play, and we didn't want to stop him from making more money." Basil added.

"I understand that but.. I do need someone who will be compatable with my own acting style". Beatrix smiled as though she wanted something from them.

Ten minutes later, her husband returned with the order. Placing the steaks in front of the men first, he left the salad for last, as he moved over Beatrix's left shoulder, to put the plate down in front of her. Beatrix looked up angrily at Claude, saying "Aren't you a bit too close to my shoulder, waiter? If my husband were here, he wouldn't like it!"

"Sorry Madam!" Claude replied.

"There you go with the Madam, again" she said in a low angry whisper.

"What would you like for me to call you?" Claude asked.

"Darling, sweetheart, for starters." she smiled. The two men almost gagged on their steaks as they watched the waiter bend over and give the star a kiss.

"What is going on here?" Basil asked firmly.

"This is my husband gentlemen Mr. Claude Rains!" The two men rose as they heard his name. In his finest English accent Claude greeted the two men. "I am sorry about my wife's behavior gentlemen but I don't know what is going on either."

"Darling, I just wanted to show Mr. Dean that you will make a fine waiter in my play." She laughed as the men joined the joke.

"We have heard so much about you, Mr. Rains. Of course you may have the role. You had me fooled completely. We must use that French accent in the play." Dean laughed. The wind was knocked out of Claude's sails as he accepted the role.

"I would be delighted to be working with my wife again." Said the happy actor.

Beatrix's joke had paid off. Her husband started his role a week later. Fans started to take notice of him quickly. So the New York Times sent a reporter to interview the actress and her famous husband. Rita Miller was granted an interview on December 1, 1926. Beatrix told Miss Miller how Claude had pushed her into coming to America to play "Teresa Sanger" He was willing to take a small part in this show, so that I would get my big chance." She told Miss Miller that her husband was like "John Barrymore" on the London stage. As the interview progressed a knock came at the dressing room door and Claude walked in. With the suavity of Old England, he charmed the reporter. He spoke only of his talented wife.

"In England... he said, "few people go to the theatre just before the holidays, But here!.. Why, we play to a full theatre at every performance" then he turned to leave, but added. "But who wouldn't go to the theatre any time to see my wife's beautiful portrayal of "Teresa Sanger". And who wouldn't give up a kingdom to let her play it!" Then he said goodbye to the reporter and let his wife carry on with the interview. Miss Miller than asked Beatrix what shows she had performed on the London stage?

"When Mr. Dean produced "Loyalties" in England, he had already engaged someone for the lead. The show had run three months, when I was engaged to take the lead. I played in that for nine months, until the show closed. Then I was in another show, "The Three Sisters" I played in "The Idiot" and "The Year Between". That was a play from

The French, but they don't mean much now, of course. They did at the time, but now I'm Teresa and I want to keep on being Teresa."

"So you like the character you play?" asked the reporter.

"Oh yes... there is something in doing a character you like, but when a show is produced as true to the book as "The Constant Nymph" and produced so beautifully there's a great deal more than something really... It's everything!"

"Are you going to stay in the states for a while? asked Miller.

"Having been in these States only a short time. The usual question as to whether I will stay, always comes up. Well if they want me, I'm going to stay". Beatrix smiled.

The New York stage took to Rains' to their hearts and on December 19th they were interviewed again by the New York Tribune. Beatrix told the reporter, that she and her husband had stayed up all night the first night the play opened waiting for the early editions to hit the stands. Then neither my husband or I knew which paper to buy! He kept ordering the same one" Beatrix told the reporter. "You have hundreds of journals haven't you?" she asked the reporter.

"Yes we do!" said the reporter. "But before I go, tell me, do you really like New York?"

"Like it! We adore it. My husband and I walk up and down Fifth Avenue with our mouths and eyes wide open. Neither of us ever saw such beautiful women. Such gowns and fur coats." Then Claude came into the room and Beatrix introduced him as "My Darling husband, Claude Rains." The reporter thought he was very young and good looking that he fitted the role of "Roberto" perfectly. The reporter thought they made a lovely couple. When the writer asked him about "New Yorkers," Claude exclaimed

"Women look at the clothes, men look at faces. New York women are the best looking in the world!" Claude exclaimed.

"Oh I do look at clothes and I adore them, though I can't wear them!" Beatrix said, then continued. "Aren't I a funny looking little dump?"

"You're beautiful, darling." Claude told his wife.

"I did have beautiful hair down to here". Beatrix showed the reporter the length.

"And I kept it for years and then I bobbed it for "The Constant Nymph". But it was down below my waist for a while. My crowning glory is now being preserved in a box, so that I may look at it occasionally. But it was worth the sacrifice to play the role....... right Claude?" Beatrix asked her husband.

"It will grow back for another role, Beatrix!" Claude reassured his wife.

"I understand you went to the Royal Academy of Dramatic Arts in London".

"Yes, Claude jumped in; "yes my wife was the school's prize pupil!"

"Yes I was but being the prize pupil has its difficulties at times!" Beatrix laughed.

George Tyler and Mr. Dean think you are wonderful in the part." Said the reporter.

Yes, they have been very good to the both of us." Beartrix smiled.

When Beatrix was at the Academy, I was one of her teachers." Claude added

"Yes he was... and he gave me a jolly hard time of it. Very demanding you know. I married him in spite of it all. We all knew he was doing it for our own good!"

"She still thinks, we use to stay up nights trying to think up ways of making it difficult for her." Claude giggled.

"Well you were tough on all of us darling."

"Can you tell me why he made you feel that way?" asked the reporter.

"I remember four years ago the school produced ' The Jest'. Claude was the director. The class room gossip had it that I was playing the lead female part. One for which I was unquestionably fitted to play, but instead, Mr. Barnes and my dear husband, gave me the role of the wicked, deep-voiced brother. I think Lionel Barrymore later played the same part on Broadway."

"Well, darling that was the toughest role in the play!"

"It was?" she asked her husband.

"Yes and you carried it off so well, darling." Claude said holding her hand.

"The next year, when the academy put on Somerset Maugham's "Caroline". He signed me for a two-year period under his direction." Beatrix explained.

"Her father was a good sport about her becoming an actress." Claude injected.

"He's a Colonel in the Twenty-third London Regiment and director of public companies. My family encouraged me to go onto the stage. Claude had a more or less negative guidance at the academy, but I prospered at the school while I studied with Claude." Bea smiled.

"When were you married?" The reporter asked.

"November of 1924! Claude answered, and we celebrated the occasion by working together in Shaw's 'Getting Married', Bea laughed.

That ended the interview for the reporter and the two players went back to work.

"The Constant Nymph" ran for four months on Broadway, before the company took the play on the road to Hartford Connecticut, for another three months. The Rains made the newspapers a few more times, which brought in more patrons to see the love-birds of London.

The couple loved the fresh air of Connecticut and decided to stay as long as they could in America. They felt free to promote their art, in ways they couldn't in London. But after the year ended, Beatrix found herself out of a job. She then wanted to go back to England to see her family, but Claude talked her out of it. He decided to make an appointment to see 'Lynn Fontanne', because he wanted to join the "Theatre Guild". The Guild was going into their eleventh year of production and he thought it was his best bet to get a job. He was given an interview at the theatre at 245 West 52nd Street. There was where the Guild put on amateur productions. For years the "Liberal Club" and the "Socialist Press Club" had put on amateur plays on the same spot.

Lynn Fontanne welcomed her old friend into the "Guild" as a guest star. She chose him to play "Arthur Logris", in "Out to Sea". Which he played at the Bijou Theatre, on December 15th, 1927. Rains had a lot of competition for roles in the "Theatre Guild". The other players respected Rain's reputation on stage but as a competing actor, he didn't need any training from his boss. In fact, Alfred Lynn asked Claude to teach his newest players the art of acting, when he wasn't in a play.

The Life and Times of Claude Rains

Fontanne was happy to be the one, who would be instrumental in giving Rains, his start on the American stage.

The Guild had a system, where they would rotate roles, with each guest star, that might be available at the time. Beatrix didn't want to join the Guild, because she thought of herself as an accomplished actress, who just had a successful run with a Broadway? play. She didn't want to compete with actresses like "Helen Nestley", Judith Anderson or "Gale Sondergaard". But her husband was willing to go up against actors like Ernest Cossart, Henry Travers, Morris Carnovsky, Tom Powers, Glenn Anders, Whetford Dane, Phillip Leigh, Earl Laremore, George Gaul, Douglass Montgomery and Dudley Diggs". Stars like "Edward G. Robinson", "Cary Grant" and "Clark Gable" were already picked up by Hollywood studios. Silent films had graduated into the "Talkies". People flocked to see the new invention that told a story with words. A ticket to the movies only cost five cents, while the cheapest ticket to a play was nearly three dollars and fifty cents.

Rains was on salary for a hundred and fifty dollars a week for six months of work. But his fans grew with every play he performed. With her play closed Beatrix shopped on Fifth Avenue or took long drives in the countryside on Sunday mornings with her husband. But she grew restless as she idly stood by, watching her husband at his rehearsals. When Claude was rehearsing in "Volpone", she grew very argumentative. Asking him to return to England with her. But he didn't want to leave America where he had found total freedom at his craft. Finally she wrote to friends in London, asking for a role in the play. The word came back, giving her a role in a new production. Claude couldn't talk her out of going back to England. He had given up everything to follow her to America, so that she could have her chance, but she wouldn't give him a shot at being a star. Now she was deserting him for her career. He saw her off at the pier hoping she would change her mind, but she didn't!

Lynn Fontanne was happy to be the one assisting Claude's attempt to conquer the American stage.

Rains thought back to his last days on the English stage. He had just given notice to his producer, that he was going to the Colonies to join his wife. The produce of "The Inspector General" needed to find a replacement for Claude's part of "Alexadrouich."

Claude suggested that Charles Laughton replace him in "Summer Stock". Elsa Laughton had suffered a miscarriage which disturbed Charles, enormously.

Claude said, Charles has just won the "Bancroft Gold Medal For Acting."

"I know of Laughton reputation, Claude," the producer said.

"He's a wonderful actor as his wife. They were my finest students, at R.A.D.A." Claude affirmed.

"We'll have to measure him for a larger uniform...but it sounds proper. Claude."

"One point...I must insist... Don't tell him I recommended him. He's a funny fellow with a lot of pride. He might take it as a hand-out from his friend.

"Fine, I will let "Theodore Komisajeusky" talk to him."

So Director Komisajeusky, nick-named "Komis" called Charles in to read for the role. Claude had followed all his student's careers like a mother watching her chicks. All of them seemed to be doing good, especially, Charles.

When Rains finished his contract, he gave up the couple's apartment, and headed for a ship to America. Their reunion on the docks of Manhattan was quiet, without the fan-fare of report-ers in tow. Beatrix was still high, from her success on the New York stage. Whereas at first, Claude couldn't even get a job washing dishes.

Then there were the problems back home, to tear at their relationship. Benjamin Thomson, wrote to his daughter to return home. Fred Rains was in a financial bind, So Claude would send him a few bucks, now and again. London was still a war-torn city, with many young people leaving for other countries, like Australia, New Zealand or America.

Many actors had set sail for Hollywood. James Whale enlisted many to "Universal Studios. The studios needed clear speaking actors for the new industry.

Claude was undecided whether the coupler should go to Hollywood. The couple decided against the move, while their bread and butter was still on the stage.

On their days off from work, the couple accompanied other actors, who had vehicles, for rides into New Jersey. His friends taught Claude how to drive a car. He loved it and wanted to buy a car, when he got a good part. He also loved the land with all its farm-land for sale. He asked Bea if she would like to live on a farm where there was peace and quiet? She answered . "No, I love the city-life."

In the space of a year, the city became very congested. Horse carts and motor vehicles didn't mix on the slippery streets. Accidents between these vehicles happened all day long under his apartment window. Since he worked nights, Claude needed to sleep during the day. It was bad enough that he suffered from Insomnia , since the "Great War" So when Rains couldn't sleep he would go on long walks on Broadway.

Collecting tea-cups was a hobby of his, so when he saw one in a store window, he would go in and buy it. The more he couldn't sleep, the bigger his tea cup collection grew.

Bea's interests were plays, parties, and writing plays. Bea's star had all but disappeared in a year's time. While her husband's acting Career took off. Bea didn't want to join the "Guild" like her husband had. Because she thought she was a better actress than, Helen Nestly, Judith Anderson or Gale Sondergaard. Of course she was wrong, because all these actresses went on to become big names in the movies.

Claude on the other hand took on actors like Earnest Cossart, Henry Travers, Morris Carnously , Tom Powers or Dudley Digger. Stars like Edward G. Robinson, Cary Grant, and Clark Gable were already snatched up by Hollywood.

A ticket to the "Talkies" was five cents. The cheapest seat at a " Guild" Theatre on 245 West 52nd Street was three dollars.

The "Guild" was going into it's eleventh year of production with Rains as a visit-ing star. Which meant he wasn't in every play. When he did work, he made a hundred and fifty dollars a week. At other times his boss talked him into directing a few plays. He even gave a few acting classes to the company actors.

Lynn came to him one day with a play, well suited to his talent. The play was called " Out To Sea" his role was that of "Arthur Logris" Claude would open at the " Bijou " theatre, starting December 15th 1927. He opened to a full house and wonder-ful reviews.

A new competitor for the public interest entered the scene at this time …Radio. It was flooding, the airwaves with Marconi's dream. A family could listen to music, stories, soap operas, Don Quixote or Shakespeare's Falstaff. Radio actors became stars over night . Every week a new star was profiled in a Radio Magazine. Radio and the " talkies" were a danger to the survival of the theatre.

The worst part of this situation was the "Great Depression". American citizens were out of work, so their money went for the necessaries …..food , clothing and a roof over their heads.

So prominent citizens of New York City, had to keep the theatres alive with their donations. Rains, was grateful he still had a job. Alfred Lunt would throw parties for rich patrons, while theatre stars signed autograph theatre books.

Claude's agent was working to find him a good radio show, most of the time the actor would turn down the program.

On June 17th, 1926 Warner Brothers had bought "Piccadilly" theatre in Manhattan. It was wired for sound and renamed "The Palace Warner Theatre". Vitaphone was producing musical shorts in Brooklyn. Warner Brothers "Don Juan" opened August 6th 1926 starring John Barrymore. The Rains' were invited to opening night. The theatre was packed with dignities including the mayor.

It was an expensive business installing sound equipment. Twenty five thousand dollars to be exact. But Warner Brothers lost $ 279,000.00 that week. It wasn't until the release of the "Jazz Singer" on October 6th 1927, that a profit was earned. The film cost $ 500,000.00 , but made Three Million Dollars. John and Lionel Barrymore films started to pay off after the "Jazz Singer".

English actors were hired in groves due to their distinct pronunciation. It was a necessity to film-making the actors be understood.

Western Electric along with its partner's, Vitophone and Warner Brothers, still Hadn't perfected on a disc method.

Sam Warner's little studio in Brooklyn was making all the musical shorts. Vitophone's instruments were very sensitive o the smallest of sound. The crew had to move around the studio in their stocking feet, to avoid noise.

Claude and his manager drove out to Brooklyn one day, just to look around. His agent wanted him to take a screen test. Rains was up for it when he met Sam Warner. Sam showed the two men around the studio saying :

"We would like you to take a screen test, Mr. Rains."

Claude hesitated before he spoke. " I tried to make a film in London a few years ago. But I failed at it."

"Times change, Mr.Rains. We have the skills to make you into a great movie star".

" Sounds wonderful Mr. Warner, but I don't know I'll be any good at it."

" Claude take the test…. I'm working here to earn my ten percent." His manager smiled.

" Where would this test be given? Mr. Warner."

" We have another studio in Queens… we can take it there for you."

" May I think about it … I have to talk to my wife."

" Sure any time you want to call the office ."

Claude wanted to take Sam's offer, but didn't know how Bea would take the news. She was hinting about going home. He knew she would become very temper mental, with him making a film. Lately he always felt like the villain, on and off stage. Claude knew the end of his marriage was near. He was thirty eight and Bea twenty nine.

Then just before he started his new play "Marco's Millions' in the role of "Chu Yin" Bea declared she was sailing for London. He tried to talk her out of going but she didn't listen to him.

CHAPTER 6

WORK, WORK, AND MORE WORK!

By the time he started working on "Marco Millions", his personal life had taken a turn for the worse. Beatrix was doing a play on the London stage and didn't want to come back to America. Claude knew his marriage was finished but he still hoped for a life and a family of his own. His family was doing well on their own and didn't really need his help But on occasion, he would send some money home as a gift.

His daily routine was leaving home early for the theatre, just to watch the people in the street, as they went about their daily work. He would find some of his characterizations to perform on the stage from the people he watched, on his daily walk to the theatre.

One day, he was sitting in the back of the theatre, just relaxing. When two figures walked onto the stage. "Hit the lights!" yelled the stage manager and the area was lit. Claude saw a new face, a young girl about eighteen uncovering white sheets from the props. She had black hair and dark eyes and she looked to be about five feet-four

"They gave me a "walk on" in this play, Hank!"

"In Marco Millions. That's great!"

"Who wrote it?" came the next question from the young girl, folding a large white sheet.

"Eugene O' Neil... some critic wrote he couldn't write a comic play, so he wrote one!"

"What's it about? I only saw my little part."

"Marco Polo, I think he makes Marco a salesman in the story trying to sell the Chinese the idea of trade."

"That's sounds interesting," said the youngster, returning to work.

"I hope so. I can use the work, to support, my family. Things are real bad out there. People are losing jobs, all over the place". Claude lit a cigar and Hank heard a noise in the back of the theatre, so he yelled! "Who 's there?"

"It's only me, Hank,. Claude Rains." the actor said moving down the aisle. For a moment the dark-haired girl, could only see the flame from his cigar, come closer and closer towards the stage. Then she saw a handsome slender man climbing the steps two by two.

"It's pretty warm in the back Hank, Maybe we should have rehearsals on stage today."

"You might be right Mr. Rains, its warmer, in the basement."

"And who is your pretty assistant?" Claude asked eyeing her slender figure

"Miss Francis Propper, meet Mr. Rains." Francis fell in love with Claude the first time she saw him, as she said.

"So nice to meet you Mr. Rains." Francis smiled at the man holding out his hand to her so gently.

"The pleasure is all mine, my dear." Claude said kissing her hand and bowing from the waist. Francis frowned. She wasn't use to men kissing her hand and didn't know how to react.

"Proper? is that a stage name?" Claude said leaning up against a piano.

"No... no it is my own name!" Francis huffed.

"Oh... I see. I didn't mean to be rude, but I haven't heard a name quite like that." Claude said watching Francis move a chair to center stage.

"She is working her way up from prop girl to actress." Hank told him.

"Well that is how I started," laughed the actor. His statement seemed to excite the young girl. "Really, you started this way too?" Claude smiled saying "Yes, but in England we are call-boys. Like you we did everything that had to be done to bring off a performance." Francis has been helping in the office too, a little typing for the boss.

"By the way... where is the old fellow?" Claude asked?

"Sleeping in his office... he puts on that radio and off he goes to sleep."

"The radio... now there is an invention I don't like." Claude said plainly.

"Why not... it has music and stories..." Francis injected.

"Yes and it is free! How do you expect people to come to the theatre if radio is free!"

"You have a point Mr. Rains, But I don't think it will put us out of business."

"You may say that now but in a few years, who knows what the radio will bring."

"I like the radio!" smiled the girl.

"How old are you, Miss Propper" asked the actor.

"Eighteen years old. This is my first real job and I love it!"

"Are you a good actress, Miss Propper?"

"I don't know yet! I've done a few school plays up in the Bronx and my teacher said I had talent."

"The Bronx... fancy that! Well we shall see little one if you can act soon enough. I have to go now for my reading. I hope to see you again Miss Propper. See you too, Hank." Claude said making his way off stage.

When he had left, Francis told Hank that she thought he was really a handsome man and she loved his voice.

"Come on Francis stop day-dreaming about that guy, we have to have the costumes cleaned by Friday!" So off she went with her boss but she sighed about the actor she just met.

"The Guild" had caught the public's fancy, as the venture continued in a modest prosperity. In the early days of the Guild, a play could be produced for thousand dollars. They had started the theatre with one hundred and thirty-five people, who subscribed five thousand dollars each. With six thousand seven hundred and fifty dollars in the bank, they had managed to rent the Garrick Theatre, which had been discarded as a theatre. They found a lot of scenery consigned to the city dump and painstakingly rebuilt their sets. The Guild believed in it's artististic merit, which the public noticed in ten seasons. Four months before, the opening of the 1928-1929 season. The Guild was obliged to close its subcription books. The Guild contracted for six plays in a season. But the small theatre, could only seat so many people before it had to move the production to the larger, Martin Beck Theatre.

By the summer of 1928, the "Theatre Guild", had become the most interesting theatre in the English-speaking world. The "Guild" had used the money-made from some of its world premiers to bring Shaw's plays to Broadway. They included "Heartbreak House", Saint Joan" and "Back to Methuselab". Rains felt, that Shaw was always part of his life whether in England or in America, because Shaw's plays were produced by so many companies, he had worked with. Another playwright, Ben Johnson was also a favorite of the Theatre Guild's audiences. He had written, ' Volpone ', which was a tremendous hit for the producers and stock holders!

The board of managers of the Theatre Guild, also thought Rains was a great boxoffice hit. Lee Simonson, Teresa Helburn (executive director), Phillip Moeller, Helen Westley, Maurice Wertheim and Lawrence Langer, were all fans of the little actor. He could charm all of them with his wonderful voice and he did.

While working on "Marco Millions" Francis found all kinds of excuses to talk to Rains. She had fallen in love with Claude but didn't know how to tell him. Rains, on the other hand, wasn't interested in starting up another relationship that might end in disaster. He hoped that Beatrix would change her mind and return to him in the United States. But the gap between the two, grew too large to be repaired. Beatrix wanted to have a career in England where she would be with her family. Claude didn't care about staying in England because he felt America was his home now. His family was still in England but he didn't feel close to his estranged father.

He gave some of the younger players at the Guild acting lessons including Francis.

But as much as he tried, he knew the Bronx girl, didn't have what it took to be an actress! But she was a friend who he could talk to about his work, or life in general.

When she told her family about Claude they weren't happy about the friendship between their daughter and a thirty-eight year old actor from England. They knew the relationship was doomed from the start, because of the difference in their ages.

Back in England, Beatrix wasn't getting the parts she wanted, so she started writing plays instead. Between acting and writing, she managed to keep afloat. But she still thought Claude would return to England. But Claude was too deeply in love with America and her freedom of expression, that he decided to make it his home.

Marco Millions was a money-maker which lasted six-months on Broadway. With, "Lally", "Volpone" and "Marco Millions" under his belt, he was a new star on the great "White Way". Francis stayed close in case, her love would love her back!

On April 29th, 1929, Claude opened the show, "Camel Through The Needle's Eye" in the role of Joseph Villim." The Theatre Guild players also contracted for this play was Miriam Hopkins, Henry Travers and Morris Carnovsky. Then he co-stared with Otto Kruger, in "Karl and Anna". He was the guest star in this production. Rains played "First Prisoner" while Otto Kruger a favorite with the Guild had most of the lines in the production. In this play, he befriended Gale Sondergaard who would cross his life again in ther future, many times at Warner Brothers. Gale was a good actress, with a good sense of humor. He would try to overshadow her in rehearsals a few times.

Gale would tell him to watch his step... he was stealing scenes from her. He would retreat from her sharp tongue with, "Sorry dear", did I cut you off again?"

Gale would give him a sharp look.... saying. "There is enough limelight for the both of us on stage!" He would smile shyly and move back on his spot. Claude liked Gale a lot because she was a professional.

The play had been translated from the German, which had taken the playwright almost a year to complete. The "Guild" thought it was a good story to open it's twelfth season with. The story takes place right after World War 1, the story tells how the city of Berlin survived the glitters of war. The playgoers are taken into a tenement dwelling where families pick out an existence. They feel the savages of war, as mystic perceptions take the place of reality.

Otto Kruger plays a German soldier who returns to his home to find a destroyed city. He has spent five years in a Russian prison camp, with other prisoners. Hearing stories from all the other prisoners about their wives and girlfriends, he finds comfort in their lives, 'one man's wife catches his fancy, a woman named Anna, who is the wife of another prisoner. Alice Brady plays the part of the suffering Anna.

The rest of the story is inherent in the Enoch Arden legend. After leaving the camp Karl seeks out Anna. He tries to pass himself off as her husband. He succeeds in fooling Anna, so that she falls in love with him. Rains plays one of the prisoners in the camp, who talks about his loved ones. Otto dominated as the romantic lead, which didn't leave much for the other actors to do. The play only lasted a month, but Claude soon found another role with the Guild.

Without taking a break, his next play opened on November 25th, with the play "The Game of Love and Death". In this play he met a young man named Henry Fonda, who was given a walk-on. The tall youngster impressed Rains very much. Fonda watched how Rains worked and finally got up enough nerve to ask him for a few lessons. They became fast friends, which would last a life time. He gave "Hank" the courage to go back to school in his home state where he excelled, with a Broadway credit and being tutored by Rains, gave Fonda an edge in his new production company.

By 1930, Claude figured his marriage was at an end. He wrote to Beatrix that he was going to obtain a divorce. Beatrix didn't answer his letter, so Claude went to a lawyer, to start proceedings to end the marriage.

In the 1930's Rains had picked up a powerful new friend, the critic for the "New York Times", J. Brooks Atkinson. The reporter seemed to like everything that Rains, performed on the stage and he would do so for the next thirty years.

On February 4th, 1930, Rains played "Proteus", a Pilgrim minister, In G. Barnard Shaw's "The Apple Cart." his co-stars were "Tom Powers", a fine actor and Violet Kemble Couper. At this point in time, he decided to go to England, to see where things stood with Beatrix and to place his name on the quota system. He stayed with his sister and her family while he took care of his business.

With his business completed, he sailed for America. Back in New York the Theatre Guild, welcomed him back with open arms. On March 16th, 1931 He signed a two year contract with the Guild. His first play under the new contract was on Sept 21st.

Rains liked this role of an elevator man, who thinks he is Napoleon. The three act play included, Violet Kemble Cooper and William Gargan. "He" the play was produced at the smaller Guild Theatre. Claude took the character and ran with it. He gave it dignity as the servant, who fancies himself the leader, "Napoleon".

CHAPTER 7

A MOVIE STAR AT LAST!

Claude was alone on his little farm in New Jersey, as he worked to nail down a new roof on his outhouse. A couple of bad storms, had almost knocked down the weaken structure. Suddenly, he heard the telephone ringing in his kitchen twenty-five feet away.

Always hoping it would be his agent, he ran quickly toward his house. Huffing, he picked up the reciever, Hearing the familiar voice of his agent, he huffed.

"Where the hell have you been? I called you a couple of times yesterday!"

"Working on a big deal for you, Claude!" the agent laughed.

"Surely, you have something for me, after three weeks!" Claude huffed.

"Yes I do!.. a film!" came back the answer.

"A film? After I made that awful screen test!"

"You know a guy named James Whale, a director at Universal Studios?"

"Yes I know him, We worked together on the London stage."

"Well. he told me he saw your test, and laughed his head off! But he wants you for his new film, "The Invisible Man".

"What?.. "The Invisible Man".. but I thought Boris Karloff was doing that film?"

"Karloff wanted a raise of $200.00 a day and they won't give it to him. So he didn't take the role in the film."

"My god! How much are they offering?" Claude said quickly

"$2,000.00 plus expenses.... hotel, etc!" his agent laughed.

"Dear God, I can't believe this. Why did he pick me?"

"Your voice! He told me to tell you.. you have a wonderful speaking voice."

"When do I start?" Claude asked almost out of breath with excitement.

"Well, there's a little hitch. You have to make another screen test, with Whale directing you. Seems the powers that be, still want another actor to play the role. They don't want an unknown."

"I'm not an unknown!" Claude huffed.

"Claude this guy knows what he is doing. Just show up at the Universal when they give me the O.K.!"

"For $2000.00 a week, I'll run all the way to California!" the actor laughed.

"Well, we just have to get over this hurdle with the head of the studio, Carl Laemmle."

A week later, his agent called to say the deal was a go, if the screen test was approved by Carl Laemmle and the other producers. Claude bought a ticket for the "Super Chief" and headed out west. A few days later, he was getting off the train with James calling his name. He drove Claude to a nice hotel, where visiting actors boarded.

His co-star Gloria Stuart, was also a favorite of Jimmy's since she made a test under the strict supervision of his friend. Whale explained to Rains, the reasons why, his R.K.O. test was a horror.

"You acted as you would on stage. The camera picks up overacting. So what you have to do Claude, is under-act! When you go before the camera, you must talk naturally. I want to hear every word but in a peaceful manner. William Harrrigan a Guild actor and I think a friend of yours, has been hired to be in the film with you! You will test together to see how the action goes. So be at the studio tomorrow morning at five thirty, to start work!" Excitedly, he took his few pages of script and spent the rest of the day studying his part. The dialogue was simple to learn. He just had to get the character set-up. The next morning he arrived at five-thirty, at the sound stage to which Jimmy had told him to come. He rehearsed with Harrigan for an hour, as the camera was set in place. Carl Laemmle Jr. still wasn't sure Rains was the actor for the "Invisible Man".

He fought with Jimmy, about getting another actor for the role. But Jimmy insisted, Claude was the man for the job. It took five takes for

Jimmy to be satisfied with the take. Claude, nerves, got the best of his stomach. As he waited until Jimmy could show the test in a conference room. All the big executives were present. Including the stars, as Jimmy yelled the cameraman to roll the take. They all sat and watched for five minutes and when it was over they applauded. Carl Laemmle offered Rains a contract, for three films at $2,500.00 a week, for three months of work.

Once the contact was signed, the actor was set to work. Jimmy told him the first thing he must do, was to have a mold of his face done up. He took the actor to a warehouse, where molds hung everywhere, from the overhead rafters. He recognized the faces of Karloff and Chaney and even Elsa and Charles 's faces, staring back at him.

The technician had him sit in a barber's chair. Placing a rubbery cloth over his chest, he asked Rains, if he had shaved?"

"Yes! Claude answered very annoyed, as the man said he had to shave him again.

After the shave, he placed a layer of vaseline all over his face and neck, than stuck two straws up his nose, as Rains asked. "What's cracking up here?" The technician laughed, because he didn't know what Claude was saying.

"What sir? he asked in a half-laugh.

"What are you doing to me?

"Oh... you have to breath sir, when we put the plaster of paris on your face."

"Thank you for telling me. How long is this going to take?" Rains asked.

"About an hour, Mr. Rains, sorry!" as he replaced the straws in his nose. It took about an hour for the plaster to dry, with Claude gasping for breath, all the way, until it was finished. Next he went to another department to be fitted for his costume. There he met up with the rest of the cast. William Harrigan, Henry Travers and Una O 'Connor, an actress, he had known in England.

In her book, Gloria Stuart, calls Claude an actor's actor.

"Twenty-four hours a day, on the set, on the stage, in a bar, going to a Loo, baking a cake, he was always giving a performance". Gloria complained to the director about everything, including her co-star. His ignorance of film-making made her very unhappy. She would tell Jimmy, He keeps upstaging me. He's blocking me being in the frame!"

James would tell his star politely. "Now, now, Claude, let's not be naughty!"

On the stage he was allowed to take leeway of movement. But making films confined him to a spot on the floor, which he didn't like. Claude understood about tempermental actresses. He had taught a few at the R. A. D. A., including three ex-wives. The trouble was that Gloria and the others, didn't know about his eye problem and he didn't tell anyone for fear of losing his job. So when Jimmy called him to the carpet for upstaging Gloria, he would just apologize to the actress.

Rains in his free time would observe everything about moviemaking. He learned about the camera from John Fulton. He was taught what the camera's eye was seeing, in a frame of action. When his face was covered with bandages, his speech wasn't clear.

So Jimmy would take him to the sound stage to watch his action, while he dubbed in his voice over his actions. The bandages, were a pain in a neck, because they would slip over his mouth and nose, which brought the filming to a stand still until the make-up men could fix it.

Each morning, Rains would show up at the studio at five-thirty, to have the bandages applied. It was June when he started the filming, in a warehouse that was so hot that you could fry an egg on the tin roof. The first week, he lost ten pounds. William Harrigan, who played Dr. Kemp, was a favorite with the crew, telling them jokes or sharing a bottle of brandy with them. They called Harrigan "Willie" on the set, which made Claude turn a head or two, thinking they were calling him, Making friends with the crew wasn't one of Claude's things to do. Rains spent a lot of time with Jimmy, Charles Laughton and Elsa. At dinner, Elsa would sometimes ask about Beatrix, which made Claude whince a little. She had been good friends with Beatrix and she always would ask, how she was doing, as if Claude knew how she was doing. Finally, he had to tell them, he was divorcing his wife.

Charles would nudge his wife, when she over dramatized situations. Elsa would then change the subject, as she told the company around the table, how H. G. Wells had written some material for her. Jimmy had made Laughton a star, with the film, "Old Dark House", for Universal.

Along with other pals like Raymond Massey and Melvyn Douglas. Whale had a lot of pals within the movie industry but when he went home, he lived a different life style with his friend David Lewis.

Claude had made a friend in his camera man John Fulton. Sometimes getting better advice, than his director friend. As film was very expensive, Fulton wanted to shoot as few scenes as possible. The real work started for Fulton in early July, with the trick photography. It took hundreds of clips to create the illusion of invisibility.

"Dont worry, John!" Claude could hear the director tell Fulton. To the producers, Jimmy would say, "Don't worry, we will finish on budget!" But it was up to Rains to pull the illusion off. He was fitted with a black pair of tights, a black hood, socks and shoes. These he would put on under his costume. Then they would place a plastic tubing from the actor's lips, down past his body, into his pant's leg and out the cuff. This tubing gave him enough air to breathe, but a few times he felt like passing out from the heat. Then they would bandage his head with long stripes of white cloth. A black velvet dropcloth was placed behind him. Then they filmed Claude disrobing in front of the black screen. As Claude's black tights appeared on camera, it blended into the background perfectly, creating the illusion. The camera's lens picked up only black on black, which made Claude appear to disappear on the screen. Claude couldn't talk in these scenes, so his voice would be added later to the action. Claude watched the takes calmly, but without much interest or so it seemed.

The most difficult shots involved having him unwrapping his head, while looking into a mirror. This required the filming and combination of four separate pieces of the film.

The wall and mirror, with the mirror's surface covered by black velvet. The character as seen in the mirrror. The front view of Claude unwrapping his head in front of the mirror. Then the room's opposite wall, as seen by the mirror. All these clips had to fit perfectly. Jimmy coordinated, matched in a view point, perspective and action to a fraction of an inch. Fulton told a reporter from the New York Times, after the film was shown to the public. "It was the most difficult shot I ever pieced together." But thanks to Fulton's great camera work, the film's illusions were smooth and convincing.

Carmella Felice

Sheriff was the screenwriter, that rewrote H. G. Wells' novel for the screen. Universal could do what ever they wanted with the film, because they had bought the rights to the story. Sheriff's work unified the action by giving characters who were involved in the film's major events, further tightening the story line. Sheriff gave Rains two dynamic speeches about plans for seizing power for himself. That had no counterpart in the novel by Wells. The vividness of these monolgues gave "Griffen", the character, more importance, in one of Claude's plays called, "He", Rains played a Napolean character. So he took that characterization mixed it with his own personality, to form "Griffen".

In one speech he gives, to enlist the aid of Dr. Kemp to his evil ways. The crazed "Griffen", says, "The drugs.. I took.. seemed to light up my brain! Suddenly I realized the power I held! The power to rule... to make the world grovel.. at my feet!..... We'll begin with a reign of terror, Mmmm a few murders here and there.. yes we make no distinction! We might even wreck a train or two..(looking at his hands) These characteristics do exist in Wells' novel. "These fingers around a signal man's throat... yes (laughs).

Sheriff's dialogue gave Rains a dynamic performance heighten considerable by the new dialogue. "Griffen".. was the main character, who had to hold interest of the public. Viewes are led to identify with him. Even though the average film-goer wouldn't tolerate someone else having the total power that "Griffen" desires!"

Gloria was very upset that all the good lines were written for Rains. She complained all the time about her lines. She didn't seem to understand that Rains was the star, she the starlet that couldn't compete with a seasoned stage actor.

Working under that tin roof, dressed in two sets of clothes, made the actor lose more weight, during July and August. Sometimes tempers flared, but Jimmy tried to keep everyone under control. Rains had to eat his meals through a straw, which made milk the main course. By the end of the third week, he was exhausted, from the heat and lack of food.

Weekends were spent mostly alone, driving along the country side. Some of the foods he ate on the weekends were local dishes, which were very spicy Mexican hot sauces. Shooting was extended into August, which was passed his ten weeks of promised work. He didn't mind making the extra money, by no means, but missed Francis very much. He would call her and tell her about the sights of beautiful California. She thought it would be a nice place to live, if she had to. But "No one sees my face in the film. Francie, till the end of the picture. So I don't know if my voice alone will make me a star" he told her.

His lawyer was having a hard time trying to get Beatrix in London, to sign divorce papers, so Francis was fearful, that her marriage to Claude would never take place.

Her parents on the other hand were happy that he was having a problem obtaining his freedom. A farmer was watching over his small farm, including the few chickens he had raised. Claude couldn't wait to get back to Francis and the quiet of his farm. Twenty pounds lighter, he was finally released by Universal. Packed with gifts for Francis, he headed back to East Coast. A week later, he had hired a plumber, a carpenter and an electrician out to the farm, building a new indoor bathroom. He made improvements throughout his house, in hopes of bringing his bride to live there.

Francis was uneasy on opening night of the "Invisible Man". Claude insisted he didn't want to see the film. He was afraid of jinxing his luck. Francis and her family went to see the film together, so that she could get some input from them. They all thought it was a wonderful film, until they showed Claude's face! The reviews gave the picture three stars, as the children flocked to see the picture. As the box-office started jumping, so did the letters asking for photos, of the Invisible Man. H.G. Wells was the author of the novel, even wrote to the star, thanking him, for a hit. Boris Karloff was even taking a back seat in fan mail to Rains.

The Theatre Guild wanted to take advantage of all the notoriety that Rains was getting, so they offered him a play so his fans could see him on stage and in person.

They gave him a little raise in salary, which didn't seem enough, after making two thousand five hundred a week, at Universal Pictures. After his lawyer obtained a divorce in New Jersey from his wife Beatrix, he asked Francis to marry him. They had agreed before they were to be married that she would not become an actress. His other three marriages were to women who loved the theatre, better than him. She agreed because she loved him so much. They were married in her parents home in the Bronx, and when the minister asked for the rings to bless them, Claude remembered he had left them on his dresser in New Jersey because he was so nervous. Seeing little silver curtain rings placed carefully on her mother's curtains. He took them off the curtain, smiled and gave it to the minister. "When we get home, I'll give you the real thing!" Her told Francis. Placing the curtain ring on her finger, they were pronounced, husband and wife.

After a small party that her family gave them, the couple headed to his newly constructed farmhouse. What Claude didn't know was his divorce in New Jersey wasn't legal in Great Britain, where he had married Beatrix. The newspapers reported a few weeks later that he was a bigamist! Francis was upset, not to mention her parents, who were fuming. Rains hired a London Lawyer, and told him to make his divorce to his exwife, legal. After three months of calls to London, Beatrix finally signed the papers, that made him a free man again. But Francis wanted everthing legal, so they were married again at City Hall, by a justice of the peace.

Francis went everywhere with her husband, as he opened a new play for the Guild. He was given the role of "George Clemenceau", in White Plains, in the "Peace Palace" He put on a heavy make-up for the part, of an old, talkative man, who loved women and France. His friend at the New York Times gave him a very good review.

Another group of people were also interested in his talents and his newly found fame. Producer-Director's Ben Hecht and Charles MacArthur. They showed up one night after a performance with their wives. Helen Hayes, now Mrs. MacArthur, carried on, how wonderful he was in the role of "Clemenceau". Then Ben asked Rains if he would like to do a film for them called. "Crime Without Passion". They knew he had just come off of making the "Invisible Man" and the public wanted to know what he looked like! Hecht had written the storyline, as the others were going to work free, but they were willing to match Claude's salary at Universal. Claude had only one question for the producers, "Are you going to be in the film? Mrs. MacArthur?"

"In a small scene" she smiled.

"That's good enough for me!" Rains smiled.

The filming was going to take place in Queens, at the old Paramount Studios just thirty minutes, where he was playing in "Peace Palace". Ben told Rains, that he would hire a man to drive to and from his theatre. The actor agreed to come to Ben's office to sign a contract, to do the new film. "Good! Ben said. "Then I will rent the studio, for two months, for our film." Rains was going to play a character named, Lee Gentry a lawyer who thinks he killed his girlfriend. They had fought with a gun, when a shot grazed her forehead. Thinking that she is dead, he tries to cover up the crime.

Rains adored the story line, so he called up Ben, to make an appointment to see him in his office. Claude was aware that Ben had a sense of humor, but when he walked into the director's office to talk over the contract Ben was standing up with his hand outstretched, He offered Claude a cigar, which the actor took then Ben sat down behind his desk. To Claude's surprise, he saw a large picture directly behind Ben of a naked woman.

"Oh" Claude said looking at the picture "Do you like her Claude?"

"Well yes... but this is hardly the place for such a picture." Claude smiled.

"Well".. Ben smiled... "I have a lot of reporters come into my office for stories about my films. Mostly young ladies. I stand in front of this picture for the interview while they are seated. They can't see the picture unless I sit down. So when the questions become a little too personal, I sit down, to reveal the picture. But the one that gets them is the one on the door you just entered. Claude turned to see another naked woman smiling at him.

"I can see why they would be disturbing to the ladies."

Changing the subject, Ben asked, "Well do we have a deal, Claude?" Claude leaned back, trying not to look at the picture behind Ben, and said. "Yes my wife thinks it is a good project for me to undertake. I just have one concern for this film, "Don't you need a hero for this film?" Rains asked.

"Hero.... why Claude... you are the hero and the villain, rolled up in one. I want that quality you are showing in your new play. That of Nathan Rubin."

"Rubin is a good character.. where Gentry is a shady type."

"That's the challenge Claude, I'm sure you are up to it. With all the notoriety you have been getting from "They Shall Not Die". You can play this scoundrel!"

"Yes... Rubin is believable! So much so, we nearly had a mob scene in front of the theatre last night. They really think I was Rubin, trying to free negroes in a murder trial.

Fifty young men stormed the theatre, asking to see Rubin! And the letters that come to the theatre.... my good God.. I didn't think I was that good!" Claude laughed.

"Yes the Scottsboro trial still lives in their minds. I heard Ruth Gordon was getting hate mail, too!"

"Yes poor Ruth, she wouldn't hurt a fly. This has been really an upset for the poor dear."

"Unbelievable! But that's what I want for my film! Then it will be a winner!"

Then the two men worked out some other problems with the script. Claude notified his agent that he had another assignment, which made him very happy. When the film started into production, Francis would drive her husband to the theatre, then a car would pick them up, to be taken to the Paramount Studios. Which they learned very quickly was in ill-repair. Or Francis would go up to the Bronx to visit her family for the day.

While Ben and Charles took turns, at directing her husband, from a chair placed on a wooden table. They were working on a small budget, where only the actors were paid.

Running between boroughs wasn't Claude's idea of fun. Soon his nerves got the better of him. All he could remember were Jimmy's words of directing. "Under act, under act!"

Sometimes the producers' directions confused him. But when Lee Garmes, the associate director, took the director's chair, he felt better. Lee brought out the best in his performances, besides being a great camerman".

Then one day, the pot boiled over, as the lights in the studio went out, the camera froze, then when they fixed the camera, the sound went out. Claude lost all his concentration, as the delays increased. He became very angry yelling. "I 've become mechanical! There's no feeling in my expression. No meaning to my lines!" The crew and directors, looked on, as the actor blew his top. "I 'm not going on with this!" Rains shouted. I 'm not a puppet!" Came his stage voice, that echoed through the open studio. The crew went silent, as they waited for Rains to calm himself. A minute passed, as he strutted back and forth, waving his arms in the air. Finally he stopped and saw everyone was watching him, he didn't know how to correct the situation, until Charlie yelled out. "O.K. My puppet, let's take a rest." Claude sighed with relief at Charlie's remark. From then on MacArthur, would always call Claude.... my little puppet.

Rains had never had a flare-up like that, it was the first time he had shown any temperment on stage. He wasn't proud of it, but letting off steam, felt good. He thought to himself.

"Sir Tree was right. Maybe you did have to curse a little to release the tension. The crew knew he was tired, from working his two jobs, so they laughed it off like Charlie did. Exhausted every night, he fell asleep, as Francis drove them home.

To make up for her husband's outbreak, Francis made some homemade angel cake, for the whole crew. Lee enjoyed the cake as he asked Francis, "What's this called?"

"Angel Food Cake." Francis replied. Suddenly Lee jumped up yelling.

"I've got it! We'll hire some showgirls, dress them in white silk body tights. Hang them from the rafters with wires, while we run a backdrop of the city in front of them.

It will look like "Fairies", bring trouble to the city. We can run the credits over the finished clip.

The next morning when the Rains' came to work, they saw beautiful showgirls, hanging from wires, as Lee photographed them on a Manhattan backdrop. A few months later, the film opened on October 4th, 1934. The critics had mixed emotions about the film. City dwellers loved the film, while country-folk didn't care for it. One reviewer wrote: "I was pretty sure I was going to find Mr. Rains acting boring, due to his inclination to strut and make fussy gestures with his arms. However as the film progresses, Mr. Rains becomes more and more interesting, as a character.... He is one of those birds, who gets under your skin. And it's difficult to explain because he's not an impressive looking man, nor is his voice particularly easy to take. Maybe it's because he is a good actor, that has something to do with it."

The producers made a little money from the film. But the best part was, both producers were offered writing jobs, with a major studio and it gave a face to the "Invisible Man".

Besides his stage appearances, Rains also was into another medium.. Radio! He had done three radio shows by 1934. "The Good Earth" on September 13th, for N.B.C. a "Bill of Divorcement", on February 13th, for N.B.C. Then the "Fleischman Hour", with Rudy Vallee, on March 17th. The networks were willing to pay big bucks for his voice. He thought radio work was fun, but not an art form. He had a script in his hands, so he didn't really have to learn the lines. Most of the time he knew the plays by heart. Only one rehearsal was needed to get his timing right, for commercials and sound effects. The N.B.C. Studios, were located in the R.C.A. Building, which was close to his theatre. There wasn't any kind of strain put on him, doing this kind of radio work and he got to meet a lot of famous people, like Rudy Vallee.

Back in England, his fame had spread, as his family sent him articles written about him in England. His father was very proud of his son, as were the whole family.

Rains was still under contract, to make two more films for Universal Pictures. This time Francis went with him to the West Coast, on a honeymoon. He was given the script for, "The Man Who Reclaimed His Head". But this time Edward Ludwig, would direct him not James Whale. Claude told Carl Laemmle Jr. he didn't like changing directors, but Junior ordered him to do the film with Ludwig. He played, "Paul Verin", a writer who is married to a beautiful woman, played by Joan Bennett. Joan came from a theatrical family, Lewis Morrison, her grandfather and her father Richard Benett, who was a matinee idol in his youth. While filming this picture Joan worried all the time about her sick father, back in New York City. Soon after this film was finished, her father died.

Claude, Lionel Atwill and Bennett, talked a lot about the theatre, because Joan didn't like the filming too much. It was a macbre tale, not to her taste. It was the first time a story was being told, about a mentally sick person. Of course, Rains was the mentally ill man in the film. But it wasn't a new thing for Claude, who was always pigeon-holed into playing those parts. He asked Junior for a new type of character, for his last film on contract.

The studio heads promptly made him take fencing lessons, with Lewis Hayward, another contract player. They were doing a fencing routine one afternoon, when Rains lost his footing as he lunged at Hayward. The point of the sword pierced Hayward's fencing pants in the crotch. Then Claude saw Hayward's sword, bounces back and hits him in the head. As Hayward gazed down to see if anything was bleeding in his crotch. Claude said calmly, "You are bleeding from your forehead, but I don't see a wound!" With that Hayward removed his toupee, to reveal a long cut.

Claude wanted to laugh, but didn't. He didn't know the handsome actor was bald.

"I thought you cut something important there for a while, Claude." Hayward smiled.

After this incident, the two men became close friends, even making commercials together. Universal had Hayward slated to be in a few sword fighting movies. Claude thought he was heading in the same direction, because of the fencing classes, which made him happy.

But Junior had him slated to play John Jasper, a choirmaster of Cloisterham Cathedral, in Universal's "The Mystery of Edwin Drood." Rains would play an opium user, who is in love, with his nephew's girl. Someone kills his nephew, why is not clear, but you are led to believe it is Jasper. The Dicken's story is very dark, as it takes you through Opium Dens and graveyards.

About a week before Christmas there was still some scenes to be shot. The final sequences were being processed so everyone could go home for the holidays. One member of the cast "Frank Sullivan". an Englishman had been counting for weeks on eating plum pudding in merry old England. Which prompted Claude to order tickets too, for the next ship to England. To reach England by Christmas, Sullivan had to leave Hollywood by plane on a certain morning. But the day before there was still another outdoor scene to shoot and finish, it meant working till dawn. The Rains' were going to England by boat, so he wasn't in any kind of hurry!

That night the Director called on Claude to perform an eight foot jump from a slanted elevator. So, not telling the Director about being blind in one eye, wasn't a smart move on Claude's part.

It was a very cold night and the outdoor scene had never been rehearsed after dark. Miscalculating the distance because of the dim lighting didn't help Claude's landing. He jumped and landed with his leg twisted up under him. He groaned a little as he rose, not showing how hurt he really was. He was such a good actor that no one knew how injured he was!

The leap was at 12 Midnight, but the cameras kept grinding away for three more hours. Claude wanted Mr. Sullivan to catch his plane the next morning and he did!

Later that morning, Claude's doctor sent a note to the studio that Mr. Rains would be detained in bed for a week or more with a badly twisted ankle. The Doctor asked the studio heads why Mr. Rains was permitted to work when he should have been sent home after the accident?

The cast and crew reported that Mr. Rains showed no signs of an injured ankle the night before. The cast proclaimed Claude a hero and a great actor for showing no pain!

But Claude being who he was, refused to listen to the doctor and hobbled to his job on crutches to finish the picture so he could depart for the east where he was tp complete negotiations for a "Stone" farmhouse in Pennsylvania, then he set sail for England.

Along with a visit to his family, Claude signed to do a picture and motored eighty miles an hour through Buckingham Shire, Devonshire, Donset, Essex, Wessex, and Sussex. Searching to renew his collection of Cromwellian egg-cups.

The Gainsborough Gaumont studio, was having financial troubles, so they contacted him to do a film. He thought it was a a good idea to do the film and have a Honeymoon too! He bought two first class tickets on the Queen Mary, the newest member on Cunard White Star Lines, The Super Liner was Christened by her Majesty the Queen on September 26 th 1934. They chose the Deluxe state room with luxurious twin beds, a sofa, arm chair, two closets and private bath finished off the room. Two round windows made you have a view of the Atlantic Ocean.

The main restaurant was huge with freash ocean air and sunshine flooded the deck. At night the ship was lit up by a vast system of indirect illumination.

They found the forward cocktail lounge a delightful place to hang out. Claude's face was still not recognized by the average person, but the Captain knew who he was! His favorite part of the ship was the Round-Bart-Lounge, with a Mural of folk dancers hanging over the bar. The only thing he didn't like were the very high red bar stools. While Francis found the ship's shops, Claude enjoyed a cigar seated in a leather armchair.

All too soon the ship docked at South Hampton, meeting with his family. Then they drove to his sister's small cottage. The next day he made his way to the studio to meet with Fay Wray, his co-star.

Claude played a phoney mind reader, whose act is booked in London. But when Maximus meets a woman named Christine (Jane Baxter) he becomes a real live clairvoyant, when she is near him. He can predict future events. He gets arrested and charged with instigating the state of panic, which leads to a disaster, but he was found not guilty.

Everyone at the studio agreed, that Claude was a natural in his role, because of his compelling steel stare, when he goes into a trance. His penetrating eyes made the film great fun. His co-star Fay Wray was asked to write an article about Rains in the "Clairvoyant". She wrote: "I found him to be rather unexpected mixture of boyishness and seriousness. He is without a doubt one of the most meticulous actor, I have ever known. He is careful and thoughtful about every scene he plays. Claude never does a thing without considering every angle of it, studying it first."

Several times during the making of the picture, he would ponder quietly over a scene. Then say, he felt that the character's reaction in the scenario and he would always be psychologically correct.

"I was particularly intrigued by his eyes. He uses them all the time. They seemed to me all the while to reflect the actual thoughts of the character. In other words he was acting with his eyes."

Claude has a queer habit in real life. If anyone is talking to him and he is tired of the conversation, he will not trouble to interrupt the conversation. He will simply look at the person in a way which seems to say, I'm looking straight at you, but I 'm not listening to a word you are

Carmella Felice

saying. And the conversation at last will falter with the person forgetting what he was talking about. Fay continues the interview. It is the ability to make his eyes talk for him which accounts very largely, I am sure for the intensity of his acting.

Claude is very quiet most of the time but some times he really made us laugh.

For instance he played a joke on us. During a scene in which several of us had to pass through a revolving door, we were told by the director in which order to go, so as to prevent any confusion. But there was a glorious mix-up just the same and Claude Rains was entirely responsible. He deliberately went through the door out of turn and in a moment we got into a dreadful muddly, with hilarious results.

Naturally, we chatted a good deal about the stage as opposed to films. Claude has been associated with the theatre nearly all of his life and is still a comparative new comer to the screen. Claude Rains is genuinely enthusiastic about film work.

He regards it as an entirely new medium and doesn't try to bring his theatrical mannerisms into his acting, which helps to explain why he has achieved success in films so quickly.

When Francis read Fay's article, she couldn't agree with her more.

"That's you Willie.... boyish.. so boyish, women just have to love you." Francis laughed.

After completing the film, the Rain's took that trip to Paris, with a side trip to Vimy Ridge, where 15,000 men lost their lives. Claude could almost hear his fellow soldier's cries in ther cold night. The French government was going to build a memorial on the spot, where bunkers and tunnels, still were in tact, for ten miles around the area. The Rain's gave a donation to a memorial, for the souls, that were killed. Claude held tight to Francis's hand, as they left the overgrown field. It still was barren of trees, as Claude had left it in 1915.

Claude was happy to be sailing back to the United States. He had wanted to see his family, before anything had happen to his father. Also because he didn't know when he would be back to see his family. While in Paris, he had bought Francis a lovely dress and for himself had a few tweed suits made to order. Claude liked good clothes and he liked shirts with stripes on them.

A month later, Claude's agent wired him saying, "Warner Brothers has offered you a two year contract. What do you want to do?" Claude wired back, "Take it!" So off the Rains's went to the West Coast to make movies. Warner Brothers generously offered him $2,500.00 a week!

CHAPTER 8

WARNER BROTHERS, HERE I COME!

But before the contract with Warner Brothers was ready, he was offered a film at Paramount Pictures, called the "Last Outpost", with Cary Grant. He played "John Stevenson", but in the film, Michael Andrews (Cary Grant) only knew him as "Smith", a British intelligence officer. Smith saves Michael's life when his post was destroyed. He carries Michael to British troops, then Smith disappears again. Michael is taken to a hospital, where he falls in love with his nurse. Of course, the nurse turns out to be Smith's wife.

Two thirds of the picture was filmed in piles of sand, which made walking in the stuff a real pain for Rains. But the worst was when they blew the sand in his face. When it came to work, acting in the morning wasn't his forte '. His best acting was done after one in the afternoon, from years of training on the stage. Cary was younger and full of pep, but very insecure about his career. Cary knew Claude was the better actor and he envied Claude's peaceful serenity. What Cary didn't know was that was an act Claude was putting on as always. Cary wanted a wife like Claude's that would help him with his career too! Between takes, Rains taught Cary a little bit about acting.

The two actors got along splendidly, coming from England with almost the same background. Cary appreciated the lessons the older actor gave him. Claude told the handsome actor he should try comedy, because he had a natural flare for it. Then once he had the timing down for the comedy, he could carry on with the real acting. When the "Last Outpost" was released on October of 1935, "Graham Greene" of the Spectator Magaine, wrote this about Rains, in his column. "Mr. Rain's low husky voice, his power in investing even common place dialogue, with smoldering conviction is remarkable.

He never rants, but one is always aware of what a superb ranter he could be in part which did call for modern restraint, but only for superb diction".

When Claude signed with Warner Brothers, he joined the William Morris Agency, located on the West Coast, but he didn't give up his East Coast agent. Cary went on to do comedy, as Claude had suggested and became a big star. He had found his timing, just as Claude had told him and he ran with it.

The Rains' decided to stay for a couple of years in Hollywood, as they went shopped for a new house, in Brentwood. Francis liked her new place, hidden away by the large trees, but she also liked the night life of the Coconut Grove. All the stars went there for dinner and for a while the couple enjoyed the night life, But Claude wasn't a party animal and he had to study most of the time for his films. Francie urged her husband to loosen up and enjoy his good fortune and to stop worrying about saving all the time.

Claude was starting to be recognized in the streets, which was disquieting. His Brentwood home was hidden away from the street, but he longed for his farm in New Jersey.

He looked forward to spending the winter time on the farm, with his wife's family. But every time they tried to go back to the farm, Claude was offered another piece of work, which he didn't turn down.

Warner Brothers had seen, "Crime Without Passion" and thought Claude could perform in a new project they had purchased called, "They Shall Not Die", but a lot of rewriting had to be done on the storyline. So the first film they gave him was, "Hearts Divided", starring Dick Powell. It was a musical, but Claude would be playing a straight role of "Napoleon Bonaparte". He met his old friend Arthur Treacher, on the set of this film and they talked about old times. Dick Powell was a very nice guy, friendly and outgoing, while Marion Davies was inwardly unhappy. William Randolph Hearst had a lot of money invested in the film, so he talked to Jack Warner into firing the actress originally slated to do the part, and replace her with Marion, the love of his life. Hearst was always doing things like that and it would upset Marion, to no end. So she vowed to make this her last role.

Powell played Jerome Bonaparte, who comes to America to sell the Louisiana Territory, to the United States. But he falls in love with Betsy Patterson (Davies). As the couple announces their engagement. Napolean gets wind of it and orders his brother to return to France. Jerome tells Betsy to come with him and that they would be married in France. But Napoleon wants him to wed the Princess of Wurtenburg. When the ship reaches France, Jerome goes to find his brother, while Napoleon goes aboard the ship, to talk to Betsy. He convinces her to return to the United States, because Jerome has to represent his country, by marrying the Princess. Betty convinced, leaves on ther next ship headed for Maryland.

But Jerome follows her back to America, and ends with Jerome singing to Betsy in her garden. All of which happened in real life, with Napoleon agreeing to the marriage of Jerome to Betsy.

Rains next film was more of a challenge for the actor. "Don Luis" was a really nasty villain, in the film, "Anthony Adverse", In this film, he will meet up with his friend, Gale Sondergaard. They liked to needle each other a lot about scene stealing. "Don't you upstage me on this set.... Napoleon! Which would crack up Claude. Sondergaard was a wonderful actress and it was a pleasure for him to work with her. Another colleague of his graced the set, Mr. Lewis Hayward, his fencing friend. They were directed by the great Mervyn Leroy and his assistant Michael Curtiz, an Hungarian.

Jack Warner had brought the Hungarian to America, because he had seen one of his films while in Europe. Curtiz was happy to be at Warner Brothers, because Hitler had come to power in Germany and was making trouble with other countries in that area. He had a thick Hungarian accent, that annoyed a lot of people. He stood a good foot over Rains. Curtiz would always talk to Claude seated, so that he could talk eye to eye with his actor. Like the actor, Michael felt the freedom to create. Claude liked Michael, because he made him laugh with his awful English accent!

"Move your bitt!" Michael would yell at the crew, or mind your peas!"

In Claude's next film, Warner Brothers, gave him top billing in one of their films, "Stolen Holiday". The actor plays Stefan Orloff, a charming crook, who enlists the help of a model, to further his schemes to steal money from the rich. He offers Nichol Picot, (Kay Francis) a chance to have her own shop, where she can show off her dress designs. For years, he uses her good reputation as a designer, to promote his own illegal deals. Years later the government of France catches up with his gang. Married to Nicole, he sends for her, to get him out of as jam, but the police have followed her to his hiding place and he gets killed.

By this time in his career, he was getting a little tired of playing the bad guy, but Jack Warner didn't want to change that formula that made money for his company. But Jack gave in a little, when he asked Claude to play the Earl. of Hertford, in the "Prince and the Pauper". Twins, Bobby and Billy Mauch, take the leads in this film, with Errol Flynn. Errol isn't seen until almost half way through the film. The Mark Twain story is about a Prince who's father dies, while he is out playing with a boy that looks, like the prince. When the real prince can't get back into the castle, the beggar takes his place. As the prince is about to be beaten by the Captain of the Guard, (Alan Hale), Errol comes to the rescue of the prince. All this time, the "Earl" wants to take over the crown, by proving the prince is crazy.

Rains wore a very heavy costume through the filming. His skinny legs couldn't keep up his long black stockings that he had to wear. He was forever pulling them up, as Alan Hale laughed at his efforts. Or when he went to sit down, the hilt of his sword would hit him on his side of his hip. As Claude would pull it straight, Hale would shake his head with a smile and a tease. "Your socks are falling down again Claude",

Flynn finally saves the new king and Tom Canty is made a ward of the King. Rains wanted to go on vacation after the film was completed, but Jack wanted him to do "They Shall Not Die" first. In this production he plays a southern district attorney.

Claude practiced at home, before a mirror, to see if he could obtain that southern drawl, he needed to do the film. But his English accent still crept into his speech. Then he tried talking with a cigar in his mouth, and that seemed to work a little better.

Under contract to do the movie with him, was his old friend Otto Kruger and a newcomer, a teenager who has a small part in the film, because she is the one murdered. That little part made a star out of Lana Turner.

The Life and Times of Claude Rains

One day he talked to Jack again, about being typed cast as a villian. Jack wouldn't give into the actor's demands and Claude drove home to Brentwood, a little upset. When he opened the door to his house, he could smell something wonderful, cooking in the kitchen. Francis was all smiles as she lit the two candles placed on the kitchen table. Claude kissed his wife and asked what was cooking, that smelled so good?"

"All kinds of goodies!" smiled his wife.

"Any thing in particular, Francie?"

"Roast Beef, baked potatoes and some red wine."

"That sounds good, after the day I had. I don't think I'm going to renew my contract with Warners, after this year is up!" He said sitting down and pouring himself a glass of wine.

"Oh, but you have to Claude.... I mean.. we need the security now!" she insisted.

"Security... the acting profession was never good about security!"

But Claude... you have to keep your job now.... we are having a baby!" she exclaimed.

Claude almost choked on his drink, as he stared at his wife..."How"? he just said.

"The regular way... we wait seven more months, and then... you are a daddy." she laughed. He slowly rose to his feet, still thinking Francis was joking with him.

"I can't wait to tell the family." she cried.... and he knew it wasn't a joke.

"My dear, you have made me very happy.... thank you." he said holding her tightly.

When her family found out she was pregnant, they were overjoyed. Claude stayed silent at work about his wife being pregnant, he didn't want to jinx his luck. For the next seven months, he treated Francis like a queen. He hired a cook, and a housekeeper, so she wouldn't hurt herself cleaning.

When his daughter was born, everyone in Francis' family came for a visit to see Jennifer. Claude was so proud, when he announced to his bosses that his wife had a baby girl. He handed out good cigars, with little pink wrappers, with Jennifer's name on them.

Claude couldn't believe his good fortune. He loved his life even more then he could have imagined. When he looked into his child's eyes, he knew he wanted only the best for his daughter. He wanted her to have, what he did not have in his youth. Two parents to love her, and schooling that would make her into anything she wanted to be. "Even a doctor, to take care of her dad!" he thought to himself, as he watched his baby sleeping in a peaceful country. After the baby was born, Claude fought harder to get better roles. He wrote little notes to Jack Warner, concerning his lines. The writers wrote him lines that weren't dramatic enough for him. He had to rely on his little tricks for him to be noticed in a film. A long stare, a raised eyebrow, the Stewart appearance, when he was walking around, with one hand in his pocket. He tried to be polite, to the studio heads, as he tried to get a good role. But sometimes he felt like a dog, waiting to be thrown a meaty bone. The scripts were inferior and he wasn't the only one complaining about it.

He had to endure standing on a four inch box, just to be the same height as the other stars, in a frame. It overwhelmed him some times, what the studio, would do to its stars. Edward G. Robinson was another star, that Warner Brothers, wanted to stand in a box. But Edward wouldn't have it, saying, "If I'm the boss of a gang, wouldn't it be more dramatic, if a little man bossed big men around?"

Jack Warner had his share of problems, with his stars. He knew the public liked Rains, just the way he was, but a little taller. He couldn't play a romantic role if he was shorter than the girl. He knew Claude wasn't the rebellious kind, but he was having trouble with his biggest star, Bette Davis. She had wanted better roles too! Jack didn't give her a good picture, so Bette sailed to England, hoping to make films in Europe, that she liked. But she had a contract with Warner Brothers. Davis had found a producer, that wanted her for two pictures, "The Garden of the Moon", and "Comet over Broadway." The European producer, Ludovico Toeplitz, loved Betty and wanted to make her a big star in Europe. But Jack hired the celebrated trial lawyer, Sir Patrick Hasting K.C. to represent Warner Brothers' law suit to get Bette to honor her contract.

Back at Warner Brothers, the newspaper put out by the studio, told of Bette's exploits.... Rains and the other stars, waited for the out come of the case, with great interest. Jack knew that he had to win the case, or half of his stars, would take to the hills, or worse Europe!

Sir Patrick went to court on October 9th, 1936. "This is a rather naughty young lady, who wants more money, my lord!" he said in his opening speech. Bette's reply was "No! It's not the money but more the roles worthy of my-fully developed talents." Bette said on the stand.

Justice Branson the judge on the case, was not use to women suing in an occupational dispute. He was an old fashion man, who believed women should stay in the home. He couldn't believe that Miss Davis, was claiming "Artistic Hardship". After a few days in court, Justice Branson, ordered that Davis should honor, her contract with Warner Brothers.

"You cannot claim "Artistic Hardship" Miss Davis, when you are so well compensated, for your services", the judge concluded. The studio's newsletter carried the account's of Davis's trial, making sure the stars knew where they stood. Claude decided he should stop his complaints, as they handed him a new script called "The Adventures of "Robin Hood" again he was to wear a heavy costume, for his role of Prince John. King Richard the lionhearted has been captured by his enemies, who want a fortune for his return. While the King was away Prince John took control of England and taxed the people severly.

Robin is played by Errol Flynn, Basil Rathbone is Sir Guy Gisbourne, Olivia Dehavilland is Lady Marian. Claude had to made his villain more nastier, than Basil's "Sir Guy". They played very well together, and on their breaks, they talked about England and her troubles with Germany again. Basil belonged to the British community, that had a country club, where they played polo together. All of the English people at the club, thought that England was headed for a war.

In the mean time, Claude was fighting a war with Machael Curtiz, just to get home at a reasonable hour, so that he could spend time with his family. Michael worked every one till eight at night, just to keep on schedule. Mike was always calling for rehearsals, just to make the scenes perfect. He yelled at the assistant director, Jack Sullivan, and dialogue director Irving Rapper, all the time about the script.

Rains had studied up on Prince John before shooting started on the film. He read all kinds of history books about the Prince. They showed the man to be cocky, self centered man, who loved clothes, goods food, and might have been a homosexual. When he first started shooting the film, Claude wanted to play him, like he had read about the character. But Mike told him, it wouldn't pass the censors,. So Rains played him like a very cultured man, to obtain the same effect he was aiming for. One afternoon after a take, Basil and Claude sat talking about the "Great War". Rathbone told him that he had been an intelligence officer, during the war, station near Vimy Ridge, with his outfit. One day his Captain ordered him and two other soldiers to go over the enemy's line, and capture a German. Basil and his friends crawled through "No Man's Land", looking for some German soldiers. Suddenly they heard voices speaking German. They were digging holes and placing something in it. Catching them by surprise, they captured the two men, and took them back to their camp. They had also taken the canisters, that the German's were burying in the ground. It turned out to be Clorine Gas. The General of the Allies, decided not to act on this information which lead to the gasing of 15,000 Allied soldiers.

Rains was mad when he heard the story. He wondered how the General could live with that on his soul. Now that the Germans were trying again to take over Europe.

CHAPTER 9

WAR AGAIN, AS HE BUY'S THE FARM!

Would America go to war? was the question uttered by Americans. "No," came the answer from President Roosevelt. "It's a European problem and Americans will stay out of it this time."

As England tried to talk peace with Hitler, he had other ideas of taking over the world. By 1939, Rains had become an American citizen, because he wanted his daughter to grow up knowing he loved the United States. His obligations towards England were ended, as he began to talk up, with the other stars, about halting trade with Germany.. stars like, Jimmy Cagney, the Marx Brothers, Gloria Stewart and the studio heads, signed petitions, to end trading with Hitler. Their petition was sent to Congress, in hopes that the people would take some action. But their cause fell on deaf ears.

A party was given to Erich Wolfgang Korngald, at the studio, for winning an oscar for his musical score on the "Adventures of Robin Hood". The Rains' took their small daughter with them to the party, where all the stars, on the lot came, even in costume to congratulated the composer. After Jack saw Claude with his small daughter, he offered him a new film, where he could have top billing. "White Banner", would co-star two teenagers, Jackie Cooper, and Bonita Granville, who played Claude's daughter.

He also had a small baby so in the film, which he handled with great care. Fay Bainter, stole the film, with her portrayal of Hannah Parmalee. In this production, Jackie fell in love with Bonita, but she wouldn't go out on a date with him. He was heart-broken, that she wouldn't return his love. Claude seemed to find himself in the middle of the affair as a mediator.

In his father-like character of Paul Ward, they came to him for advice. But Claude told the boy, to let it go if the young lady didn't want to return his love. Jackie threw himself into the part of Peter Trimble, to forget what he felt for Bonita. Most of his scenes were with Rains, as Bonita kept out of his way. Claude plays a teacher who is also an inventor. He and Peter, invent an icebox. The parts for the machine are madeto-order, by a man in the village. One day the man comes to the house with another piece for the invention. Peter shows the man the machine by mistake. The scrupulous mechanic, steals the idea, and copywrights Ward's invention. But Hannah helps the two, with her kind words, and they discuss inventing the refrigerator, Hannah is Peter's real mother, who gave him up for adoption, to a rich family. Peter's biological father gives them money to produce the refrigerator. It was a nice little family picture, that would lead Rains on a new path, playing a father type.

Rains' fans enjoyed his role, but Fay Bainer was nominated for her role as Hannah. She also was nominated for her role in "Jezabel" for supporting actress for which she won her oscar. With the huge success of "White Banners", Jack Warner started looking for another project where Rains, could play a father. Jack Warner offered him the role of Adam Lemp, which Rains accepted. Lemp is a music professor, who has four daughters. They are played by three sisters, Lola, Pricilla, and Rosemary Lane. The fourth sister was Gale Page, with May Robinson as Lemp's sister, Etta. Newcomer John Garfield was signed by Warner Brothers, after seeing the actor in a Broadway play.

John is "Mickey Borden". After this film is released, Garfield will rise to fame quickly, but in the Lemp storyline he is killed.

John, or "Jules", as he preferred to be called, became attached to Rains, because they came from the same background. Poor and with a very bad speech impediment.

If it wasn't for the principal of his school, taken an interest in John, by giving him diction lessons, Garfield, would have ended up, a hoodlum. Next his teacher talked him into doing a school play. Garfield took to it, like a dog takes to a meaty bone. After the showing of his first film, he became an overnight sensation. Fans wanted more Garfield and Rains.

Director Michael Curtiz, brought out the best performances in his actors. Claude had a few scenes left to do with Frank McHugh, and Dick Forman, before the family could head back East.

The Rains family hadn't been back home a couple of days when the storm from the North East sent a lightning bolt, striking his farmhouse, destroying all his prize possessions. Lucky the family was in town when the storm from the North East hit!

Calling his agent he related this at three o'clock in the morning. Jimmy was still sleeping when Claude roared over the telephone.

James, This is Claude.

Yes Claude said the agent quietly

Claude's booming voice.... yelled "Did I tell you James, That I, intended raising Chickens on my Farm?"

Yes Claude, James said faintly

Well I can't! Claude........ Boomed again

That's too bad Claude.", James said almost asleep again

Claude yelled louder. "Well, why don't you ask me why?"

Irriotable James asked why?"

"Because there aren't any Roosters left and the Hens are dead too! Well what I mean is.... The farm was struck by lightning last night when I was in town and the farm disappeared. Demolished! Gone! Gone up in smoke! All of it. Not even a tree or candlestick left standing. My mugs, All my collections, My books, scripts!

Claude!... James yelled! Are you all okay?

Yes, Yes we were in town!

So rebuild, buy a new farm house

Buy a bigger one, but just let me go back to sleep."

Claude hung up the phone repeating Jame's words, buy a new farm"

So when Jack Warner sent him a new script called "They made me a Criminal", he took the role. Even though he didn't want to play a New York detective with an English accent. John Garfield had the accent and so did The East Side Kids. But he couldn't fake that kind of accent. The more he thought about the role, the less he liked it. So he decided to write Jack Warner Vice President of Warner Brothers a letter, First National Pictures.

> Dear Jack,
> Having thoroughly enjoyed my association with the studio, and towed the line to cooperate, to the best of my ability. I feel that you should know my, inability to understand being cast for the part of Phelan in "They Made Me A Criminal". Frankly, I feel that I am so poorly cast that it would be harmful to your picture. You have done such a good job in building me up that it seems a pity to tear that down with such a part as this, and I am confident that your good judgement will recognize this. Dogs delight to bark a bit and I think I have been a good dog for three years, so perhaps you will give me five minutes to talk it over, Claude.

But as always Jack didn't listen... casting Claude in the film. So Rains had to try every trick he knew to cover up his English accent. He would practice in front of his wife, with a cigar in his mouth, talked out the side of his mouth like Edward G. Robinson. But he couldn't obtain that substance he needed to make the character work. Then he thought maybe, if I make the character really look ridiculous, Jack wouldn't hand him these parts anymore. But deep down he knew the director wouldn't make him get away with it. Now he knew how Errol Flynn felt working for Michael Curtiz.

His friends Garfield and Wong Howe the cinematographer, got him through the picture. But he wasn't satisfied with the results. Even though the picture did well at the boxoffice, Claude went again to Jack about a better role. Curtiz than approached him to do a twenty-two minute short called, "Sons of Liberty". He would play Hagm Solomon, a Polish-Jewish emigrant that saves the American Revolution.

It was a good part for a film short, as he co-starred with Gale Sondergaard, who plays his wife.

Solomon helps George Washington and the Continental Army, fight the British.

Solomon becomes a spy for Washington, when the British find out, he is quickly captured. In prison he meets Nathan Hale then escapes, making his way to Philadelphia. There he helps raise money for Washington's army. He addresses other Jews in many synagogues, to go out and raise money for Washington. A grand total of $400,000, is raised to outfit the war, which causes General Cornwalles, to surrender to Washington at Yorktown.

The twenty-two minute film short won an Academy Award for Best Short Subject in 1939. Curtiz had finally won his oscar and a bonus of $3,000, from Jack Warner. Claude's reward was the part of Napoleon III in the film "Juarez". It was a Paul Muni project with Gale Sondergaard playing opposite Rains. Jack never broke up a good thing, but used it over and over. Gale and Claude were a good team, which Jack thought was perfect.

At this point in time Rains had never met Bette Davis. But he had a scene with the actress towards the end of the picture. Davis didn't want to rehearse with Rains, so she came in blind to Claude's scene with her. He had played Napolean so much, he felt he had that character down pat. Davis wasn't on the set, as Claude lit his cigar, and placed it in his mouth. Gale stood waiting as Rapper called for the star. Davis was late and Rains didn't think that was very professional of her. A few minutes later, Davis rushed into the studio. "Sorry, sorry, but they just couldn't get this dress on me". Claude glanced horrendously at picturesque Gale. Finally he took his seat, when the director called, "places". He took a puff from his cigar, as he waited for the action call. The call came, and Bette was announced. The actress sailed onto the set.

She took one look at Claude's glaring eyes, and she turned and ran towards the director yelling. "Oh my God! His eyes his eyes.. they scare me to death!" Claude jumped up, to see what the trouble was? "It's your eyes, they scared me for a second.

"Sorry Miss Davis, but my wife says I have that effect on women!"

"Bette looked straight into his eyes, and said. "You're not doing it now.. that look!"

"Oh I was acting, dear lady.. I did want to rehearse with you, before we did the scene.

"Sorry, so sorry.... they had me doing another scene in another studio."

"So I was informed. Are you alright now?"

"Yes! Now that I can see you are a very charming man." Taking their spots again, the scene was done in two takes, which pleased Rapper. In those few minutes Bette knew they would make a good team. She went to Jack and asked if he could find a story, that she could play with Rains. After seeing the two in the scene, Jack agreed that there was flame there, that could be kindled, In the film Davis plays, Carlota, wife of Maximillian (Brian Aherne) while Paul Muni was excellent as Benito Juarez. John Garfield was a spanish, soldier, under Jaurez. Garfield seemed out of place in this film, but like Rains, he was under contract to do the films that Jack wanted them to do. When the film was released, Bette gave this interview with the press, when she was asked about her co-stars, Bette pointed out Claude Rains's "Napolean", who began as a revolutionist, then the President of the French Republic, finally the head of the Second Empire.

Rains makes him proud, vain, crafty, elusive and cowardly. His scenes are relatively few, but Rains makes them vivid!" This coming from the Queen of the Movies, put a seal of approval on the actor. The fans took another look at the film, and realized what she meant. She probably fell in love with Claude, the first moment, that they met, but Claude always told her, how much he loved his wife. She respected him and his family, and they became great friends. At first Francis wasn't too happy with Claude's new friendship, but she knew her husband loved her, and she trusted him.

Many organizations were formed between 1936 and 1939, to stop Hitler. On June 9th, 1936, Rains had joined a group of Hollywood stars, calling themselves, The Hollywood Anti-Nazi League. Gloria Stuart had started the group at Universal Studios. Carl Laemmle Jr. also was in the group. The document stated that the United States should stop all trade, with the Nazi government of Germany. They weren't taken serious by the President, or the Congress. What the Stars didn't know was that the United States wasn't prepared to fight a war, so the President didn't want to cause any waves, that might bring America, into a war too quickly.

Jewish actors like Paul Muni, Edward G. Robinson and John Garfield, gave their time and money to organizations, that told the stars, they would help fellow Jews. But they were only fronts for the communist party. With England at war, Claude felt helpless because his family, didn't want to come to America, to sit out the war. He sent them money to buy what they needed, but life in England became very grim. Rains was still working in Hollywood, when he was approached to play a role in, "Mr. Smith Goes To Washington". Director Frank Capra's first duty was to get permission from the President, to measure and film the Senate floor. He wanted to reproduce it on a studio lot, and he needed the exact measurements. While he was in D.C., President Roosevelt invited him to a press conference. Roosevelt was already seated at a desk, when the reporters, came into the room. When they all left, the President rolled himself in his wheelchair to greet the famous director. Most Americans didn't know that the President was in a wheelchair, because of his bout with Polio. He didn't want to be seen weak in the eyes of other governments, so he never had his picture taken in the wheel chair, Capra told Roosevelt honestly.

"I didn't vote for you Mr. President, but I feel, you have done a good job."

Jimmny Stewart the star of the film, wanted to join the Air Force, after the film was finished. Most of his buddies had already gone to England to join the R. A. F. But Jimmy wanted to be in the American counterpart. Jimmy was always nervous with his lines, because he told everyone, that it would be his last film before going away and he wanted his fans to remember him in it. Stewart played Senator Jefferson Smith, to Claude's Senator Joseph Paine. Their co-stars were Edward Arnold, Thomas Mitchell and Jean Arthur.

It took months before, Capra could build his own Senate floor and upper gallery, where Miss Arthur and Mr. Thomas would do most of their acting from. No one in the administration, knew what the picture was about. But if they did, it would have made life uncomfortable for the studio. Claude had to calm down Stewart, with funny stories.

Great tales about his almost favorite director Michael Curtiz.

"You think Capra is strict! Jimmy... you haven't worked with Michael Curtiz. He works you to death! In my contract it is written, that I stop working at 6 P.M. But Curtiz was working us till 8 P.M. at night to stay on budget, costing me time with my family. I wanted to be home with my daughter, before Francie put her to sleep. But Michael wanted to complete the work ahead of schedule, to save the studio money.

I couldn't take it any more! On my way home one day, I stopped at the local drugstore, and bought the biggest alarm clock, I could find! The next day I set it for 5:59 p.m. and placed it in my costume. I told the other actors, that we were going home on time that day, and not to be startled, when they heard the clock go off at the appropriate time.

At 5:59 P.M., the alarm in my pocket went off. We all stood still, as Curtiz went crazy with the noise. "Vhat is that noise? Stop it! Stop it? Where is it coming from?" Curtiz asked. Then I stepped forward smiling and said. "It's my new clock! I said taking this large thing from my pocket. The crew started to laugh, as Curtiz walked towards me.

"Vhat is this about, Claude?"

"My contract says I go home at six o'clock Mike, and you kept us here till all hours of the night. We have families, we have to go home too! Well, Mike smiled and hugged me saying. "You're right. My mind floats vay vhen, I am having fun." After that we went home on time every day, and I was a big hero to the stars but not to the crew, who made the overtime." Claude laughed. Jimmy laughed saying. "I didn't think you had it in you to pull a stunt like that." Claude. Claude grinned, saying.

"Oh a dog can take so much from a cruel master, then he will bite the hand that feeds him!"

"I guess your're right, but this scene is getting me down. Capra doesn't like the way I play being hoarse." My voice can just do so much, before I really get hoarse.

"Well then he will have what he wants!"

But they took two more takes, and Capra still didn't like the way Stewart was doing his lines. That night Jimmy went to see a doctor-friend of his and asked. "I'm doing a scene in my film, where I am suppose to be hoarse, but I can't achieve it. Do you have something that will make me hoarse?" The doctor answered. "In my eighteen years of practicing, that is a new one. I don't think I can do that, Jimmy."

"I'll pay you for the day, to come with me to the studio, so you can watch if I get sick."

"Well, Bichhoride of Mercury, can induce, that effect, but I will have to spray it into your throat."

"I'll pick you up at five tomorrow morning, and I will drive you to the studio.

The Life and Times of Claude Rains

The next morning Jimmy picked up his doctor and they went together to the studio.

The doctor sprayed his throat then waited while Jimmy went to put on his make-up. At 7 A.M. Jimmy picked up his doctor at the studio's cafeteria, and took him to the studio.

Jimmy asked the doctor to spray his throat again, because it didn't sound hoarse enough.

After he started coughing a little, but the doctor told him it was just a side effect. Capra came on the set, with the other actors, as Jimmy took his spot on the floor of the senate.

Claude sat down in his Captain's Chair, to await being called by Capra. Stewart was still coughing when Capra took his position near the camera.

"Well Jimmy, do you think we can finish, this scene today?" Jimmy smiled and waved. "O. K. let's try it!" Capra said "Action" Jimmy just stood standing for a while, then he spoke with a very hoarse voice, that Capra couldn't understand.

"Cut! Jimmy, I can't understand, what you are trying to say! Let's try it again."

Jimmy started coughing as he spoke his lines. Claude watched as Jimmy's voice faded out to a whisper. After an hour, Jimmy finally confessed about what he had done. Claude couldn't believe that an actor, would do that to his voice. "Mercury!" Capra yelled. He sprayed "Mercury on your vocal chords?" The doctor stepped forward saying. "It will be all right. It wears off in about three hours!"

"Capra yelled. "Get off my set doctor and don't you ever do this again to any actor!"

The doctor left in a huff, thinking that his name would be brought up in a lawsuit by the studio.

Claude and Edward Arnold, just shook their heads about the incident with the "Mercury".

"This studio has a million dollars, wrapped up in this film, Jimmy and you play a prank like this!"

"I am sorry, Mr. Capra. I just...... cough... wanted to get.. cough, the scene over and done with. "Do you feel like doing this scene again?" Capra asked. "Yes".... coughed Jimmy.

Carmella Felice

Capra set up the scene again, and it was a take for Capra. The director didn't want to hear Jimmy's hoarse voice again. Stewart walked over to where Claude and Arnold were seated and shrugged his shoulders saying.

"Guess, that's over... cough.. with."

"Jimmy, why would you do such a foolish thing as to spray a chemical, in your throat.

That spray could have scared your vocal cords for good." Claude huffed.

"Yes dear boy, why would you take such a chance?" Arnold asked.

"This might be my last film... cough.. I wanted my fans... to remember me!"....

"Remember you, I don't understand?" Arnold asked puzzled. "I enlisted into the Air Force, last week. The government is going to give me a commission, in a few months. If something happened to me.. cough.. I wanted.... people to remember..... my name!"

On July 7th, 1939 Rains completed his part in the film. He had the summer off, as the family returned to the new farm, to see how the farming had progressed, with all the lime he added to the soil. The budget of the film exceeded by $288,660.

Months later the preview was a dazzling social event attended by 4,000 guests. Among them 45 Senators, including Majority Leader Albert W. Bankley, 250 congressman, the Speaker of the House. William Bankhead, Majority Leader Sam Rayburn, Secretary of State Cordell Hull, Attorney General Frank Murphy and many other famous politicians. They watched the picture and were insulted by what the film implied. The next day the newspapers carried the resentment of all the politicians that attended the affair. The critic of the "New York Sun," called the film superficially polite. The "Chicago Tribune's press service blasted the film. William Edwards wrote the members of the Senate were writhing in their seats."

Rains didn't attend the showing, but read about it the next day. He thought for sure the picture would be a flop, but all the publicity made the public want to see the film. Then after they saw it, they told their friends about the film, and more people went to see the picture. Letters and telegrams flooded the studio about how wonderful the acting was in the film. Then Claude read how Majority Leader Rayburn had remarked in the papers.

"It won't do the movie industry any good." Then Leader Barkley said.

"The very idea of the senator walking out at the behest of that old crook! Claude Rains.

"Rains couldn't believe that the country's leaders had taken it to heart. Like it was personal afront to their characters. He called Capra long distance to complain about the negative publicity. Capra laughed at how up-tight Rains was. So Capra said.

"It only goes to prove what a wonderful actor you are Claude, that these fools would believe you are really a Senator."

"Well you might be right Frank, but I'm still worried about this affair. I just became a citizen a short while ago, and I don't want these people to take that away."

"Don't worry Claude... we'll take care of everything." Capra promised. But things only got worse for Capra the film-maker. On October 27th Capra shot back in the newspapers.

"With all those things they got to do, down there in Washington D.C with the Neutality Bill and Social Legistration with the war breaking out in Europe. The whole U.S. Senate has to move against one motion picture and it's actors, It's amazing!"

The studio had been urged by the government not to send the film to Europe. Joseph P. Kennedy, England's U.S Ambassador, offered to buy the negative of the film, so he could burn it. Capra replied to the U.S Ambassador to England. "Nobody should be able to buy a book to burn it, nor a film to burn it. What is this... Nazi Germany! The actors have given their all for this film and you want to destroy it! Why? Mr. Ambassador? And where will you get the money to buy it? Mr. Ambassador!"

After all that trouble, the film was released to the European market on November 11th. The production made a lot of money for it's backers, because of all the bad publicity. Showmen 's trade Review wrote: We are beginning to wonder whether the whole controversy about the film wasn't just a publicity ploy to sell tickets.

"To this day, the film's rentals alone amassed $6,467,801, and it climbs everyday as a big money maker of all time.

Claude was surprised when he was nominated for Best supporting Actor for that film. But didn't win the Oscar losing it to Thomas Mitchell for his performance in "Stagecoach". For Claude it was an honor just to be nominated. Big time scripts started to come his way plus a raise in his weekly salary.

Warner Brothers sent him six scripts for him to inspect, three of which he didn't want to do and two that he thought his fans wanted to see him in. "Four Wives" was just a continuation of the Adam Lemp adventures, with his four daughters, and "Saturday "Children", Ann Shirley plays Claude's daughter this time. They were family pictures, where Rains thought he wouldn't get into any trouble, like with "Mr. Smith goes to Washington." Claude didn't mind that his good friend John Garfield had top billing this time, so long as they paid him at the end of the week. By now the Epstein brothers knew how to write for their favorite star. He also was working with his best Director of Photography, James Wong Howe. Howe was a genius with the camera and lighting on his stars. He always brought out the best in Claude's face.

One day Howe announced to Claude and John, that he was going to open up a Chinese restaurant. That they and their families were invited to opening night on the house. Rains liked Chinese food, so he and Garfield were taught to cook it by James Wong Howe. Claude really respected his cameraman. When ever he planned the scene he knew just what Claude liked.

Claude was also doing a lot of radio shows between 1936 and 1940. It was the only means that the poor had to entertain themselves. Now with a war in progress, Americans were glued to their sets. On October 14th, Rains performed with a little girl by the name of Shirley Temple, for C.B.S, on the Lux Radio Theatre. The story was "The Littlest Rebel", and Claude plays her father. Seemed everywhere he went he was listed as the father type now. He got to meet some of the funniest men in radio, like Jack Benny and Fred Allen. Rains didn't like to listen to the radio himself, and he didn't want one in his house, but as time passed he relented on that decision for his daughter's sake.

With Europe at war, things in England were slowly going downhill. The English community was getting worried about their families overseas and started sending for them to come to America. But Rains's family were sticking it out in their home, now that German submarines were trying to sink England's ships.

The atmosphere in Hollywood had changed in the space of a few months. Many men had left to join the Canadian Army or they went to England to join their Air Force. War talk was spreading all around North America, but Roosevelt still held out as an isolationist. Stories of Concentration camps started to spread on the radio as Claude started his next picture the "Sea Hawk" Back to costume parts went Rains, as he played "Don Alvarez", Ambasssador from King Phillip of Spain. The actor's costume itched him like crazy, because of the hot lights, shining on him. His bouts with his saber left him all black and blue. But than there was Michael Curtiz, being his old "Pain in the Neck" self, working the crew long hours, to make up for the lost manpower!

Many actors in the film were either an emigrant or naturalized citizen like himself. So all they talked about was the war, and how their old home lands were fairing. Some even had maps to trace the battles, like Errol Flynn, who was himself a Tasmanian. Donald Crisp an Englishman and Michael Curtiz a Hungarian, talked about the war constantly. Brenda Marshal who played "Dona Maria", Flynn's love interest in the film, held her own in these conversations. The budget for the film was approximately $1,400,000 a great sum for a film made during a depression. Claude recieved almost $40,000 for his role in the film. His popularity in full swing, matched that of Errol Flynn.

Warner Brothers had purchased a new water tank that had just been constructed on stage 21. The tank was literally a man-made lake, to sail the Spanish toy-ships on. The tank was capable of holding water four feet deep. Many carpenters were set to work building the ships that would sail in the small lake. After the models were finished, they were mounted on platforms which were connected to hydraulic jacks, that produced the rocking motion of the sea on the ships. Claude would bike out to the sound stage to see how far the carpenters had gotten with the work every day on his lunch hour.

Flynn in the meanwhile was taking fencing lessons from his teacher Don Turner, who was also Errol's double in the film. Claude wasn't sword fighting in this film so he didn't have to practice his moves with the sword. So he would take a sandwich out to the pond and watch the ships bounce on the water. He loved the little Spanish galleons which were built to scale. Everything was made in detail to the original ships that sailed in those days.

Little cannons all in position to fire, lined the deck of the ships. The sails full out in their splendor, blowing in the soft breeze, were magnetic to look at.

One day as Claude watched from his bike and eating his sandwich, Curtiz came up to him saying. "Vhat do you think of them? Claude."

"Give me a couple of those ships and I might win a war!"... Claude smiled.

"They cost enough to feed an army!" Curtiz replied. Claude nodded his head in agreement, but wished Mike would leave him alone to enjoy his lunch break. Curtiz pointed to the bigger of the two ships and said. "That one is $4000! The two others are $3,000, each.

"Why didn't you ask me to build these ships, I could have done it for less Claude kidded his boss.

"You can build ships like this?"

"Are you kidding me, Mike?.... I built the ship that sailed on the Nile, for my boss in England. Sir Herbert Tree!" Rains laughed.

"Vell next time I need a ship to sail the Nile, I will get you to build it, smart man."

After he finished his sandwich, Claude lit a cigar up and watched Mike direct a scene, with the ships rocking back and forth. Handymen waded into the tank to set the action for the fight scenes between the ships. With their pants rolled up to their knees, that attached the ships to the jacks. Curtiz yelling all the time on where he wanted his camera set up. Suddenly, Rains felt a hand on his shoulder, it was Errol, finished with his lessons.

"What's the cow up to now? Claude?" Errol asked.

"Going to do the fight scene, with the Spanish Galleons!" Claude said puffing on his cigar. "Good.... anything to get that jerk out of my hair!"

"What's he done now? Errol"

"He went to Jack about the fencing lessons. He told him I couldn't do the scene. So what if I can't sword fight with the best of them. That's why they hired Ralph Faulker and Ned Davenport!" Errol carried on.

"You make him get on your nerves too much. With Mike you have to fight fire with fire."

The Life and Times of Claude Rains

"He wouldn't treat John Barrymore like he does me! Errol sighed.

"No... maybe not... but after this picture you might be a force to reckon with! Mike sees things as a director, who has to bring his film in on a budget. While Jack just sees dollar signs. We are just the dogs that do the hard work look easy!" Claude sighed.

"How come you didn't have to go for sword fighting lessons? Claude."

Claude gave Errol a long stare and whispered. "Ask Louis Hayward he should know!"

In 1940, the Prime Minister of England, Winston Churchill, was begging President Roosevelt to enter the war. But as much as Americans wanted to help England, they felt it wasn't any of their business. They had helped Europe in a World War, which made many families lose their loved ones. Roosevelt's answer was "No, we are having troubles of our own."

Rains was handed a few more scripts, which he and Francis read over. But he was more interested in his farm. They had pumped a lot of capital into the small farm, with no results. After reading farm magazines, and reports from the Agricultural Department, they came to the conclusion the farm was too small to produce a profit. So the Rains' hired a realty service to find them a large place, about one hundred acres.

In their free time, they scoured the countryside looking for a new place, while asking big farmers how they ran a place so large. They told them how the Government was beefing up productions of certain grains, to be sold to England, so that they could feed their armies. This interested Claude very much, as he expanded his search for his promised land.

"Lady with Red Hair" wasan't much of the script, but it wasn't controversial either. He didn't want another film like, Mr. Smith goes to Washington!" Francis thought it was a woman's story, and she was right. Claude plays "David Belasco", the great producer-director of the early part of the century. Claude had seen him once at one of the theatre's that the Guild played at. Belasco was a very strong character to play, as he fought his way in the theatre with everyone. In the story, Mrs. Caroline Carter (Mirian Hopkins) comes to Belasco seeking to be an actress. At first, he doesn't want to teach the widow. But slowly he changes his mind, because he sees she has talent. As the years pass, she becomes a great actress, but the two always fight about parts. Belasco doesn't want her to act in any other plays but his own which finally breaks their friendship for a while.

The film wasn't a great hit, mostly because people were suffering with a depression and money was tight!

A month before Christmas, Warner Brothers shut down the studio, claiming lack of funds. The Rains' spent that winter at their farm in New Jersey, with most of Francis's family. Jennifer was almost three years old, and excited about Santa Claus coming down her fireplace.

Around the 12th of January, the realtor called to say they had found an exciting piece of property in Philadelphia. They rode down the next day to see the farmhouse and the land surrounding it. As they approached the farmhouse the Rains' could see the place was in ill-repair. But Claude liked the large house in Romanville Pennsylvania and asked who owned it, He learned that it belonged to a Quaker Church but that the taxes were too much for them to keep up with. It had three hundred and twenty nine acres, with a huge house and Barn up the hill from the main house. After talking with the owners, they decided to buy the property. He had falling in love with the place at first sight.

Compared to his first farm in Lamberville New Jersey, this place was a "Kingdom", he could rule over.

CHAPTER 10

FILMING CASABLANCA

It was summer time in Brentwood, where the Rains' lived while he worked on a picture. He had just finished making " Now Voyager", with his friend Bette Davis and her new discovery Paul Henried. When Jack Warner sent him a book called " Rick's Place" Jack was going to make it into a film with Ronald Reagan. A little note came with The book which read, "Would like for you to play the French Captain."

Keeping up two homes and four hundred acres of land was very expensive. The farm was starting to show a profit because of the United States buying up most of the farmer's wheat, to sell overseas. France and England were having trouble feeding their people because of the war, so Claude decided to take the role, at his wife's insistence.

A week later Claude made the 45 minute drive to the studio. Parking his car he unchained his bicycle and pedaled to lot 8. As he pedaled he wondered where Frances was spending his money. He knew she love Hollywood because of the excitement of the town and it's night life. But most of all she loved all those wonderful shops.

Soon he came to the construction site of "Rick's Place". The workers were nailing the last wall up as he heard the Director Mike Curtiz yell to him.

"Where is your friend Henreid ? Paul is suppose to be here today."

"He's on the set of "Now Voyager". He had some retakes to do." Claude answered.

"No, No, No he called in sick, vants more money. New guy and he thinks he is a big shot. That's your friend's Bette's fault. Makes him a Fat-head!"

Claude rubbed his chin as he followed his boss into the sound stage. As his eyes became accustomed to the darkness of the large warehouse. He spotted the actors seated around a round table.

Ronald Reagan had turned down the role of Rick, so Jack Warner slated in Humphrey Bogart for his first real romantic lead.

Hal Wallis, the head of the studio had spent months trying to get Ingrid Bergman for the female lead. Finally her studio released Bergman to perform in the Warner Brother's film.

The rest of the cast were contract players, Conrad Veidt was also a big headliner in his own right. Co-stars Rains, Peter Lorre and Sydney Greenstreet were always in "A" film. The Epstein Twins, Julius and Phillip were writers assigned to rewrite the storyline for the film Michael Curtiz the director was a very nervous man as he greeted his new cast.

" Hello, Hello, Hello, My Darlings". Then he introduced Ingrid to her fellow co-stars, then continued in his Hungarian accent.

"Ve have a great actress vith us. I don't vant anyone to fool around with my star. Second ve have changed the name of the film to "Casa Blanca".

"Whitehouse" Lorre laughed.

"Am I suppose to be Roosevelt? " Bogart asked.

"That would make me Churchill." Claude huffed.

"Stop it!" Mike ordered. Look in front of all of you, the Epstein Brothers have typed out a few pages for each of you to read.

"That's it." Greenstreet said picking up the five pages of script.

Then we don't have a completed script to study Mike? Claude asked.

"Soon ,Soon, ve vill!" Mike snapped.

" All I want to know is who gets the girl at the end of filming?" Bergman asked trying to brake the tension.

"The husband of course. At Warner Brothers we stick to values or the census will have our heads." Greenstreet said.

"Our dressmaker Miss Susan Veils vill be in to measure you all for your costumes today at 1:00 p.m."

" Do I have to wear that Nazi uniform? I hate it! Veidt said.

'Yes, of course Mr .Veidt. Ve are a veek late into production. Now Paul Henreid wishes to play some game vith me. He vas to be here this morning, but he vants more money."

" I told you Mike, he had to complete some scenes from our last picture, Claude reminded the director.

"That's Vhat you think,....1 know better."

Suddenly the side door opened and Jack Warner walked in with a pretty young girl on his arm. When the cast recognized their boss, they all rose to greet him.

As Claude rose he whispered to Sydney "Mike is right about Paul. Paul is mad because the studio won't give him a raise."

Greenstreet's eyebrow arched as Jack introduced Miss Joy Page," She is going to play the role of "Annina Brandel." Jack said as Mike pulled out a chair for the starlet and motioned her to sit down.

"Aaaah a protegee, Mr. Vanner ? Curtiz asked.

"My step-daughter Mr. Curtiz ! Jack snapped back.

"Right, Right, a lovely daughter." Mike said as the cast smiled.

"Mike put his foot in his mouth again." Rains thought.

" It's always nice to have new blood at Warner Brothers." Peter said.

" Watch out for that one Joy. He likes to play jokes on people. " Her father warned.

" I'm sure Mr. Lorre is a perfect gentleman" Joy said.

No, he isn't!" Bogie added. " You are better off staying with Mr. Rains or Mr. Greenstreet." Jack kissed his step-daughter on the cheek and left.

" We read Jack had recently married, but we didn't know about you Miss Page. I'm glad he has a daughter. I have a daughter too. Would you like to see her picture ?" Claude asked.

" Oh yes, Mr. Rains" Bergman injected.

So Claude took out his pictures of Jennifer to show off his daughter, Peter told Claude he had a young son and took out his pictures.

" Maybe we can make a match here" Peter laughed. Soon everyone was talking about their children, which upset Mike to no end !

These rehearsals would continue for another two weeks until the sets and costumes were ready. The writers had produced a couple of scenes, but not the whole storyline. Rains and Conrad Veidt had the hottest uniforms to wear. Conrad hated the Nazi uniform because it brought back awful meories, why he left Germany and escape to England. When the war broke out he was in England, becoming an

English subject. He had given the English government most of his fortune to fight Hitler.

Most of the time for Bogart was spent playing Chess. The cast would line up trying to beat the actor, at his own game.

Everyday the writers would come in with a scene or two and the actors had to learn their lines on the spot. Claude complained about it everyday but it didn't speed up the Epstein twins.

The war in Europe was raging, bringing death notices to many families that worked for Warner Brothers. England was being bombed almost everyday. Paul worried about his family living in England . Claude worried about his sister's family and his father in London.

Paul never received a raise, which made him difficult to work with. He believed he was a leading man and should be getting stars pay.

The crew and cast was made up of all kinds of nationalities. Everyone read the papers every morning in disgust. So when Peter Lorre, the prankster would set up jokes on members of the cast. It would distract them from their problems for a little while. One of the biggest pranks was played on Mike Curtiz, who liked to tell starlets he would make them into stars.. .If ??? Peter knew Mike had a eye on one young woman in particular. So he paid the crew, to hide a microphone in Mike's dressing room. During lunch time Mike told a lovely girl." It vas fun time !" The microphone was attached to loud speakers, that could be heard all over the sound stage. The cast and crew could here the moans and groans and pleas of" Oh God Yes !" coming from the speakers . Claude was appalled that Peter would do such a thing. But the others just laughed at the joke. Mike was never told of what Peter had done to him. But everyone from that point on, would laugh or giggled when Mike walked by.

Everyday the writers would come down with new lines, which the actors had to learn on the spot. Each scene had to be measured before the action could be filmed so that it would match the scene before. After each measurement was taken ,chalk marks would be put on the floor to show the actors where to stand. Lorre would come and rub out all the chalk marks and add his own.

The cast and crew knew what Lorre was doing but they didn't say anything because it made for more overtime.

The Life and Times of Claude Rains

Even Claude wasn't beyond pulling a prank or two. Like the one he played on Mike one morning in July. Claude didn't feel like rushing about because of the heat wave . But he had a scene with Bogart, which consisted of Bogart opening a door to Captain Renault. Claude supposed to rush in asking for the "Exit Visas." Curtiz wanted Claude to enter quickly , for the action. Claude took four takes, which Mike thought were too slow. " Faster. 1 vant you to do that entrance faster. Claude." So Rains had an idea. He ran and got his bike and brought it back to the set. He told Bogart." When you open the door... Step back fast! "Action". Bogie opened the door fast and steeped back quickly. Claude rode in on his bike waving his hat yelling. "Is this fast enough for you Mike ?" Curtiz gasped, not believing what Claude had done. The crew was in hysterics, that the mild-mannered Englishman would be so bold.

Claude had many visitors on the set of Casa Blanca. Evelyn Ankers, his co-star in " The Wolfman" Invited Abbott and Costello to the set. Lou was a big fan of Claude's. They all laughed when Evelyn recalled the day, she was to shoot a scene with Lon Chaney Jr.

" They had flooded the set with this thick fog. Right Claude? "

"Yes my dear I remember."

Well we had a trained bear on the lot. The director called for action and I started the scene by walking through the fog. Well the fog made the bear irritated and he broke his chains. All I could see was a bear standing in front of me on his back legs. The Trainer finally got the bear to calm down, but I had passed out in the fog. It took them thirty minutes to find me . Right Claude ?"

" Yes dear. and how about the time I hit Lon a little too hard, with my cane. I thought I would die. I felt so bad when I saw that blood come out of his eye."

" Boy you people play rough ! Costello laughed.

"We might be making another " Invisible Man " picture Mr. Rains, we wonder if we could put a photo of you up on a wall, when we film our first scene? " Bud asked.

"I'm very honored you would do that!" Claude replied.

Claude liked Lou and Bud, for they seemed to be down to earth people. He would bump into the comics when he would perform on some radio shows, like the Fred Allen Show.

Claude was also visited by the English Community of actors. One day Herbert Marshall, C. Audrey Smith, and Basil Rathbone visited the set. They came to ask Claude if he would perform, free of charge, in a new film called "Forever and a Day" ? Rathbone said. "We are trying to raise money to buy airplanes for England."

" It will only take five days of your time, dear boy and it would mean so much for our Airmen." Herbert said.

"We have hired one of the sound stages at Warner Brothers for the filming." C. Audrey Smith informed Rains.

"Who's going to be in it? " Claude asked.

"Well Elsa and Charles, Cedric, Ray Milland and Merle Oberon so far Claude." Basil said.

"I have to wear a costume I suppose?

"Yes, dear boy... .but it's for England." Audrey urged.

"We have a script for you Claude. The part is all marked out for you. Basil smiled.

"All right I'll do it, for England. Besides how can I turn down three English war heroes ?" Claude winked.

" But I don't think my agent is going to be so happy, losing fifteen percent!" Rains couldn't stand injustice, where ever he found it. One day he was waiting to play a game of Chess with Bogie. Paul had just finished his game, when the men heard loud cursing coming from one of the sets. He was still dressed in his French white uniform as he made his way to where the argument was taking place. Curtiz was cursing out a German refugee from Nazi Germany. The actor, who will go un-named, was an aristocrat who had fallen on bad times. He had lost everything under Hitler's regime. He had made his way to the United States, with some help of from American friends. Curtiz had formed a great dislike for any German. The poor actor was standing with his head down, as Curtiz called him all kinds of nasty names.

Claude couldn't take the indignant actions of the director, so he yelled back at Bogart " Are you hearing this ? Bogie."

Still playing his game Bogie turned to Claude and said. " Yah.... It's a shame!"

Curtiz was now calling the actor, "A Stupid Son Of A Bitch ! Who can't understand English. Which was funny because Curtiz's diction was terrible. Claude marched up to Curtiz saying.

Stop. I order you to stop! Now! Bogie, Paul, Peter, come here at once! The actors came running to Claude's side.

"Well chaps... .what are we going to do about this situation ?" Claude asked. The three actors turned to Claude as though called to battle.

"What do you suggest ? Captain." Bogie asked. Claude thought for a few seconds then said.

"We are going to walk off the set unless this kind of behavior stops !" Peter and Sidney had just returned from lunch and joined the party.

" Are we going to war Captain? Peter injected.

"Did you hear us Mike? We will not tolerate your abusive languages on a fellow actor !"

"Go avay....you bother me!" Mike answered.

"When we all walk out of this picture, we won't bother you anymore." Rains replied.

"Go valk out! Mike yelled.

"OH ,OH, I think the Captain went too far." Peter said.

"I can suspend all of you! "Mike Yelled.

Calling Mike's bluff Claude said. "Your values in the last few years have gone down the sewer. I for one don't care about being suspended. But I don't think Jack will like losing money over this situation. We do not have a union for just this type of confrontations."

Suddenly hearing Jack's name Curtiz changed his tune. Saying." You are right Claude, I made myself get too upset. Don't walk out on me please."

" So be it. Let us forget and all be friends again."

Claude said turning and taking his troops with him to play another game of Chess. For the next few weeks, the set was wonderful place to work in.

But at the end of July, Curtiz reared his ugly head again. It was hot on the sound stage as the end of filming was in sight. A special set was built to resemble an airport. A fake plane was placed in the shadows of the hanger. Midgets were hired to walk around the plane. Which gave the appearance of distance. Then the set was flooded with chemical fog, so that every thing else couldn't be seen, like the back wall of the sound stage.

Carmella Felice

All four actors are in a car as the scene takes place. Bogie and Claude in front, while Paul and Ingrid are in the back seat.

Claude has to drive slowly onto a white mark on the ground, so that all four actors are in a full shot after sitting in the hot car for ten minutes. Curtiz yelled "Action" Claude slowly drove the car, but he couldn't find the white line on the ground through the fog. Six takes later Rains still couldn't find his mark.

Under his breath Bogie would try to help Rains, but Paul and Ingrid in the back seat were giggling all the time.

" Do you always have this trouble finding the mark ? Claude. Bogie laughed.

" Leave the poor man alone Bogie. He is trying very hard "Ingrid said.

" We all might drop dead from the heat before Claude finds it! "Paul said.

"Hush now. All of you. And watch for the line! Claude ordered. The next try Bogie said "stop"

All four actors got out of the car to act in the scene. Claude walked over to the actor who was playing the soldier on duty at the airport. Standing at attention, the German actor muffed his lines. The actor was the same one Claude had saved a few weeks before from a tongue lashing by Curtiz.

Claude looked over at Curtiz as from his perch over the set Curtiz yelled. "Cut! Cut! Cut! you stupid bastard ! Ve finally get the car to the white and you can't remember your lines? " Mike cursed.

The commotion was heard all over the set. Even the midgets came running over to the car. "Lets just do it over again! "Paul said.

But Curtiz was in a rage. As Mike turned to yell at the actors again. Claude said. "We are walking off the set!"

All the actors hid for two hours in Ingrid's trailer playing Chess until Mike sent for Jack Warner.

They found the players and Curtiz promised to hold his tongue until the film was finished.

Claude and the others returned to the set got into the vehicle, hit their mark and the little German spoke his words perfectly.

At the end of June, Rains was released from making Casa Blanca. By September of 1945, the film was opening up in movie houses all over the United States. The fans went wild for Bogart and Rains. They asked the studio for a new ending. The fans wanted to know what happened to Rick and Louie after they disappear into the fog.

So Jack called back the actors and offered them six thousand dollars for a week's work. Rains and Bogie returned to film the new footage. It shows Louie and Rick escaping to Lisbon to join the French army.

But Curtiz didn't want the ending to change. He fought hard and won out in the end. Keeping the last scene with Rick saying." I think this is the beginning of a beautiful friendship Louie! "

Curtiz went on to win the Oscar for Best Director for "Casa Blanca". The night of the Academy Awards the Rains' had returned to the East coast. But Bogie went to the Award's in case Rains won for " Best Supporting Actor" he would have accepted it for him.

When Curtiz was named Best Director, he ran up on stage. Stepping up to the microphone he said excitedly.

" So many times I have a speech ready.. .but no dice. Always a bride's maid never a mother!" Thank you my vonderful stars."

Claude didn't win the Oscar, but he was proud to be nominated.

CHAPTER 11

$1,000,000, AND GREAT BIG BUZZ BOMBS!

The Rains family took the Super Chief train back to Stock Grange, to gain a little peace and quiet.

One day Claude was pitching hay, when Francis came running out to the field with a cablegram in her hand. "Shaw wants you!" she yelled out of breath. "Take is easy Francis, I can't understand you." he said leaning against the wheel barrel.

"Shaw wants you for the film called Caesar and Cleopatra!"

"Now?.... In London? In the middle of a war?"

"Oh I didn't think about that. I was so excited about Shaw sending you a cable. I forgot the war!" Claude read the letter, than called Levee up, to tell him about the offer.

"Find out what they want and get back to me."

"A few days later, Levee called to tell Claude that the production company was offering one million dollars, for his services in Caesar and Cleopatra."

"A million dollars.. why, no one gets paid that kind of money to make a film."

"Well you just did!" Levee laughed. And I get ten percent of that!" added the agent.

"But there's a war going on. How would I get to England?" Claude asked

"You leave that to me. Claude." replied the agent.

143

"I have to think about this Levee. I have a wife and child to think about. They will have to stay here in the United States. I don't think I can talk Francis into this kind of commitment."

"Claude, you will be the first actor in the world to be offered such a price."

"If I do take it.... I want all the taxes I have to pay in England to be paid by the studio. If I have to pay taxes here in the United States and England, I won't make anything! But you will come out with a pile of money as I risk my life!" Claude said dryly.

It took a lot of persuasion to let him go to England. It would mean he would be gone for at least four months, while he made the film in London. Francis at first didn't like the idea, of her husband going to a war-torn country. Daily bombings were going on in England, which Francis didn't want Claude to be caught up in. But finally, she gave in because Claude wanted to do it so much.

Before Claude signed the contract, the studio had agreed to pay 1.2 million dollars to Rains. Then he had to get permission from the United States government to leave the country. He would have to take a train to Canada, then take an English Transporter to New Foundland, then another aircraft to an airfield outside of London. It would be Claude's first trip of this kind. He didn't like to fly, but the government had told him that it was the safest way to get to his destination. Subs were blowing up liners in the North Sea, so that was a dangerous route to take. Flying over the Atlantic was the only safe way. So Rains said a long goodbye to his family and started his forty hour trip.

In the plane ride over he talked to English and Canadian soldiers, about his war in 1915. They enjoyed the actor's stories and bits of information about their favorite movie stars.

Rains stayed with his sister's family in their Surrey house while waiting for the studio to call him to work on the film. It was good to see all of his family. The O'Connors treated him with great respect, as he visited with his father. Fred was very proud of his son and he couldn't believe that he had braved a war, to come to England.

Warner Brothers needed him back by January of 1945, as he waited for the studio to start work. Finally Gabriel Pascal called to say he was sending a car for him the next morning at six o'clock. Claude agreed and the next morning he was up at five, moving around the small kitchen making himself breakfast. His sister heard him moving around her house. She came into the kitchen, as her brother was making himself a cup of tea. When he saw his sister, he told her he was sorry if he woke her. He made a little breakfast for both of them and they sat and talked until the car came to pick him up. They talked about their families, their homes, and their sick father. Finally the car came up the trim suburban street, to his sister's little brick house. He kissed her goodbye and got into the car. As he left the neatly tree-lined streets, he soon found himself, riding over bombed out streets The driver avoided the the bricks, and parts of houses that had been bombed the night before. He couldn't believe the devastation the Germans had caused during the night.

The first thing he needed was an apartment, closer by the studio. Gasoline was rationed and he knew the government wouldn't let him have a car. The driver kept apologizing for the bumpy ride but Claude told him, it wasn't his fault. Soon they reached the Rank Studios. Even in the walls of the studio and the roadway were terrible he thought to himself.

"What have I gotten, myself into!" The driver showed Rains to Rank's office and left him with his secretary, who just kept smiling at him. Soon he was shown into Rank's office to a happy Arthur Rank. Photographs and newspaper people came next, as Rank handed Rains his first $100,000 check, which the British government quickly claimed as it's own.

All the stars were introduced and the studio took them all to lunch so that they could get to know each other. Rains found out that he wasn't the first choice for the role. It had been offered to John Gielgud, but the actor turned it down, because he had called Pascal. "An Hungarian Horsethief!" Claude found out later from John that he didn't like the way Pascal drove his actors like a complete dictator! He wouldn't listen to any actor on how an actor could create his character more believable.

The studio had found a small cottage near the studio, that they rented, for him. It was small, but a pleasant house and suited him just fine, while he worked on the film. Shaw's play Caesar and Cleopatra, had always been a favorite with the English theatre-goers, but would it make a good film? In all the newspaper articles, they mentioned Rains was personally chosen by the playwright, for the role of Caesar, Rains didn't know the real story, until he went to see his friend Gielgud, backstage of where he was doing a play. He told Claude that Shaw had come to the theatre, where he was playing in "Love for Love", trying to get him to do the role. Gielgud refused because of Pascal.

After being measured for his togas, Pascal told Claude that Shaw wanted to see him. So Pascal, Rains and a photographer drove to the remote village of Ayot St. Lawrence in Hertsfordsire. There, the eighty year old writer, lived in seclusion, since the death of his wife. The famous philosopher-dramatist wanted to make the acquaintance again of the little boy he knew in 1914. He had viewed selected parts of Claude's past films, but he still wanted to talk to the actor.

Shaw was writing in his one room shelter, which he had made separate from the house, to listen to himself think. There was only a small desk, a swivel chair and a cot in the room. He worked there for six hours a day, mostly attending to business matters, although he did have a play he was working on spreading over the top of his desk. As he emerged from the hut, he appeared taller than Claude had remembered him from his youth. He had on a brown tweed suit and tweed tie. His long white beard covered the top of his tie as his white eyebrows looked the two men over through his rounded glasses. Shaw had knickers on, as though he was about to go hunting in some woods. He looked like the total Englishman in that outfit. He was very gracious, as the photographer took pictures of the three famous men. Shaw walked the men to his main house where his cook had prepared a small lunch. They talked about the play and that Shaw knew that Rains would do his best with the role. After lunch he asked Claude if he would like to see his farm, to which Rains answered,

"Yes very much! I have a farm of my own in the states."

"That's wonderful!" Shaw said picking a walking stick out of an umbrella holder that had about twenty walking sticks in it. On top of the walking sticks, hung many caps, including a steel Blitz helmut, just in case the farm was bombed. The Germans were coming closer and closer with their raids about the countryside. Shaw showed Claude his prize hogs, that he had raised from piglets. He was very proud of his farm as was Rains as he told the author about his hogs. He told Claude that he and Tycoon J. Arthur Rank were counting on him to bring life back to films in England. Since the war, the industry had gone down the drain and Claude said he would try his best to do credit to Shaw's Caesar. He showed the actor a tulip bed, that his wife had planted and said.

"I miss her very much."

"I remember your wife as a child coming to the theatre one day, Mr. Shaw."

"When was this?" Shaw asked with interest.

"You had a box at one of Grandville's plays. I was the assistant manager at the time. Then after the play, you both came backstage to say hello."

"Dear Lord.... yes.... that was a long time ago. Granville was like a son to her. She loved him very much, until he divorced his wife!" Shaw added "Your wife came to the Haymarket Theatre a lot, when I was the stage manager there." Rains smiled as he remembered Shaw's wife.

"Yes I remember that! She had a soft spot for that theatre," Shaw winked.

"You and Mr. Barker, gave me my first role on the American stage, in 1914.

Shaw brushed his long fingers, through his white hair, saying. "Yes, those were very interesting days. Painful for some people, as you know!" As the men walked, they talked about the theatre. Shaw recalled his fights with Herbert Tree and his great respect for Miss Terry.

"She was a wonderful actress, don't you think? Mr. Rains!"

"Quite, outstanding sir!"

"Yes she was! Now.... every one is gone!" Shaw said softly.... sighed and continued. Caesar was bald, Mr. Rains, that's why he placed a Laurel Wreath on his head to cover up the missing hair!" Shaw instructed.

"We will take care of that Mr. Shaw. The make-up men will bring out his nose a bit, so that he will at least look Roman! Pascal jumped in.

"But he has my Caesar profile already, Mr. Pascal!"

In the days to come Claude would spend a lot of time with the make-up men, shading his nose to make it longer and shaving his hair on the sides of his head, to show a receding hairline.

Pascal had put together a great cast of English players, Vivian Leigh was Cleopatra, Cecil Parker, Brittonus, Flora Robson played Ftatateeta, a name Claude hated to pronounce. The actors all became great friends in a very short time.

Soon every one on the set, believed Pascal was a crazy tyrant. Claude thought he was ten times worse than Michael Curtiz. The actors would complain about him all the time, when they went to lunch in the studio's commissary. The food was rations, that the British Army had provided, which tasted "dull, bland and unattractive." At his little cottage he had a cook come in to serve two meals, which were a little better.

When he went to lunch in costume, he made a striking appearance, dressed in his toga with his legs crossed, reading his lines. At lunch one day, Arthur Rank came by to tell his stars, that he had set up an interview with the press on the following day. Claude took the assignment in stride, as the reporters, descended on the stars. Most of the reporters wanted to know how his visit with Shaw had turned out.

"Was Mr. Shaw happy to see you?" Mr. Rains, asked a reporter.

"Mr. Shaw didn't show like or dislike, we just talked about our farms."

"How is Mr. Shaw doing these days?"

Pascal jumped in to answer the question. "He looks fit and he talked about the old days, in the theatre!" Then the reporters turned their attention to Miss Leigh.

"Miss Leigh, how do you feel playing Cleopatra?"

"With Mr. Rains, as my Caesar.... It's wonderful!" Claude laughed saying.... "I hope my wife back in America doesn't read this interview! with that Vivian's husband, Larry Oliver came into the room, in full army uniform, and stood in the back of the room. He had a four day pass and was sticking close to his wife. After the interview, all the stars signed autographs for the reporters.

Larry invited the cast members to his club, where a little better food was being served to the officers, Rains had arrived in England the day after D. Day, but the Germans were still bombing England, with great precision. But Larry informed the group, that he thought the war would go on till the Allies, reached the borders of Germany.

That night Claude was in his bedroom, smoking his pipe and having a glass of scotch when the sirens, went off all over the city. He knew he was supposed to go down to the basement or to a local shelter. But he decided to watch the show from his room. He closed the lights, and pulled up a chair, near an opened window. Putting out his pipe, he sat down and saw the search lights move back and forth on the skyline. Small blimps rose to the sky, on long lines of metal wire, just in case enemy planes wanted to drive on the city.

The planes would hit the thick wire and get tangled in the wire. England had run out of bombs and had to rely on Americans to bomb the hell out of the enemy. But that didn't mean that they didn't bomb the enemy. But instead of bombs, they would use melted down gates, old cannons, anything that would cause damage to the Germans.

His building shook a few times as the bombs landed a few miles away and he wondered why he had risked his life! When the all clear sounded he tried to use the telephone, but damage was done to the lines and he couldn't get through to America. It was a couple of days later that he could place a call home, to talk to his wife and daughter. Francis told him every thing was fine with the family except Jennifer was being a bad girl because her father wasn't home. Claude promised his daughter anything she wanted if she was a good girl. Jennifer wanted a dog!

A few days after their interview with the reporters. The articles started to show up in the London Times and other newspapers, that still had a press. As Shaw read the interview, he became very upset. Because the reporters had mentioned that Rains was second choice and that Rains, didn't think Shaw was thrilled in having him instead. Shaw sat down at his desk, pulled out a post card, and wrote to Pascal.

"I remembered Mr. Rains and made up my mind about him the first second of our meeting." G. B. S. A few days later, Pascal recieved the post card and showed it to Claude.

"What does he mean?" Claude asked. "I think he read the interviews and this is his way of telling us.... you have his approval!"

During July, the smell of gunpowder filled the air. It was the worst Summer, England had ever seen, as Vivien slowly became ill. Shaw would be sent the completed rushes every day. In one scene, Vivian says the line to Caesar "you are rather thin and stringy." Annoyed, Shaw thought Rains was a pretty healty looking man. He wanted that line replaced to fit how Rains appeared. On a postcard, he wrote to Vivian the corrected line. "You are hundreds of years old but you have a nice voice. I think this is the only personal remark that needs to be changed!" G.B.S.

Vivian wrote back on her own postcard the following. "When Cleopatra confronts Caesar with those words, I can make the public believe Claude is thin and stringy!"

Upon recieving Vivian's postcard, Shaw wrote back. "No, Rains is not stringy and would strongly resent any deliberate attempt to make him appear so. Besides, you are hundreds of years old is a much better line, as it belongs to the child-like Cleopatra, in the first half of the play. I never change a line except for the better. Don't be an idiot!

G.B.S. P.S Why don't you put your address on your letters?"

Vivian was very upset at Shaw's constant interference, but Pascal reminded her that Shaw was the man with the money to produce the film. That the film would make or break, the movie industry in 1944. Claude smiled at Vivian, when she showed him the postcard. Vivian was upset, that she might have caused Shaw to pull out his money from the project. Claude tried to calm her down, as she broke into tears. "Now.. now.... you know... when I was a young man, Granville Barker, who was like a son to Shaw, told me. "His bark is worse than his bite! Money can't buy him happiness or unhappiness. It can cure your hunger or maybe not in war time! he smiled, he corrected himself. But food can satisfy the appetite, but not the soul, which deliberates. Don't take Shaw's remarks on the postcard as law, He is granted the greatest writer, England has ever known and we have to respect his position in life."

The actresss finally gave in to Shaw. But she still questioned everything that Pascal and Shaw asked of her. Everyone couldn't understand why Vivian was becoming a shrew, until later in the filming, when Vivian told Pascal she was having a child.

To get away from the pressures of work and the bombings, Claude decided one Saturday evening to take in a play, at his Majesty's Theatre. Twelve years had passed, but the old place looked the same. It's marble pillars and gilded mirrors, brought back memories of his youth. The plush red chairs, were a little faded, but still held his weight. As he sat in a box seat watching a gay modern musical, he wondered what had happened to those old melodramas, that Tree loved so well.

After the performance he couldn't resist going backstage to congratulate their performances nostalgically, he wandered backstage before the stage manager stopped him. Recognizing the famous actor, even with his hat on, he shook his hands vigorously. Soon all the actors were crowding around him, asking him all kinds of questions about Hollywood. The actors asked Claude, to join them at the bar, in front of the theatre, for a drink. He agreed and followed them to the front of the building. At the bar, leaning up against it's railings was dozen of Americans. When they saw Rains, their eyes lit up, to see a movie star from home. The airmen offered him drinks, just to listen to him talk.

He told them stories about his farm, because most of the boys came from the heart land of America, where their parents were farmers. One of the airmen, was from South Caroliner, and he said to Rains. "I read an article about your farm..."Stock Grange".... wasn't it?"

"Yes.... how kind of you to remember that fact."

"I miss the smell of hay, sir I wish I was home again."

"We all wish that." Claude said.

"Did they draft you too? Mr. Rains." asked another soldier.

"No.... they say I'm too old for this one. But I did serve England in the last war!" Rains said proudly.

"I saw the "Invisisible Man" eight times, when I was a little younger. I was trying to figure out how they made you invisible." said another soldier.

Rains stayed for two hours just talking to the men, before he left feeling very good about his talks with the soldiers. The actors invited him to come back any time he wanted to, which he did the next weekend. He felt closer to home, when he talked about farming with some of the soldiers. Some of the men knew every picture he had done, including "Phantom of the Opera". Jeanette MacDonald was a big favorite of the boys, and they wanted to know why she wasn't in "Phantom of the Opera".

"Why, didn't you like Susanna Foster?" Rains asked.

"Yah, she was alright, but Jeanette is beautiful." sighed a navy man.

"Well Miss MacDonald's contract wasn't renewed. She wanted to take a year off, to get to know her new husband."

"I liked the part where you cut the lines to the chandelier!"

"That's my favorite scene too! I like playing those nasty characters." laughed Rains.

"Tell me.... I didn't know that film had been released as of yet."

"Ah.. Mr. Rains... we always get the good films first.. and we don't pay either. Laughed a soldier. Claude raised one eyebrow when he heard that. "I guess the studio loses money on you guys." He said dryly. Rains became a one man show every Saturday, at his Majesty's after the play. He would recite to the boys, or show them how to grow hay, It was a way to forget how lonely he was in England, without his family. One day he even took a ride on the red bus to his old neighborhood, to see the house he was born in. But the whole block had been bombed out.

Back at work on Monday, Vivian became very argumentive. Shaw finally sent for her and she asked Claude to go with her, because Larry had gone back on duty. Shaw was kind, but firm as he asked her, why she was causing such a fuss? In tears, Vivian cried.

"I don't mean to be, but we can't talk to Pascal about our parts. He doesn't understand me as an actress!"

"Well, my girl.... most of England doesn't understand me either. It is impossible for an Englishman to open his mouth, without some other Englishman despising him for it!

But we have to live with the condition of life. Good money has been poured into this film and I expect the actors to be cooperative, for the sake of the studio."

Vivian didn't like Shaw's politics, because he was a communist most of his life and she blamed the Communists for starting the war. Then Shaw turned his attention to Rains.

"You thought I didn't remember you, when you came here, a couple of weeks ago.

But I did. You might remember, but I collapsed at His Majesty's theatre, when you were about sixteen."

"I recall the incident, Mr. Shaw."

"You wrapped me in a warm blanket, than ran ten blocks to get a doctor to come to the theatre. I had gone to France the week before and had cut my foot on a sea-shell. That caused a blood infection that almost took my leg, and my life. You extended my life by forty years by your fast actions. So when I picked you to be my Caesar, I knew exactly what I was doing. Herbert was right about you. He told me you would be a gractor one day, but he had to cut you loose from his apron strings for that to happen.

I will always remember you, as a thin child with a horrid voice.... now look at you. When I die, I wanted children like you to get a break. That is why I have bequeathed part of my fortune, to the British Simplified Spelling Society. I have fought the P.S.P (Public School Provication) in 1940. They too wrote bad things about me. But that will not stop me." Shaw huffed.

"That is very generous of you Mr. Shaw, I'm sure children like myself, will gain greatly from the funds, and all your plays!" Rains said proudly. Shaw walked around the room, waving his wooden cane, yelling. "I'm glad Gielgud turned the role down. Why should I hire the student, when I can have the teacher. I needed to see your boyish face again, Mr. Rains. With you as my Caesar, we will have a good film." Claude's soul filled with pride, at the words of the great playwright.

A couple of days later, Oliver came in to see his wife. Seeing Rains he said. "I've come to fetch my wife." She was just here, Larry.... maybe she went back to her dressing room."

"How are you doing Caesar?." Larry asked.

"I could do without the bombings!"

"But you are the greatest general the world has seen!" Larry kidded him. To which Claude replied. "I am just a humble soldier whose sandels are a bit too large! Larry laughed saying. "I hear your're having trouble getting some good help around here!"

"Yes, everyone it seems has gone to fix this damn sandal" Claude huffed. That last bombing last night scared them off. Now I can't get anyone to fix this thing." Claude said pointing to a broken sandal.

For a while the two men talked about Larry's days at the Old Vic. Then Vivien came onto the set in a huff. "I can't take that man.... thinks he knows everything about acting."

Claude rolled his eyes as Larry tried to console his wife. He seemed concerned about her health, so he said. "Listen dear.... I have a three day pass. Let's go away for a little carefree weekend." Smiling.... she kissed Larry and shook her head... yes!"

Three days later, Pascal came on the set in a nervous state.

"She has done us in! Larry just called me to say that Vivien had a miscarriage. She is in the hospital, pretty bad off."

"My god.... she was pregnant!" Claude exclaimed.

Stewart Granger was standing off to the side anbd heard the bad news about Vivien.

"How is she doing?" Stewart asked.

"Bad.... badly!" Pascal said excitedly.

"My wife is pregnant too. It's the lack of fresh food, that made her lose her baby!"

"She's been very nervous for the last two weeks, these bombings didn't help either!"

Claude pondered.

"God.... what am I going to tell the "old man!" Pascal closed his eyes at the thought of telling Shaw about Vivien.

Vivien wouldn't see anyone and Larry was given time off to take care of his wife.

But the loss of her baby had hurt her mentally. Larry told Pascal she was having a nervous breakdown, so Pascal had to work around his star. The production company was then moved to the back lots, where a makeshift harbor had been built. There they tried to complete the rest of the film for a while. There's a scene in the picture where Claude is about to jump into the ocean, so that Caesar can swim to his ship. Suddenly the sirens went off in broad daylight. Pascal said, "I don't think the Germans are going to make a day time run.... do you Claude?"

Granger jumped up unto a wall to see if there was any bombing going on. Seeing nothing he yelled. "I don't see anything from here."

"Don't take any chances with our people's lives, take cover! Claude yelled to Pascal. Every one ducked for cover, as Rains and Stewart, made for a nearby doorway, to a small brick building. Before the others could run to a shelter, an enemy plane came whizzing over head and they could hear the bomb, being released. Pascal froze in his tracks, when he heard the plane, Claude kept yelling at him to take cover. The bomb hit two hundred feet for the "Harbor" set, causing great damage to the props. Pascal got hit in the head, with flying pieces of the set, and went down on his knees. Claude ran out to help the director to the safety of the doorway. He was bleeding from his head, but it didn't seem to be life threatening. As Rains looked back towards the "Pharo Set", it was badly damaged. Twenty minutes later, they got Pascal to the Army infirmary, in the front lot of the studio.

Shakened by the experience Rank released the cast and crew for three days. They all promptly went to the nearest pub, to get drunk! The dressmakers were saying they weren't going back to the studio, but the actors took it in stride. Costumes had to be remade, the set had to be plastered up and repainted. All of which would cost the studio, time and money. Rains started to think, the whole picture, was jinxed! Vivien was out for five weeks and when she returned to work, Pascal noticed she hade lost twenty pounds or more. The takes she had completed with Rains had to be redone, because the public would notice how thin she had gotten from one frame to another.

Which meant Rains was stuck for another month's work.

Way past the completion date on his contract, Claude started to argue with Arthur about the extra taxes. Claude was very upset that it was taking so long to finish the film.

His wife was complaining why he hadn't returned on time. She thought something bad had happened to him and he wasn't telling her. Arthur explained that the dressmakers and other employees, didn't want to return to the studio, after the bombing. That Shaw had asked a friend of his at a near by farm to house the dressmakers till they completed their work. Transporting all the costumes, and sets, back and forth, was taking a lot of time.

Francis pleaded for him to come home, but he was under contract and could be sued if he left. He soon learned the million dollars, wasn't worth all the aggravation. He found himself drinking more and more, just to get the day's work done. Finally in October Rank, released him from work. Now he had to get back home, without losing his life.

After saying his goodbyes to all the O'conners and his father, he left on an English transporter, that was taking wounded Canadian soldiers back home. Claude huddled in a corner of the cold plane with an old army blanket thrown over his shoulders. The sight of the wounded men touched his heart and he wondered when this crazy war would end.

Francis's family was at the farm to greet the conquering hero. Francis wouldn't allow him to go to work for a month, while he rested. He cooked everyday to put some meat on his bones. Eating rations for six months had dulled his senses to good home cooked meals. Francis showed him the books, and how the farm had shown a profit in the summer time. Claude was very proud of her for taking charge of the estate. Warner Brothers had postponed the film he was to start in January. His agent sent him a couple of scripts, for radio shows. Claude accepted them, because he didn't want to be away from the family.

Then a man from General Motors contacted him, to do a short film, for his employees only. The name of the short was to be "Strange Holiday". The film was produced and directed by General Motors. As Paul Garrett, explained the plot of the short, Claude talked him into making it a feature film. Which today is a lost film, as far as the works of Rains is concerned.

It was a mystery, with Gloria Holden co-starring with Claude. Claude's chartacter is in a plane crash, with his friend Sam Morgan (Milton Kibbee). After awaking in the middle of of a farm, he makes his way home, to find his wife and three children missing.

Nazi types are in his home waiting to take him to jail. He is almost beaten to death, then wakes up to find that this was just a dream.

The script was filled with deep thoughts about war, and messages to people to be aware of governments who want to take over the world. But after five years of war, the public was not interested in seeing another war picture. It was a flop at the box office, because it was made by amateurs, on a very low budget.

Then Universal offered him a small role in "This Love of Ours" Rains plays a cafe caricaturist, who has hooked up with a piano player, Karin Touzac (Merle Oberon). She is a lost soul, who was married and had a little girl, in Paris. After two years of marriage, her husband is still studying to be a doctor, so Karin makes extra money, giving piano lessons. Her husband hears untrue rumours, and follows her to the house of the man she is giving lessons to. Thinking she is having an affair, he takes his child, and disappears, leaving Karin alone. She goes back to work playing the piano, as she meets Joseph Targel (Claude Rains). Twelve years later, her husband is a reknown doctor, and he finds himself, in a cafe in which his wife is playing. She tries to commit suicide, by shooting herself in the head. But her husband saves her and takes her home, telling his daughter he has remarried. Her daughter doesn't want any part of her new mother, until the daughter's birthday party where she asks Joseph, to draw her a picture of her mother. Joseph draws Karin 's face and then the daughter realizes, who she really is.

The Life and Times of Claude Rains

Jennifer while at school had many conversations with her friends, who went to see the movies in the town. They told her that her father was a big movie star, but Jennifer didn't believe them. Asking her parents about it, they sat her down to tell her what her father's real job was.

"Your friends are right, dear I make my real living working in the motion pictures and radio, stage, and personal appearances."

"Aren't you a farmer, daddy?"

"Yes.... yes I am a farmer too! But we make our money in the acting business."

"May I see you act one day daddy?"

"Well.... when you are a little older.... maybe?" Claude winced.

"But my friends all see you act in the movies, why can't I?"

"Yes.... Francis.... why can't she?" He asked confused.

"Sometimes, the stories aren't for young people. So when daddy makes a funny film, we'll go see it!"

Slowly, her parents allowed their daughter to go see her father in a film. In the meanwhile,"Caesar and Cleopatra" had been released in America and Shaw wrote to Claude the following postcard.

> "The troops stationed near our paper mache "Sphinx" discovered the shields, that covered the statue, was edible. That the fish glue varnish made an appetizing snack. They ate three hundred shields. So they had to make up new ones in Egypt, to supply the deficiencies, caused by the outbreak, of shield consumption! Hope you like the completed film!" G. B. S.

CHAPTER 12

BOY.... AM I LUCKY!

After Germany surrended, Japan did not. Newspaper reports of the United States having a secret weapon to end the war started to appear. Claude had planted two thousand Pine Trees, to stop erosion of his land. He cleared the fields of all Poison Ivy and Oak that would harm, his daughter, or his animals. Like the shepherds of old, he cleared his land of anything that would harm the animals. Jennifer was given a pair of cow girl boots, for riding her horse but Claude still worried that her horse might trip in a hole on his land. He ordered her to stay on the paths, if she went riding with her friends, under the supervision of a farm hand if he wasn't there.

The Rains' had decided to keep their daughter in school, while Claude went to work in Hollywood. He didn't want to keep pulling her out of school everytime he had to go make a film.

Alfred Hitchcock had written a story, filled with mystery and intrigue with Ben Hecht rewriting it for the screen. He wanted Claude for the bad guy. His co-stars would be his old friend, Cary Grant and Ingrid Bergman. He loved the script and signed to do the film on the west coast.

In Hitchcock's office he was served tea and some English cookies, Hitchcock's wife had made. The tea was properly served on a wonderful looking silver set, which Hitchcock had specially made up for him. They agreed on a salary of $5,000 a week for a two month period. He was going to get the girl for a short time only, than Grant would really get the girl. He told Hitchcock it was a let down after having Cleopatra.

"Notorious" had a big budget, but not as big as "Caesar and Cleopatra"

Hitchcock knew what actors, he wanted for his picture, the first time he logged his storyline. Hitchcock was in love with Ingrid, but Claude didn't know that till half way into the filming. Hitchcock had written the story with Ingrid in mind as the star. Ingrid would play "Alicia Heberman", Grant was an American intelligence agent named "Devlin". After Alicia's father is convicted of being a Nazi spy, Devlin talks her into being a spy for America. Alicia agrees to find Alexander Sebastian (Rains), and renew their love affair. Sebastian marries Alicia and she starts her spying around his house. She and Devlin discover, Uranium is being kept, in wine bottles in the cellar. Sebastian finds out he's married a spy and late at night he goes to his mother's room, to tell her about his mistake.

She tells her son to slowly poison his wife, so that the other spies don't become suspicious.

Alicia becomes very ill, every time Sebastian's mother hands her a cup of tea with poison in it! A few days later, she is in bed and cannot move because the poison has taken hold of her. After five days of not hearing from Alicia, Devlin goes to Sebastian's home looking for her. The house is filled with German spies, as Devlin picks up Alicia and carries her down the winding staircase with the Nazi's looking on. This finishes Sebastian as the leader of the spy unit operating in Rio de Janeiro. In some ways, Hitchcock was difficult to work for than Michael Curtiz. Hitchcock was relentless when he wanted something done his way. Rains couldn't talk him out of anything once he had his mind set about a scene. At least Curtiz would take his suggestions once in a while. But Hitchcock, had a plan set up in his mind on how the filming should take place and that's the way Rains did it. Hitchcock was living the lines that Claude would speak to Ingrid like. "You always affected me like a tonic. I knew if I saw you again, I would feel what I used to for you. The same hunger... you're so lovely, my dear!" Claude was playing "Cyrano DeBergarac". A mouthpiece, a puppet for Hitchcock to say what he wanted to Ingrid.

Claude didn't like it, but it was a job. Hitchcock would see the takes every night, and run the ones with Claude and Ingrid over and over. It frustrated Rains, but felt sorry for the director. Hitchcock didn't like the actors in general. He called them "exhibitionists" which underminded his performers. If the role hadn't been such a good one, Claude probably would have passed on it. Claude's height cause Hitchcock no end of trouble. But Hitchcock thought a romance between a short man and a beautiful women was intriguing, but a problem for the camera.

In one scene, Claude and Ingrid have to walk side by side, toward the camera as they talk. But as Claude approaches the camera for their close up, he disappears from the frame. "Cut, cut!" yelled the director from his position near the camera. "I can't find you in my lens, Mr. Rains. This will never do! Pacing the floor for a while, he got an idea and called for some carpenters. He ordered them to build a ramp, that sloped four inches upward, toward the camera. When it was completed he told Rains to walk on the ramp toward the camera still saying his lines. Claude didn't like the idea, but for the sake of the film, he did it. Hitchcock called the ramp. "The shame of Rains." If it had been Edward G. Robinson, instead of Claude Rains, Hitchcock wouldn't have gotten his way. These kind of insults to his height took place all during the filming of the picture. During a take one day, he told Hitchcock. "If I was four inches taller, I could have saved you twenty thousand dollars in wood alone."

In mid-December, Alfred threw a large party on the set for his leading lady. Bergman's films, "Spellbound" and Saratoga ruck", had opened at the same time in New York City, breaking all the records. In February of 1946, Notorius was completed, but before leaving for his farm. Hitchcock invited him to lunch. He wanted to do another film with Rains in the near future, but Rains wasn't too receptive to that idea.

"What are you going to do on that farm of yours?" Hitchcock asked.

"Cleanse my thoughts and soul of this film." Claude sighed.

"You make money off of this farm?" Claude.... I mean how much does it cost to run a farm?" Hitch asked calmly.

"Nothing!.... I mean we go to town to buy wholesale meat, from our local farmers.... but it's not much. The expense is the cook and my two farmhands, that live on the farm."

In the long run the crop money pays for their salaries. Why are you asking Hitch? Are you thinking about buying a farm?"

"No.... no.... my wife spends a hundred dollars, just going to the beauty parlor!"

"Then why all the run around? What's up Hitch?" Rains asked in a low voice, Hitchcock said. "A couple of weeks ago, Ingrid came to me in tears. It seems, she recieved a telegram, from a Mr. Smith. She showed it to me and I was apalled. This man accuses Ingrid of being a Communist." Smith.... a man named Smith, sent Jules a telegram, saying the same thing. This Smith guy, wrote that he had informed the F.B.I."

Reading the rest of the telegram, it claimed that Ingrid attended a rally for the "American Youth For Democracy". But a few months back, it was called. "The Young Communist League."

"She might have been tricked into going to this rally!" Claude said taking a sip of brandy.

"She didn't investigate the people, who sent her the invitation. I told her not to go anywhere, unless she tells me first. Then I can check them out for her." Hitch admitted quietly.

"She is running scared! That's no way to live." Claude said angrily.

"Smith I found out, is demanding an investigation of Ingrid, Jules, Sinatra and Wells!" Hitch added.

"Well the government can't be that stupid, to believe this man. He 's a crack-pot!"

"I'm not sure about that. Did you recieve any communication from this man? Claude.

"No. But look at George Bernard Shaw, who has been spouting Communist ideas for years. The English government hasn't stopped him."

"That's England Claude.. Ingrid isn't a citizen here! She can be accused of trying to over over throw this government!"

"I still think this man is a crack-pot but you advised her properly." Claude sighed in disgust.

At first the American government, didn't take Smith seriously. But after years of writing to the congress and the F.B.I. The UnAmerican Activities Committee" was formed to investigate these complaints. Smith had been the instigator, and fear had done the rest.

To his good luck, Claude wasn't the type to join clubs. Especially when the organizations asked for large sums of money.

The Life and Times of Claude Rains

After a few radio shows, his agent obtained him a script at United Artists, Paul Muni and Anne Baxter were to be his co-stars in a new production of "Angel On My Shoulder."

"Rains is the Devil, "Mephistopheles"... "Nick" for short, Paul Muni plays "Eddie Kagle, who is killed by his own gang member so he can control the gang. While Eddie is in hell, the devil calls him into his office. Nick is dressed in a black suit, with a large T on his right sleeve, which stands for Trustee. The devil offers Eddie a deal, that he will let him go back in human form to kill the man who killed him. Smiley Williams (Hardie-Albright), if he will corrupt the soul of a good judge. Eddie agrees, but falls in love with Barbara Foster (Anne Baxter) and doesn't go through with the pact, making the devil very angry.

Rains fitted the bill exactly, as the devil, in his sharp business like suit. Both actors have some very funny scenes in the film, making this one a winner. As the devil he is compelling, that a sweet looking man, could be so evil. After the first week of filming, Muni came down with influenza, which quickly spread to Rains and other cast members. It took almost two weeks, for the flu, to run it's course on the set.

Rains spent one third of the film on the "Hell set". The walls were all made of Paper-Mache. The director told the actors, to walk carefully around the set while the production set was under repair. The set was located on the "General Service Studio" but Claude named the set, "The Inferno". The production was beset with delays, as bad luck continued on the filming.

Bella Muni, Paul's wife made life miserable for director Archie Mayo. She called the shots on how her husband would do his scenes. It caused everyone to feel sorry for the "Hen-pecked" actor. Bella was fearful of Claude's abilities, to take over a film. She didn't want her husband overshadowed by the cheerful Rains. But with all her medling, Claude still stole the show.

The producer, Charles R. Rogers had purchased the rights to the screen play called "Me And Satan". Later he would change the title to "Angel On My Shoulder" because he knew people wouldn't go see a film about the devil. The director tried to get Bella off the set, but as Paul's agent, they couldn't do that. Claude wished that Robert Montgomery had taken the role, so he wouldn't have to put up with Bella's interference. Paul would keep quiet through all of the arguments.

Claude stayed with the charming Anne Baxter, most of the time, talking about her famous grandfather Frank Lloyd Wright. Claude loved good architecture and Wright he thought was a genius. He knew a lot about architecture and if he hadn't become an actor, that would have been his next love. He told Anne, he had bought a few rundown houses in Pennsylvania, which he rebuilt himself to resell for a profit. He and Francis had studied many architectural works in Philadephia, home of the American Revolution. Claude invited her and her grandfather to come for a visit, to see his old house, built during the Revolution.

"I think my grandfather would love to see your home, Claude."

"We took a ride once to see the Hollyhock House". Claude grinned with pride. It was really out of this world! It looked like an Egyptian monument. I didn't see any windows from the roadside, but knowing your grandfather's work. I knew that inside of that house must be plenty of sunlight. We even took a ride to Pasadena one day to see the residence of Mrs. George Madison Millard. Now that was a house! Japanese style, with a glorious garden, that made my wife want one of her own in the same style."

"Yes grandfather, is a great one for building hidden windows on the roof's of his creations. You should see his studio in Tallesin East Spring Green Wisconsin. He built it in 1923, but it has the look of a modern day home. I loved to spend time in that house as a child." Anne said quietly.

"Good God!.. I wish I could design homes like that! I have rebuilt my home in Pennsylvania. But I wish I could paint or draw some wonderful things I have seen in my life time." Rains sighed. Then Anne asked, "Have you ever seen the residence of Edgar J. Kaufmann? It's called "Falling Water". It's in Bear Run Pennsylvania!"

"No. I've never been in that part of the state. But I will make a point to take a drive there, to see it."

"Well in my opinion, it is the most beautiful house ever built. It's three stories high.... built with stone and concrete, White concrete balconies surround each floor. There is a staircase that runs from the first floor to the third floor balcony. The wide windows fill up the walls with airy light. Skylights.... from above.... you know! I wanted my grandfather to build me a house like that and he told me., I couldn't afford his price to build it!" She laughed.

"Well I guess I can't afford him either, Claude smiled.

"I just read an article about the "Johnson Wax Building" in the Reader's Digest." Anne said pulling out the small booklet from her large bag. Showing it to Rains, he saw the pictures of the new building. "What's this "Pyrex Glass"? Claude asked.

"It's a tubing which allows daylight to pour down into the work area below. It's almost like a "Flash Gordon" movie, ...but better!" Anne exclaimed with pride.

"What is he working on next?"

"It's a building for V.C. Morris. Mr. Morris wants his home to be built on the side of a cliff, near Golden Gate Bridge. Last time I talked to him, the cliff was being cut to form the foundation, for the underpinnings. Morris wants the house to be part of the cliff. So the ground work has to be perfect, to hold up such a house in place. The floors will be stacked vertically, to create the rest of the house. On the top level, the edges are upturned, so that it can hold a ton of dirt, for a roof garden. His plans for this house is absolutely fabulous Anne said with pride.

"If I wasn't a man of simple tastes in homes, I would have your grandfather design one for me" Rains smiled.

"Well, if I read what was true about your salary for "Caesar and Cleopatra" is correct you probably could own one of his buildings"! Pressing his hands together, he said.

"A million wasn't enough to do that film. Have you ever worked while being bombed? I lost ten pounds the first week, from lack of food. The English Army was feeding us at the studio with part of their rations. Sometimes I would annoy my fellow actors, by talking about food that my wife served me on my farm. I would talk of fresh milk from my cows, fresh eggs, from my chickens and they would start throwing things at me to stop talking about good food!" Rains laughed.

"Oh.... you are a rat! Claude.... those poor people!"

With lunch over with, the stars returned to the set. Bella was up to her old tricks, of telling Mayo she didn't think her husband should kiss Anne, in the scene. Mayo tried to do it a few ways, when Claude became angry. Going up to Mayo, who was next to a camera talking to Bella. Claude said. "Good God man, you direct us like a Big Boy-Hamburger, instead of a fine "Weiner Schnitzel" This isn't a supermarket, Mr. Mayo.

We are artists. We need to create. Not be rushed from hider to John. Turning to Paul he said, in a manner saying. "(Why don't you control your wife!)" I don't know about Mr. Muni? But I for one would not stand for it!" Mayo knew Claude wasn't talking to him, personally, but to Mrs. Muni, so he just smiled at Claude's temperamental outbreak. Finally the love scene was to Mayo's liking and the actors were finished for the day.

With the completion of the filming, the director gave a party at the studio on the last day of shooting. A bar was set up in the middle of the "Inferno Set", along with table and chairs, brought in by a caterer. Francis showed up in the late afternoon and sat with her husband, Anne Baxter and the director's family. The party lasted for several hours, then everyone went home, leaving the caterer to clean the mess.

Waking up early the next morning, Claude brought in his newspaper. Francis was still asleep, as he sat down and opened his paper. The headline left him stunned. "Stage Hand Found Dead On Set Of Inferno." at United Artists" Claude couldn't believe it, as he read on. "It seems that on April 4th 1946, a real life slaying climaxed the party celebrating the conclusion of the gangster movie. It seems as the caterer, was cleaning up the stage, he heard a moan coming from behind one of the sets. There he found a man dying.

The studio called for an ambulance, but the man died on the way to the hospital. The police were called to the scene of the crime, where thirty one year old Edward W. Grey, was found near death. He wasn't part of the crew of "Angel on my Shoulder" but worked at United Artists, as an electrician. Grey succumbed to his injuries which was listed as murder, with the L.A.P.D. Police doctors after examining the body a few days later, found his skull was fractured, his jaw broken and his palate pierced.

The Rains' couldn't believe any one could have murdered the young man, but the police still called the people who had been at the party down to the policestation. Mayo was very upset at all the bad publicity generated by the newspaper stories. No one called Rains down to be questioned, but they did call Paul Muni down to the police station. Claude and Francis searched, their minds if they had seen Grey around the tables, but they couldn't place him.

The Life and Times of Claude Rains

Francis became very worried about the investigation, which continued for several weeks. Till the inquest came out with the true story of the affair. It seemed Mr. Grey liked to drink a lot. He was assigned to another film production but he had heard, that Mayo was having a party. So he crashed the party on the set of the Inferno. The bartender reported that Grey, had at least eight drinks, before he disappeared. Grey might have wanted to see the stars up close, by climbing up a scaffold over the set. He must have fallen asleep on the rigging, than rolled over in his sleep off the edge of the scaffold to his death!.

But Grey's wife didn't want to believe her husband died that way. She hired a lawyer to sue the studio and all the stars for the accident. United Artists settled out of court and his widow was given ten thousand dollars. After the death, United Artists ordered that after a film was finished, no parties were to be given by the artists. With that ordeal over and done with, Claude started a new project at Warner Brothers. He joined his olds friends, Bette Davis and Paul Henried in a film called "Deception".

On August 6th, 1946 the first Atomic bomb "Big Boy" was dropped on Hiroshima, Japan because the Emperor of Japan wouldn't surrender to the United States. Then on September 25th, "Fat Boy" was dropped on Nagasaki. President Truman finally had his truce, without the help of Communist Russia. With the war over, all the soldiers came home, to start their lives again. The actors on the set of "Deception", couldn't believe that the President had dropped such a horrible bomb to end the war. But some said it was the only way to make the Emperor, who was a god to his people, end the war. A lot of the actors in the service returned to their studios, and were given a hero's welcome. Stars like Captain Clark Gable, Captain Jimmy Stewart, Mickey Rooney and Lieutenant Robert Taylor. The studios turned out to welcome all the soldiers, back from the war.

The first day he parked his new car, in his assigned spot, someone played a joke on him. He was called off the set, because someone was messing with his new Buick.

Rains ran out to see what damage was done to his new car, he found a large sign under the wipers, which read: Your truck is worth more than the seconds saved in jumping a red light. Be more careful! Rains always thought that Davis was behind the joke, because she always teased him about the accident he had with his old car.

For seven years, Bette Davis was contracted with Warner Brothers, while Rains had gone independent. Her films were among the most popular moneymakers, than any other star on the lot. But being a strong minded woman, she decided to get in on some of the money made at the movies. So she started her own production company, called B.D. Productions, so that she could invest in her own films. Like Rains, her fans preferred her to be the "Meanie", so that's the roles for which she contracted for.

"Deception" the film, was a remake of a Broadway play called, "Jealousy". Davis always liked to work with friends, but ones who she could steel the scenes from. With Rains that was impossible and she knew it, as she watched the rushes every night. Slowly Claude had taken a small role and developed it into an Oscar winning performance. During the filming of the film, Davis kidded Claude unmercifully. She tried to make her friend "Fluff", his lines any chances she got. "Come sit on my lap darling," She" She would yell at him, or "Why don't you come nearer, so that I can give you a big wet kiss!" Most of the time, Claude would keep a straight face, but at other times, he would lose his concentation and crack up in laughter.

It was fun filming this story for director Irving Rapper. Paul Henreid for instance couldn't play any instrument. But in the film he was supposed to be a concert cello player.

An orchestra was hired to accompany Paul, who was suppose to fake the bow action of the cello. But Irving didn't like the way the finger action was taking place. So he hired a real cello player, cut slits into Paul's tuxedo. Then seated in a chair, the real musician, would finger the instrument. But Paul was moving around too much, trying to make out he was fingering the cello. Irving called "Cut" again and walked around the set. Claude and Bette had been laughing at Paul's plight, as Paul gave them a dirty look. Claude finally called out to Irving. "Why don't you tie him down in the chair". The director thought that was a good idea, but Paul didn't. But finally the director won out. Paul sat down in the chair, as he looked at his fellow actors. A stagehand tied Paul's arms, behind the chair, as the cello player, slipped his arms through the slits in Paul's tuxedo. The stagehand placed the large cello in the hands of the musician. It was a take on the first shooting.

"Paul you look like you're in pain!" yelled Bette, after the shooting was completed.

Paul yelled back, "Wait till I have my arms back, I will get the both of you! My hands are numb! complained the actor, walking toward his co-stars.

"Oh you poor baby, let me rub your shoulders for you!" Bette smiled.

"Did you see that cellist fingers on that cello? My God.. I'm a good musician."

"You looked like Charlie MaCarthy, Paul." Claude giggled, while Henreid only replied with a cold stare.

A few day later, a pregnant Bette Davis came to work very upset, because, her little dog "Tibly", had died during the night. Bette became overly sensitive at the sight of the small animals kept on the set in small cages. Snowball a white cat, was to be in a couple of scenes, with both stars Bette made sure they were all fed and watered, as she watched over them as her own.

A few hours later, Irving ordered Snowball be brought to the set, for a take with Rains. The actor was seated on a large sofa, while Bette kneeling at his feet. She was to plead to Claude's character not to tell her husband about their relationship! The stagehand had finished measuring the distance, between the actors and the camera, as Snowball's trainer, placed the cat in Claude's lap. Irving yelled for "Lights", which scared the cat. The animal dug her nails into Claude's hand and climbed up his chest, and over his head.

"Dear Lord!" What a bloody mess!" Rains yelled, covered in blood. Irving yelled for a doctor, as Bette began to cry.

"Are you O. K.?" asked the director.

"Just peachy! Boy, she has sharp nails!" he said looking down at his blood covered hands. The trainer ran after Snowball, finally catching her and placing her in her cage.

The doctor treated Claude for cuts on his wrists, chest and hairline. The doctor bandaged his hands, as the director told the whole cast to go home for the rest of the day.

Bette was visibly distraught by the incident and she called Claude at home, to make sure he had gotten home safely.

"He's fine. I've seen him cut up worse on the farm." Francis told Bette. The next day Rains removed his bandages, but his hands were still covered with scratches. His wife thought no infection had set in, so off he drove to the studio. He put on a clean tuxedo, then went to the make-up man, to cover up the cuts on his face. "What are you going to do about your hands? Mr. Rains."

"I'm going to wear my white gloves, to protect me from that animal!" Everyone on the set asked him how he felt, before they started work.

"Fine.. fine.. not to worry." He took his seat on the armchair, as Bette kneeled before him. This time the trainer, had drugged up poor Snowball. He placed the cat on the actor's lap, as Bette said. "Now now Snowball, you be a good girl."

"Don't worry, Miss Davis... she has been sedated!" said the trainer. Then Irving called for another take with the cat.

"Good girl, Snowball." Bette whispered to the sleepy Snowball.

"Please Bette.. try not to wake the sleeping tiger." Claude smiled, petting the animal. The camera moved into position, as Irving made sure every thing was in proper order. For some reason more people than usual crowded the set. Claude counted almost forty people mulling around watching. Claude thought. "Have they come to see more blood run from my veins!" They all stared at him holding and petting the cat gently. Irving in a soft voice called for the lights, The bright lights flooded the set, Snowball ears moved slightly, as the crowd watched intensely. "Action!" called the director and all was quiet, but as soon as Bette began to speak, the cat woke up and dug her nails into Claude's legs and jumped down on to the floor.

"Good Lord! Not again!" Claude grunted in pain. The crowd stood in silence, as Bette asked in a weak smile. "Where did she get you now, Sweetie?"

"I don't want to look at the wounds with so many people around, Bette!" Claude said raising one eyebrow.

"I just want to know if she got something important?" Bette smiled, rising to her feet.

"The area is important to be, dear girl!" he said which made the crowd laugh as Irving called for the doctor. After treating the actor in his trailer, he returned to the set.

This time the crowd had doubled, as he took to the sofa again. The cat had been drugged and almost looked dead, as the trainer placed her in the actor's lap again.

"Everything in it's proper place?" Bette asked.

"Yes, quite superficial. It seems Snowball is a real bitch!"

"Tempermental.... maybe... but no bitch.... she has papers to prove it, Claude." Bette laughed out loud.

"Really?" he smiled.

"I told the trainer to give that cat a good dose of drugs, to put her to sleep." The director tried to reassure his actor.

As the trainer placed the cat on his lap, the animal didn't move. "Is she dead?" asked the actor, moving her limp head.

"No.... no she's just sleeping". answered the trainer. This time the cat stayed in place and the actors did the take in one shot.

Two month's after the film was finished, Bette gave birth to a baby girl and she named her Barbara. Bosley Crowther gave this review of the film, in the New York Times. "In the play, the man who is bumped off, never appears on the stage. Miss Davis might have wished that in the film too, he was kept more discreetly concealed. For the mephistophelian performance of Claude Rains in this villainous role makes her completely childish and, from the view point of logic, absurd. As a famous and worldly composer with some vicious attachment to a dame, he fills out a fascinating portrait of a titanic egoist. And all the cynical analysis which he so expressively speaks on the subject of female behavior strips Miss Davis 's character of appeal.

On October 19th, 1946, The New York Post's Archer Winsten wrote:

> "Claude Rains, it must be admitted, goes to town with his characterization of a highliving composer and genius. If you wish to call his flamboyant measures hammy, you must add that they have quality, flavor and so-called inner flame.

When Bette read a review in Collier's, she knew her friend had stolen the picture, but she didn't mind. The article read: "It was a scene involving innumerable nuances and innuendoes, delicate shading subtleties, the whole made more difficult by the many "hand props" required wine glasses, wine lists, a cigarette, napkins. The principal burden was on Rains, in close up, for six and one half minutes and eight pages of virtual monologue. Rains did it to perfection, in one take the crewmen actually cheered him, Bette kissed him, and Rapper and Henreid pumped his hand!"

He was very proud of this film, because he had to convey to his audience, that he was having an affair with his pupil, without actually saying it in words. In the 1940's movie studios, didn't have the freedom of saying or doing what they wanted on the screen. Later in the century, the censors lifted their rules a little, which left very little to the imagination. As Bette would say late in her life, "Showing your butt isn't acting!"

In 1945, the Garfields' had lost their six year old daughter, Katherine, to a devastating infection. Soon after, Robbie and Jules reconciled and in 1946, they had another daughter, Julie. It took a while for Jennifer to forget her little friend as her parents helped her forget, by keeping her busy all the time, with dancing and piano lessons.

One day at the farm, his agent called to say that the Rank Studios wanted him for another film called "Passionate Friends". The novel was written by H.G. Wells in 1913.

By 1922, it had been made into a silent film by Maurice Elvey. The novel was a difficult book to read, let alone to be filmed. It's a story about a father who writes his son a letter, telling him about a woman he had an affair with, not his mother. But the rewrites only dealt with the last few chapters. Rains was to play Howard Justin, a rich banker, who marries a woman who is in love with another man. Ann Todd plays the wife who only cares about money and not her true love.

David Lean had sent over a script for Rains to read. His wife thought it was a very good script, and besides they would have a chance to go to England and Europe.

Claude's father Fred had died, after the war ended but his sister's family were still going strong. Besides that he wanted to buy some good English stock and maybe a few pigs.

They took an ocean liner to South-Hampton, where they were met by newspaper reporters. The Rank Corporation had sent a limosine for the family, to take them to their hotel. Where a representative explained to Claude, that Arthur Rank, wanted to see him the next day at ten.

The next day he went to his appointment to talk to the head of the studio. He learned that David Lean, had taken over as director, because they were having trouble with the script. Arthur told the whole cast at that meeting that the filming had been postponed for two weeks. That they would all be given two weeks pay to wait for a call. It was a costly deal for Arthur, but it guaranteed the actors would stay in town. And it was a chance for Jennifer, to meet her side of the family. Buildings were still bombed out! Streets were slowly being repaired, to move produce into the big cities. His sister had an old motorbike on her property, which he and Jennifer repaired. Then father and daughter rode it through the countryside, looking for cattle to buy to bring back to "Stock Grange".

He visited his parents graves and took Jennifer to see Shaw's grave too. Two weeks later, he was called to the studio, to have his clothes tailored for the film. A new script was given to him by Ronald Neame, who was assisting David Lean, who never seemed to be around. Ann Todd, Trevor Howard and Rains went to lunch together to get to know each other, while a press conference was being put together for the next day with all the stars in the film. The next day reporters asked Claude questions about Shaw. Claude was asked questions about Shaw. Claude's only response to their questions was.

"Shaw.. was the greatest English playwright the world will know this century. Not Since Shakespeare has a playwright accomplished so much. He was a great man, who cared for the children of England!" He was also asked about his farm. "Not only have we come to England to make a film, but to buy some good English cows and pigs." He smiled broadly.

Rains found Ann Todd to be very temperamental, the few days he spent with her rehearsing their lines. The studio had put down the red-carpet for her, now she was using it to make life insane for the studio. The Rank Production Company had given Rains star billing, which he loved. Most of the shooting was to be done at Pinewood Studios, with a side trip to the Swiss Alps, where Francis was happy to go vacation. Arthur paid for the actor's trip, but not his family's. Everyone was busy at the studio doing their jobs, except for the actors. John Bryan had joined the group of set designers, while Neam and Ambler were flown over to Lake Como to look at locations. The crew that went to Lake-Como, were happy to be out of war-torn England for a while.

The production had switched hands from Neame directing, to Lean who no one saw.

David was in hiding trying to finish the script as the filming date approached. Finally the actors were called to the studio, to start the first days filming. Ann talked mostly about her recent success: "The Seventh Veil" with James Mason. Mason was being offered a lot of roles, which Rains was normally asked to do. Some of the studios thought Mason was the second coming of another Claude Rains. She talked about the great Alfred Hitchcock, who had directed her in the "Paradine Case", with co-stars, Gregory Peck and Charles Laughton.

Still, the cast hadn't met their director David Lean. The first scene was a sequence at Albert Hall. Everyone was in costume for a New Year's Ball, being held there. Ann Todd's work began with this one scene. David Lean was seated high on his perch on a camera crane. As he called for action, the crane swooped down as Lean watched them from his seat on the camera. Ann didn't like that Lean hadn't come to rehearsals, which was left to Neame to take care of.

After the scene, the director met with his stars. He explained his feelings about how each character should be played, and would hear if they had any ideas about their characters at a later date. A week into filming, Claude heard crying coming from the dressing room next to his. It was Ann crying about an incident she had just had with David Lean.

"I'm not allowed to take off this costume while on a break, Claude. So I was just resting when a knock came to my door. It was the call-boy saying, Mr. Lean is getting very angry that you are not coming down to the set on time. I ran down to the set and told Mr. Lean I was sorry for delaying the take. Mr. Lean, I said. I'm sorry! There was a muddle and I didn't get a call" Ann cried. Stiffly, Lean said to me. "That has nothing to do with it! As an actress it's your obligation to come down on time!" Lean yelled at her.

"Now.. now, you're a bigger person than that! what's the fuss about! Surely you know we are working in a factory. You get to the job at eight and you're paid for it!. Don't make such a fuss! Ann." Ann picked herself up, and never forgot Claude's words.

The next big crisis came in the first week of filming too. Trevor Howard was given a very small dressing room. Being very hot in the room Howard tried to open the window. He broke the glass, which cut an artery in his hand. He staggered into the hallway, with blood spouting upwards of six feet. Rains and Lean came to his aid. While Rains held the wound close, Lean sent for a doctor. Dr. Phyllis Shipman came on the run, to quickly stitched up Trevor. David asked Trevor if he could complete the shot at Albert Hall, because he was behind schedule.

"I guess so." Trevor said as Rains looked in disbelief. "But your arm is all bandaged up, Trevor." Claude said.

"I'll take an overcoat, and my white scarf, to cover up my arm." Trevor said, still weak from losing blood. Claude couldn't believe that Trevor was going back to work.

After that Claude started to study Lean, as a future character he might use in another film.

Lean had a lot of odd habits, that he found very interesting. He hated noise on the set!

So he had a grand piano brought onto the set. A pianist was told to play music quite softly to cover up all the other noises. One of the tunes the pianist played over and over was, "People will say we're in Love". Claude had thought Hitchcock was strange, but Lean had a pair of shoes, especially made for Rains, that had a two inch lift to them, so that he was the same height as his co-star. Well he thought "at least they didn't spend the money on a bloody ramp!

Claude gave an effortless performance every time he came before the camera. He had perfected his timing to the tenth degree. His scenes were played by the numbers....

"Yes.... pause, one, two, I'm not so sure.... cross legs, three, four,

"What do you think?"... five.. six... etc.

"Let's have dinner.".. pause.. lit a cigarette, with a stare.... seven, eight." Timing was everything to Claude once he had the timing down pat, he could play the scene. Except for one scene, which Claude had studied on the ship over to England. His character finds out that his wife is seeing Steven (Trevor Howard). He returns from a business trip, to find his wife isn't at home. The maid tells him that she has gone to see a play. After pouring himself a drink, he sees the tickets for the play on his coffee table. It bothers him so much that he takes the tickets and goes to the theatre to find his wife. The usher shows him to the seats, but finds them empty. He wonders where his wife could be, as he returns home. Hours later, Mary (Ann Todd) and Steven returned to the house. She is greeted at the door by her husband, who is coldly cordial.

In the next scene, Rains stumbled out of character. Lean called. "Cut!

"You're not playing that scene right, Claude." Lean yelled.

"I don't understand, David. I've studied this scene very closely."

"This is the way it should be acted. You have just found out your wife has spent the night with her old lover. You have carefully planted the unused theatre tickets on the coffee table so that your wife can see them. As you offer a drink to them.... your wife sees the tickets and knows that you know about her love affair with Steven. You are playing a cat and mouse game with your prey. When you say the word "Ice". I want to see that angry, in a cold manner. It is a rather sadistic scene. You are being very cruel, with that one word. The wife gets it, but the boyfriend doesn't... understand?"

"Yes.... I'm sorry.... I had it all wrong. Give me an hour to practice the scene."

"Good.... we'll take a lunch break!" Lean ordered. When Claude returned onto the set, he did the take in one shot, causing the cast to give him a large round of applaudes.

When the company was moved to Lake Como, Francis noticed that Ann was in love with David Lean. "You're seeing things, that's not there!" Claude told his wife. But Francis was right. When the production moved to the Hotel Des Alpes, on Lake Annecy, the crew noticed the difference, between in how lovingly Ann and David treated each other.

Claude wasn't involved with the shooting at Chamnix, so he stayed with his family in his own hotel, just enjoying the wonderful warm weather. When the crew returned from Lake Annecy, the romance between actress and director, had been established. The majestic mountains and beautiful lake had added to the romance between the two artists.

When Rains returned to the Pinewood Studios, he had a wonderful scene, where he saved Ann's character from committing suicide, by throwing herself in front of a moving train. Toward the end of the filming, Claude allowed his daughter to go to the studio with him. He told her to sit on his chair, until he was finished with a couple of close ups.

She sat down in the captain's chair, all dressed up in her blue dress, pattern-leather shoes and white bag, to wait for her father to return. In her bag, she had put almost a dozen pieces of bubble gum and popped one into her mouth. She became bored, and jumped down from the chair to go exploring the rest of the large studio. About a hundred feet away, she heard voices and she found herself drawn to them. She spotted a small hole in the roof, and one man on the roof, another one on the ladder and a man holding the ladder still. Suddenly, she heard the man holding the ladder, yell out to her.

"Watch out little girl, you're going to get hurt." Calmly Jennifer said. "My father fixes our roof too."

"Does he now. And where is your father?" asked the forman. Blowing a large pink bubble, it busted and Jennifer giggled.

"My father is back there a little ways." Jennifer pointed. One of the men on the ladder climbed down to find out what the little girl was doing. Jumping down the last few steps, he walked over to the girl, staring at the bubble in her mouth. "What is that, Lassie?"

"Bubble gum", his foreman told him, as though he knew it all the time.

"Do you want a piece?" she said, opening up her little purse. Handing the gum to the men, she taught them how to blow bubbles. It was a strange sight watching grown men trying to make pink bubbles. The third man had also climbed down to see what was going on. He smiled at the child, showing only a few teeth in his mouth. Jennifer looked at him for a second, then asked. "Did you have too much bubble gum when you were a child? My father says I'm going to lose my teeth, if I keep chewing it!"

"No, I lost it in the war. But I'll take a piece of gum, if you have extra." said the young man, with a large mustache.

By this time, Claude had finished his work, and went to find his daughter. She was gone, and he panicked. He ran around the studio, asking the people mulling around if they had seen his daughter. He ran looking all over the large warehouse until he heard his daughter's laugh. Seeing her with three men he ran toward her yelling "Jennifer.... Jennifer!" His daughter hearing her father's voice turned and waved, as she continued to laugh. Reaching his daughter's side he picked her up saying. "I told you not to move from the chair!"

"I'm sorry daddy, but I got bored." Claude turned to the men, and saw the youngest pulling pink bubble gum from his mustache.

"Sorry, Mr. Rains, we didn't know who the child belonged to! All she wanted to do was teach us how to blow the pink bubbles."

"So long as she is fine, It's O.K. But she sure gave me a scare!"

"I know.... I have a daughter of my own. She would love some of the bubble gum, Jennifer." With that Jennifer gave all the gum in her purse to the foreman.

"Here, take it to your daughter. I have lots more back home." Jennifer smiled.

"Why don't we send them a couple of boxes for their children when we get back home!" Rains volunteered.

"That would be very kind of you, Mr. Rains. You have a lovely child there!" said the foreman. So Claude asked for the names of the men and their addresses to send them the Bubble Gum. As they walked towards the set, Claude said to his daughter.

"That was very kind of you Jennifer, giving those men, your last pieces of gum."

"Mommy says I should share with my friends."

"Mommy is right....... but you have to be careful not to talk to strangers. You never know what is on people's minds."

"Bubble gum daddy.... they wanted to see how I blew up such big bubbles." Jennifer giggled.

Before Claude left for America he had purchased some of the biggest hogs, he had ever seen, from the "King Farm". He couldn't wait to get back home and integrate the English stock with his own. The trip home was peaceful and quiet, just what he needed for a while.

When the family returned to "Stock Grange," his agent reminded him that he had a big rally to do in Philadelphia. After sending two packages of Bubble Gum to England, he drove his family to the "Freedom Train Rally" in Philadelphia. He was to be a prominent part of the proceedings. He had the organization checked out by his agent for fear it might be one of those Communist Rallys. Levee assured him that it was a simple rally with noconnection to Russia. He wasn't taking any money for the appearance just in case.

When they arrived at the scene of the rally, they found five thousand children cheering in the streets. They were mostly from public and parochial schools in the area. The family was sitted on a wooden deck with a bunch of political leaders. The crowd had grown to ten thousand. And Claude was overwhelmed at the sight! It gave him a renewed hope in America. Finally at the end of the program he was introduced to read a pledge.

As he moved to the microphone, he waved to the children, who were cheering.

"Hello children of America!" Claude yelled, as the crowd yelled again. As the cheers quieted down, he thanked the Mayor for inviting him to speak at the rally. His fans cheered uncontrollably.

"We have come here together.... to pledge ourselves to America. he said, as the crowd cheered again, he took out his dark-rimmed eyeglasses and a piece of paper from his pocket. "Every one please repeat after me. I as an American... he paused to make the children repeat after him.... am a free American. Free to worship my own God... he sighed. Free to stand for what I think is right... he paused for the children to repeat. Free to oppose those who govern my country!.... This heritage of freedom I pledge to uphold....

For myself and all man kind! As his speech ended, he removed his glasses, to a cheering crowd, singing "God Bless America!"

The ceremony was broadcasted to all parts of America by radio that day. Rain's voice was carried to schools, homes and churches, as everyone took the pledge. The country was whole again as far as the people were concerned. Claude thought it was just marvelous. He hoped that World War II, would be the last war to be fought, for the sake of his child and the children of the world.

After returning to his farm, Claude found a bunch of scripts in his mailbox. But they weren't grade A films that he liked to make. James Mason, with his handsome features and perfect diction was now getting the roles, normally slated for Rains's style. But one script caught his eye, just because old friends were going to star in it.

Burt Lancaster, a handsome young actor, would star in the film with Paul Henreid (Paul Vogel) who plays a bad guy, plus Peter Lorrie (Toady) who would be his old smiling self, in the film, "Rope of Sand". Henreid had separated from under Bette Davis's shadow, by going independent.

Television was stealing movie-goers away from the studios. "Get New Blood", was the call of the studios. Teenagers were the new hope of the producers. Scripts were written for teenagers, to make money at the box-office. Some studios were even think ing about making films, just for television. All they needed were the sponsors, to support their projects. The Rains's socialized with their West-Coast friends, during the filming of "Rope of Sand". Paul invited the Rains's to his home, to meet his mother and brother, who had come to live with his family. Paul had four rooms of his own house remodeled, to resemble his mother's home in Austria. She was so happy to see things, she thought had been lost to her forever, in her native land. Bette had helped Paul find a lot of the old furniture in little shops near her home on the East Coast.

Vincent Sherman another old friend would often join the Rains's for a drink or dinner, along with his present director, William Dieterie. Vincent first met the Rains's, when he was an actor, in the production of "Volpone" and "Marco Millions". Then again Vincent met Claude, when he came out to make the "Invisible Man" The two men were staying at the Chateau d'Elgee. Claude was shining up his brand new car, a little Red Ford Roadster, with red wire wheels. When he spotted Vincent and he asked his friend to have dinner at "Musso and Frank's", then they went on a long trip to the Pacific Ocean, to test out Claude's new car.

In 1937, Vincent chose Claude to play the part of Anne Shirley's father, in Saturday's Children". Claude always kidded Vincent about the dinners, paying off in a big way. When the Rains's brought Jennifer to the set, Vincent fell in love with the child,

"She is so lovely. My wife and I have been trying to have children for years, with no luck." Claude looked at his wife, and started to laugh uncontrollably, pointing to himself. "Me too." Claude giggled.

"Maybe we were trying too hard." Vince laughed.

Vincent use to watch Rains on the stage of "Marco Millions", when he understudied for the "Guild, for $20.00 a week. He remembered, how quiet Rains was.. very quiet.

He stayed in a corner of the theatre, and studied his lines. He would learn one line at a time to perfection, then go on to the next line. Starting out slowly in his acting, then building to a big finish. The action was the last piece to be acted in his equation.

The Garfields were also included in their dinner parties, along with his old friend, director Michael Curtiz. Mike was the oldest in the group. He had been a student at the "Budapest Royal Academy For Theatre and Art". He had directed in Denmark for a while, then went to war. He was in the Austro-Hungarian artillery. Mike was married to Bess Meredyth, a screenwriter, and close friend of Francis. Bess had a strong character, and knew all about her husbsand's little affairs, with the Warner Brothers starlets.

But she wanted her marriage to work, so she looked away from that part of Mike's persona. Mike was a six-footer, muscular and kept fit, by playing Polo, on the Warner Brothers' team. In 1912, he went to the Stockholm Olympics, as a master fencer. He was very proud to have met the American Jim Thorpe, and talked about it all the time.

When it came to sword fighting scenes, Curtiz was a genius.

On the East Coast, his friends came to his farm for weekends, like Bette Davis, and her family. He had friends from other fields of life, his doctor, his banker, and some of the parents of his daughter's friends. While the women talked about womenly things, the men would have their cigars, and a brandy, while playing pool, or table tennis.

The actor loved to play these games for fun, along with telling them stories about the theatre. He also recited poems and stories to them. He told a story one time on how Pool became so popular in England. "It seemed Queen Ann went to France to visit the court, and she saw them playing a game called Pool. When she got back to England, she had a Pool table built from ther finest English oak. The master carpenter, engraved all kinds of scroll work on the table, including the Queen's name in anagram form. When the King had his wife beheaded, she asked for her pool table to be placed in front of her.

Carmella Felice

The headsman made a bloody mess of the execution, that he pulled the purple cloth from her Pool table to cover her shoulders." This story would always leave his guests, a little woozy.

CHAPTER 13

BIG STARS IN TROUBLE, OH MY!

After signing a three picture contract, with Paramount Pictures, Rains began the first of these fiilms called, "Rope of Sand". It was a strenuous experience for the sixty year old actor, especially working with a young energetic fire ball, like Burt Lancaster.

Hal Wallis the producer and the director William Dieterie, with a company of one hundred, drove to the vast California-Arizona dunes twenty miles from Yuma Aririzona.

Burt ran through the deep Yuma desert like a duck in water. While the rest of the company were calling the doctor to their trailers to remove sand from their eyes. Sometimes the wind blew up so fast, that shooting had to be postponed. Then the stars would go into Yuma for a few drinks.

The dry air bothered Claude's stomach and lungs. It was very hard for him to breath in the hot climate. Paul Henreid and Peter Lorre were his only concillation, as they talked about old times at Warner Brothers. Corrine Calvet a French actress, was making her debut in this film, and played Lancaster's love interest. She was very charming and a funny lady, as she told stories about her experiences during the war.

The topic of conversation would always rotate, to how the studios were treating it's writers, and actors. Anyone accused of being a Communist, was being let go until they could clear themselves of all charges. Lorre told his friends that he had given money to some of the organizations, named by the Congress as being Communist, but he had his lawyers take care of the matter. Paul also had given money to many clubs who were supose to fight the Germans, in World War II. Paul told Claude that a group was being formed to fly down to Washington

D. C to talk to the Committee. But Rains didn't want to get involved in that sort of protesting. Bogart was heading the group that was going to ask the senators to stop their harassment of his fellow artists. Rains was in the middle of promoting a Vice-Presidentential flag, which was being created by a women's club in Philadelphia. He didn't think talking to the off-the wall senators in Washington, would listen to Bogart and his committee.

Peter also declined to go, fearing foreigners would be the senators first targets!

He had a family to think of and his wife didn't want him to get involved in any group.

Peter told Paul. "Let Bogart, an American, fight it out! We three are transplanted Americans and as much as we love this country, our tails will be on the line first.

Sticking to his guns, Claude kept out of the fight with the government, as he started his next production of "Song of Surrender". He took second billing to Wanda Hendrix, with actor Macdonald Carey coming in third. The location for this film was much different, as his trailer sat on green grass this time. The cool fresh air was more to his liking. Henry Hull, a great stage actor, and beautiful Ava Gabor, co-stared.

Claude's character was called, Elisha Hunt, curator of the General Tyler Winthrop Museum.

The story line is much like "The Passionate Friends". Older man, Elisha" is married to a younger girl, who falls in love with a younger salesman, on route to the big city.

While playing in a scene with Eva Gabor (Countess Marina), Claude and Carey saved the beautiful actress's life. Gabor was seated on a tall horse waiting for the director to call for action. She was suppose to ride up to Claude and Carey, but when the action began, something ran in front of Gabor 's horse, forcing the horse to rear-up on his back legs. When all four legs were on the ground again, the horse took off towards Claude's direction. Everyone stood frozen, except Carey and Rains who rushed to the aid of the actress. Claude yelled, "Whoa.... girl.... take it easy, as he tried to grab for the loose reins. Finally getting the horse under control, Carey lifted the actress off the upset animal. The crew started to cheer as the three walked back to where the cameras were.

"I'm not getting on that foul animal again!" Eva yelled at the director.

"Something must have scared the horse.... maybe a jackrabbit." the director said.

"Well that rabbit wasn't in the script!" she yelled. "Get me a gentle horse that like rabbits!" she cried.

About this time, The House on UnAmerican Activities was about to call before it's committee some of Hollywood's biggest names. Francis was upset that John Garfield was on their list. She talked to Ronnie, John's wife and she was near a nervous breakdown. Claude called his friend to see what he could do for Jules?

"Let it alone Claude.... it will blow over.... but thank you for asking." came Garfield's reply. But it didn't blow over, it just got worse for the handsome actor.

The Rains' had gone to do a film in the Swiss Alps, called "The White Tower", Francis loved that part of the continent, so Claude took his family with him on location as a vacation. Glenn Ford, a wonderful actor would be the star of this film. While Sir Cedric Hardwicke (Nicholas Radcliffe) and Lloyd Bridges (Hein), would co-star as character actors in the film. He knew Bridges from making "Here comes Mr. Jordon." Bridges was the pilot of the airplane that took souls to heaven. But in this film he is a bad guy, who plays a ex-nazi soldier, who wants to get to the top of the mountain first.

Oscar Homolka was engaged to play Andreas, the groups leader of the climb. Claude's character is a drunken writer who has given up on life because his wife doesn't love him anymore. Glenn's love interest is Alida Valli who plays on the emotions of the men, to get her to the top of the mountain, because her father had died climbing the White Tower. The cast never gets to climb the mountain as the real mountain climbers are filmed doing the rough stuff. But the cast is taken to the first plateau for a filming on that level. Most of Claude's filming is done inside of the small hotel, or at the foot of the mountain. The saddest part of the film is when Claude is left on the mountain because his character has gotten drunk. As the rest of the group goes on without him, a snow storm comes up suddenly, as you see Claude disappears off the side of the mountain to his death.

After returning to the United States, Jennifer went back to school and her father took on another film. "Where Danger Lives". With Robert Mitchum as doctor Jeff Cameron. At first Rains didn't want to do this story, because it was such a small part.

But the director ordered a larger role be written in for him, because Robert Mitchum wasn't a big name as yet and Rains lent credibility to the production.

In his next production, Rains plays a Nazi captain, by the name of Skalder.

Skalder is a German, impersonating a Dane who speaks perfect English, with a British accent. Talk about confusing the actor! Claude goes back to playing a meanie in this film, something he does well in this World War II film. Dana Andrews is the star (Captain Pat Bannon), who finds out the ship he has towed into a small port on the coast of NewFoundland is a Nazi ship. Finding a secret compartment on the Nazi ship, Captain Bannon discovers that Captain Skalder's ship is loaded with bombs, meant for German submarines. The whole village plans to defeat Captain Skalder, and his crew from blowing up a coastal town in the United States.

With his portrayal of Captain Skalder, Claude hits the nail right on the head. Happy with the successs of his part in the film. Claude goes back to Pennsylvania. But his friend John Garfield is not doing so well with his career. Jules had signed a petition in 1947, along with a many Hollywood stars which supported the rights of witnesses called before the "House on UnAmerican Activities Committee". It stated the right not to answer any questions set down by the Committee. By the end of 1948, Jules name appeared on papers of the Federal Bureau of Investigation, along with Paul Henreid, and many others. It claimed that John, was a supporter of Leftist causes and gave money to many of these organizations. Then in March of 1951. John was supeoned by the Committee. He testified for four hours, as the Senators, questioned him about being a Communist. Ronnie had told him to cooperate with the government for the sake of their children. So Garfield was a friendly witness. The Senators asked him why in war time, he gave a performance for Yugoslav partisans, and why he supported Yugoslavian relief after the war? After explaining why! He told the Committee, that he loved the United States, and how he was suffering at the hands of the

Senators. The strain of it all, lead the Garfields' to be separated again. Paul Henreid had also been caught up in the investigation, but Bogart pulled out in the clear, by saying.

"I made a mistake in interfering with things, that didn't concern me or my family."

With all the intrigue in Hollywood, Claude left for the safety of his farm again. He decided to do radio and television work for a while, till things calmed down with the investigations. When he recieved a call from Sidney Kingsley, producer of "Darkness At Noon". Edward G. Robinson was having trouble with the "Committee. The next actor to come to mind to perform the role of "Rubashov" was Claude Rains. Kingsley invited Rains, to read for the part. Francis didn't want her husband to do the role, because it dealt with a Russian character. She knew what Robbie was going through, with Jules being called, before the "House on UnAmerican Activities", and she didn't want her husband involved. But he loved the role, and thought it was a good way, to tell the world what was going on in Russia.

Arthur Koestler's novel had been translated by Kingsley and it was a powerful play.

Koestler, was a native of Budapest and as he traveled through Europe, he wrote for a chain of Liberal German newspapers. When Hitler came to power these publications, were abolished by the German government. As the writer traveled eastward to Russia, he gained intimate knowledge of the emotional Moscow trials. The play is about one character, by the name of "Rubashov", who was the people's Commissar. He is charged with plotting against the state.

"Rubashov" is an old Bolshevik and is finally charged with being a traitor, and imprisoned. Rains loved the story line, which parallells what was happening to many artists in Hollywood. By doing the play, he felt he was helping his friends, who had been sent to jail for writing a story. He was sick about good friends that had given their hard earned money, to these clubs who didn't represent themselves in a proper light, being accused of being traitors. Some gullible actors, who had felt guilty, about making huge sums of money, wanted to give back to the world, a little of their good fortune. Claude had guilts too, but he had learned from a young age, to save his money for a "rainy day."

At a meeting with Kingsley, he signed a contract for a four month run with the play. But before he signed, he wanted a few changes in the script. Sidney was frightened that people might think it pro-communist, not anti-communist. But Sidney went along with a few changes, bring the necessary humanity to the character that he needed to perfect the role. The New York Times asked Rains on his thoughts about the role and he told them.

"This Rabashov is the first character, I 've portrayed on the stage since "They Shall Not Die"! I find it quite a job, after seventeen years of murmuring my way through movies, to push out the intensity of the play. The other Russians I've represented were complicated but they weren't in a class with this one. Today I would probably regard the mad poet in Tolstoy's "The Living Corpse" or Chlestakov, in the "Inspector General", as fairly light assignment, although when I played them, they seemed formidable.... What a hell of a fine thing to come back to the stage with!"

CHAPTER 14

AT HOME ON THE FARM, BUT NOT FOR LONG

With Claude home for a while, Francis decided to do a little spring cleaning, starting with his library. She wanted him to check through his bookcases to see what he could get rid of. He had contacts and scripts, that dated back to the 30's, Without an agument, he set to the task of packing away, some of his things. With his pipe lit and a record of Thomas Morley's Renaissance music, playing, Claude started with the top shelf. Morley was a favorite of his. A composer who lived in Shakesphere's day, and who wrote most of his music for his plays. Morley had translated magical Italian music, to fit the tastes of the English people. He was also a favorite of the Queen, who went to see most of Shakespeare's plays. His music was called "Heavenly Music", because the audience couldn't see the musicans and the sounds came from above their heads on the balcony, behind a curtain. As Claude listened to the record, he wished he had been there to be directed by Shakespeare.

Pulling down a batch of interoffice memos, from the top shelf, he laid them down upon his desk. He picked up one memo written to the production crew which included Michael Curtiz. Puffing on his pipe, he sat down to read one dated December 3, 1937.

"To Henry Blanke.... from Mr. Wallis.
Subject: "The Adventures of Robin Hood".
    There is one thing that we will have to watch with Mike. In his enthusiasm to make great shots, and compositioin and utilize the great production values in this picture he is of course,

more likely to go overboard then anyone else because he just naturally loves to work with mobs and props of this kind.

I dropped in on him last night and he was shooting a close-up of one of the knights who was in a scene with Prince John (Rains). The knight had one line to speak which probably took ten seconds and which will probably run six feet on the scene. Instead of shooting a close-up of this man, as he should have done, with a couple of squires in the back of him, or perhaps a piece of wild wall, he shot it at an angle, with the man in the foreground and shooting across the entire room, so that the entire room had to be lighted and approximately one hundred people were in the scene backing up this knight for his one line. These, of course are the things that cost fortunes and by the same token, these are the same things where if a little judgement was used, we could save fortunes!"

Claude laughed as he remembered the memo. He continued to read:

"Had he moved in and taken a close-up of this man it would have taken a fraction of the time, and we could have utilized the couple of hours last night for more important shots, getting into the light etc. As it is, Polito was running around having lights changed to get proper highlight on one of the bowmen in the extreme rear of the set, which, so far as I am concerned is a lot of hooey! Can't we make make these people realize that a little judgement can save the company a fortune and when they have this sort of a shot, they should do it as a close-up, not a production shot. After all, the man speaking the line is an extra man, and instead of cutting to him in a close-up as we should have done and getting back to Prince John immediately, we go into this huge production shot which took all of an hour ot two to get, and used valuable time.

I don't have to tell you again that the cost on this picture is mounting at a tremendous rate, and it is up to us to see that we economize where economy is possible. I did not try to stop Mike yesterday when he was on the crane and making beautiful production shots, because they were establishing shots and they moved up to our principals and we immediately got into the story, but I do object to wasting time and money on un important characters and unimportant action.

I talked to Mike about this when I was on the set, and I wish you would follow through and see that he carries through accordingly. I need your help on this, because I know that you see Mike several times during the day and you are at all times in touch with what he is doing, but you must be in accord with my ideas and must be thinking the same way, not along the lines that Mike is thinking and that is how big he makes every shot.

Also, when he gets into the fight stuff, please be sure that Mike doesn't over-shoot and get a thousand daffy shots of impossible gags, which as you know are liable to boomerang and make our scenes ridiculous. We must be very careful not to make the thing too wild with Robin escaping from a hundred men, so the quicker he gets out of the room and up on the balcony, the better and don't let him have Robin holding off a hundred men with a bow and arrow, or the audience will scream and from that point on you won't ever get them back into the story again. This must be handled very carefully and worked out very carefully. Hal Wallis.

Claude thought to himself after reading the memo. "I remember that day.... Mike went crazy with the overtime, and we stayed on the set until nine at night." Then he picked up another memo dated February 10, 1938 it read:

Cutting Notes by Hal B. Wallis. Copies to Errol Flynn, Patric Knowles, Basil Rathbone, Claude Rains. Shorten the last two credit cards. After "Much" the Miller shoots the arrow at the deer, cut right to Gisbourne saying "Come on men, follow me." Take the cuts getting him out of the tree. Fade a little quicker after the line "Fetch the deer then," don't wait until they exit from the shot. When Flynn runs across the banquet room, let him run right up the stairs and climb over the balcony. Take out the business of grabbing the shield and catching the arrows on it and throwing the torch at the men.... all those cuts that go with it. There's a little trimming that can be done on all of Flynn's cuts firing the arrows at the men in the chase, after he runs up on the parapet.... the beginning and the end of each cut.... of Flynn's and the other people. It may be just a few frames here and there, but keep it moving from one to the other in action.

Trim on the outside shot where the door finally opens and Rathbone says "You internal idiot". Pick that up a foot or so later so that the door opens right up on the cut. Trim a little on the men chasing, two cuts before the bridge cut. Cut a little on that chase shot just before Flynn and Knowles. Take out the four cuts in the chase where Flynn shoots the knight. Have Rathbone come right in with the line "The ransom, your Highness," After Rains hesitates the first time. After the cut of Will strumming, come right back to Flynn on the line. "You need a merrier tune, etc... When Flynn exits from the scene, take out the man saying "The Black Arrow". End the scene with Flynn riding out and go to the next cruelty.... the hanging, and pick that up a couple of feet later with the noose already around his neck reading the line. The long shot of the caravan under the bough of the tree is to long.... a couple of feet off anyhow. After the line, "Look, the Guards, quick," on the next cut, trim the last part after the line "They'll think they fell into a hornets' nest," cut to a long shot of the caravan, then back to the two in the bushes, "There they come". Trim on the long shot just before Flynn says. "May I serve you, M'Lady?" When Harry Carding gives the signal for the men to close in, cut, Don't have him ride out of the shot. Take out the second cut of Carding, not the first. Come right to Claude Rains' line. "You're a very rash, young man." Take out Flynn laughing and kicking the men in the stomach and all of that. When you cut back to Best, have Rathbone already with the door open, and he says "Guard." right on the cut.

After the escape through the city gates, we'll fade out. We will fade in on Flynn climbing the wall, and then cut to the two women sitting at their embroidery work, and pick it up on the line as discussed. Hal Wallis.

"My goodness.... how did I survive that film?" Claude laughed to himself, as he picked up another memo from Wallis. This time for the "Sea Hawk" dated March 9, 1940.

> I am writing you Michael, separately about the boat shots that were made yesterday, the breaking up of the Spanish ship. In connection with the action, we will have to get a punchier faster tempo with these shots on board the ship. Here is the ship supposedly sinking and Flynn and the other principals walking around speaking their lines as though they were in a drawing room and have all the time in the world and Flynn particulary has no drive in his performance and his delivery of lines. I don't know whether or not he knows his lines, but if he doesn't, we had better stop the picture until he learns them, because the stuff as it is..... is not good. We are putting a fortune into this picture, as everyone knows, and if the actors are not prepared to do their scenes properly, then I am not going to start any more pictures of this kind with Flynn, or with anyone else, who won't cooperate. Certainly, their responsibility is not greater in view of the tremendous difficulties under which we are operating, and it seems little enough to ask an actor to come prepared so that he can do his job properly.
>
> I want you to have a talk with Flynn and tell him of my complaint, and that I expect him to do better. The scenes on the boat where they are getting ready to board the Albatross, are not good and the reason they are not good is because the actors are fumbling with their lines and there is no drive or no certainty in their performances. Instead of thinking of the action, apparently they are thinking of what they are going to say, and the camera photographs this. Hal Wallis."

Rains thought for a moment, then said aloud to himself. " Yes.... yes poor Errol, always in trouble with Curtiz! Hated the man! That was the problem Mr. Wallis.... Errol wanted Mike to look bad, but he did it the wrong way. The next memo was also to Michael Curtiz dated March 10, 1940

Carmella Felice

The Sea Hawk:

> Dear Mike,
>
> The long shots for the big crowd yesterday's dailies were on the whole very good. There are some very effective shots and they will undoubtly help a great deal when cut into the picture. There are two or three things which I want to comment on, however The first is, that the crowd was too big. The people looked like they were packed in like sardines. There was no room for anybody to move around and no feeling of the conflict because they were packed in so solidly, that when they swang from one boat to the other, they landed right in the middle of a group of swordsmen, which in every case could have made mince meat out of them. However, in the action, the people just land and go on about their business, while the Spaniards are busing waving their swords in the air all through the scene. The swords themselves looked very proppy and fake. They looked like painted, wooden knives, and looked very bad in the scene, and there were so many of them waving in front of the camera that it looked like a forest. It really killed the illusion.
>
> I hate to criticize this stuff in any way after you worked so hard and got such fine long shots, for on the whole, they will work out well when we cut in our close action and I am only calling this to your attention so that you can correct it when you move in for your medium and closer shots, and don't have this fake action going on with those wooden swords waving around in the air in the closer shots. In other words we can use the long shots up to a point, and then when we get to out closer action, Let's shave it a little more realistic. It also bothered me that in every shot the Spanish ship was rolling while the Albatross was stationary. You got the definate feeling that the camera ship was motionless, while the other was rolling with the sea and it seems to me that it would have been much better had we had both ships rolling. I don't understand why you didn't have that. It would have been so much more effective and so much more realistic.

As Claude finished reading the last of the memos, his wife walked into the room, carrying a silver tray, with two tall glasses of ice tea.

"Are you finished yet?" she asked putting down the tray, and handing him a glass.

"Not quite! I'm not Superman! I was sitting reading these old memos, while I was making "The Sea Hawk".

"Memos?.... I thought you were supposed to throw out all that stuff a while ago! reaching in the pocket of her housedress, she handed him his mail. Flipping through the letters, his eye caught an English stamp, and opened that one first. As he read out loud he said. "Oh this is interesting. It's from the Merely Society of London. Listen Francis.... They want me to perform in a Gala Performance in aid of Theatrical Charities. It will be held on Sunday March 30th 1952, at the Royal in Drury Lane. They want me to play Casca, in Shakespeare's Julius Caesar. John Giegud is going to play Casius, while Godfrey Tearle is going to be Brutus. This is wonderful Francis. Shall we go?"

"England in the winter? Can we make a side trip to Paris for some clothes?"

"I don't see why not. God it will be good to see the old crowd again. Shall I accept then?" he asked his wife.

"Why not! You know that part backwards and forwards. And you want to do Shakepeare again. This is the perfect time to do it! Francis agreed.

In February of 1952, The Rains's left for a short trip to England. He studied Act I Scene II of Shakespeare's play, while on route. Claude was happy that he was going to see old friends at the Royal Theatre. Many new actors were there to greet the Tony Award winnning actor, along with old friends from the R.A.D.A.

After that engagement was completed, the Rains's returned home to do some radio shows. In early May he recieved a letter and a script from his old friend Robert Nathan. He had written a play especially for the actor, and it was called, "Jezebel's Husband". While Jennifer went away to camp for six weeks in New Hamphire her father rehearsed his play. The story line was very unusal, as it dealt with a bibical story of the prophet, "Jonah". The character had a shrewish wife named. "Jezebel", who wanted her husband to become rich. But Nathan updated the story so that it takes place in modern times. At an old theatre near his home, the cast met for the first time. They were slated to perform the play in summer stock, in three states. It was the first time he would meet, Ossie Davis, Vinnie Burrows, Ben Gazzara, Ruth McDevitt and Robert Emhsardt. Nathan had hired the talented Carmen Mathews to portray "Jezebel", in the light hearted comedy. Claude had a lot of fun with his character, as a comical figure, being dominated by his crazy wife. He hadn't met Claudia Morgan, who played "Judith", but found her a charming girl. She plays the girl next door, who finds "Jonah" pleasing. Francis accompanied her husband to all the small theatres, her husband played that summer. Friends, producers, writers were still writing to Claude, asking for him to be in their films, after his success with "Darkness at Noon". It was Francis's job to sort out the mail for her husband, so he could keep a clear mind for his performances. The only job he kept was keeping his accounting books. In it was listed income from the farm, his plays, his radio work and his films. For relaxation, he would take his books to his room, and figure out his gains and loses. He enjoyed his quiet life style, even when he was on the road. The producers of the show took care of all the publicity for the tour, so all Claude had to do was show up at each theatre.

As the production company reached the last stop in the tour, it was time for Francis to go to New Hamphire and pick up their daughter from camp. Theatre by the Sea, was a small hotel, with a theatre in the round. Francis was gone for two days, when the director informed Rains, that he had set up an interview for the local papers. Claude agreed, then went out side to watch for his family, who were over due. He paced in the parking lot waiting for their car to turn the bend in the road. Francis had called him that she was on their way, but they still hadn't arrived. An hour later, a worried Claude saw his car drive into the lot. He walked towards the car smiling as Jennifer emerged yelling "Daddy.... daddy!"

"Hello.... my girl!" he waved. Jumping into her father's arm. Jennifer gave him a big kiss.

"Did you have a lot of fun, at the camp?" Claude asked.

"Oh yes.... I did a lot of swimming, see my tan?" she smiled.

"Yes.... you look very healthy!", he replied as a small bark, came from the car.

"Oh I left Hiedi in the car." she cried

Running back to the car, as her mother was getting out, she opened the door and pulling out a small brown dachshund. Kissing his wife hello, he told Jennifer to keep Hiedi in tow. "Jennifer, this is not the country, we have a lot of cars, on the road around here. So we'll have to find Hiedi a leashe." he ordered.

When they walked inside the hotel, he asked the bellboy, for a piece of rope.

While having some lunch the bellboy, brought him a long piece of clothes line.

"Will this do, Mr. Rains?"

"Oh yes, thank you." Claude said giving the boy a tip.

"Now Jennifer I'm going to tie this rope to Heidi's collar. You make sure you keep her in tow." Claude ordered. He liked the dog very much. When he couldn't sleep on the farm, he would go for long night walks with Heidi. Sometimes, Francis thought it was Claude's dog, because Heidi, would follow Claude all around the farm, while Jennifer was at school. Claude had never owned a pet, until his daughter asked him for a dog.

He found the dog's love refreshing.

After lunch the family went to their rooms to take a shower, and get ready for the show. Before the show, they went backstage, so Jennifer could meet the cast. The little girl was impressed with Ben Gazzara, who was a handsome young actor. At Six, dinner would be served, and at seven the play would take place. So Francis and Jennifer headed for their table, as Claude got ready to do the play.

The stage was a small one, but what it lacked in width, it gained in height. Built in three step-tiers. So the actors, had to step up and down the different levels, which added depth to their performances. Jennifer was worried about Hiedi, up in the hotel room, but her mother assured the youngster, that she was alright. She had walked Hiedi and she was set for a few hours. The play was a total success. Afterwards, Ben Garzara signed Jennifer's autograph book, along with the rest of the cast. Claude never saw his daughter take to an actor so much. "I think our little girl is growing up Francis. I never saw her swoon over an actor like that!"

"He is a doll, Claude. I think he'll be a big star one day."

The director walked over to Claude's table to say hello to the family and to tell Claude an interview was slated for him, in the dining room at nine the next morning.

Claude agreed as Jennifer asked her father if she could go swimming in the pool the next day.

"I don't see why not, if it's okay with your mother?" Jennifer looked sorrowfully at her mother, as Francis Agreed.

The next morning, the owners of the hotel had a small part of the dining room, cut off from the main room for the interview. They served breakfast to the reporters, just before the Rains's came into the room. A long table was set up for the family with the waiters ready to serve breakfast to the family. Claude and Francis just wanted some coffee, while Jennifer was served a glass of milk. Most of the reporters had seen the play the night before, so that they were ready with their questions. Some told the actor how much they had enjoyed the modern production od "Jezebel". Some had all ready written in the local papers their reviews of the play, that takes place in the palace of the Great Hall of Zebillion, in the year 731 B.C.

The reporters represented Matonach Rhode Island, and some of the surrounding areas. Claude had decided to take Francis and Jennifer to the interview for moral support. He didn't dress up for the press conference because it was hot. Francis had put on a cotton print dress, while Jennifer wore shorts, with her swim suit underneath her play clothes. Claude in his light weight tan slacks and white shirt, with his collar opened to reveal his neck.

Francis was annoyed with her husband for dragging her out of bed so early in the morning. But she gave the reporters a broad smile as she lit a cigarette. "Good Morning gentleman". Claude said, then introduced his family.

Claude sat down in the middle of his two women, as Jennifer pulled Hiedi up onto her lap. Hiedi gave out a small bark, as Jennifer pulled on her collar.

"What's the dog's name?" asked one of the reporters. "Her name is Hiedi! She is a minature Dachshund!" Jennifer informed the reporter without fear in her voice. Turning his attention to Claude, the reporter asked. "How did you start in show business? Mr. Rains?"

"I was a call-boy at her "Majesty's Theatre". The first year, not such a good one.

My boss.... a great actor, Sir Herbert Tree, sometimes forgot his lines. The director of our plays, decided to place me in the orchestra pit, with large cardboard cards, with his lines written on them. The first night Mr. Tree, forgot a line and I was in place with my cards. But he walked over to right-stage, to ask the director his line, in his loud stage voice. The director whispered, the boy has the words in the pit.

"I know that. but the stupid boy has the cards upside down."

With this the reporters all laughed.

"Does that mean you played hookey to go to work, Mr. Rains?"

"Yes.... you could call it that! I had a terrible speech problem, that took years to correct!" he said sipping a cup of coffee.

"Daddy couldn't say "R"s or any vowel.... none at all." Jennifer explained. "Could you daddy?" She asked her father in a voice whose accent was unmistakably Pennsylvanian and a New York mix.

"I couldn't pronounce "R"s or little else." He answered in his best British accent. "I had a lazy tongue, but my mother thought it was pretty. So it wasn't corrected early in my life."

"Hooky, isn't so easily codoned today." Francis said taking a puff from her cigarette.

Claude turned to look at his wife for direction saying. "It's true!"

"How would you feel if your daughter Jennifer played hooky?" came another question.

"Oh never!" Jennifer exclaimed.

"Jennifer would never play hooky. She loves her school she goes to a wonderful school at home." Claude added.

"Right pop".... his daughter agreed. The reporters laughed when they heard the great actor called, "Pop!".

Claude patted his daugher on the shoulder, as the child's tan face turned to her father with anticipation. As her father smiled at her, she pushed her soft brown hair back off her face. She was a typically American teenager, who was hugging her dog. She is enthusiastic about the many things that compose the routine of her life. "You must be very proud of her Mr. Rains?" came a voice from the back of the room. Oh yes.... she goes to Quaker School and her desire is to dance. She has just returned from summer camp in New Hampshire!" Francis injected. "Jennifer lives in the present and loves it. She likes to wise crack her old dad a lot. I guess she has my dry sense of humor". Claude said proudly.

"We enjoy her social life so, in a small town. It's very down home America." Francis added.

"We understand you own a four hundred acre farm in South Eastern Pennsylvania?" A women asked.

"Yes..... yes.... I'm very proud of my farm. It's been operating in the black for a long time now. I've planted twenty-five thousand white pines and spruce trees, to combat soil erosion. I have seventy-five head of cattle, hogs and we raise wheat, barley and some hay." Rains said proudly.

"I take care of the vegetable and flower gardens, plus administer to the eleven room farmhouse. It was originally built in the 18th century." Francis reported. Lucille Elfenbin a reporter asked, "Were you in the Theatre originally? Mrs. Rains." The question seemed to surprise Claude, and waited for his wife's answer, but before she could say a word, he answered for her.

"No!" Claude exclaimed quickly as Francis simutaneously said "Yes!"

"We met twenty-five years ago. I was working for the Theatre Guild's production of "Marco's Millions", by Eugene O' Neil." Francis said annoyed that her husband didn't remember.

"Oh yes, that's right. We met on stage of the theatre.. right Francis? he smiled.

"I had absolutely no talent, so my husband told me." Francis said taking another puff from her cigarette, as the reporter laughed.

"She wanted to do nothing for something!" he said dryly and moved his eyes toward his wife. Francis eyed her husband with indifference.

"So she hooked him!" Jennifer wised cracked, as the reporter laughed.

"She didn't hook me, Jennifer. I persued your mother." Claude said crossing his arms as though upset at his daughter's remarks.

"See" Francis said pointing at her husband and daughter. "They have the same eyes and moves.... Don't you think? They see everything.... very observant. I've never seen anything like it." Francis said watching her family.

"But she is a wonderful cook." Jennifer smiled, trying to get into the good graces of her mother again.

"My wife lives in a dream world, but she is a wonderful cook. She cooks everything in butter." Claude huffed.

Looking over his black-rimmned eyeglasses, with a small smile on his face.

"Yes.... and she makes great apple pies!" Jennifer injected.

"The moment she brings something to that table.... she makes us say.... how good it is right away. Otherwise she won't make it again." Claude laughed with Jennifer giggling along with him.

"I have my own kitchen that Claude built for me. So I don't get in the way of the cook.

Who's regular domain is the main kitchen. She cooks all the time for everyone on the farm. So I don't think it's fair for me to get in her way. For instance, I never get up for breakfast. I have breakfast in bed. Claude just has a glass of orange juice for his breakfast, then he goes out to dig in the fields. The cook gives Jennifer breakfast, then she's off to school. I like to work and cook, but not early in the morning.

Claude is the early bird. He gets up at five." Francis smiled, took a breath and continued. So when I cook I want them to enjoy it!"

"Life on the farm is not quite what one might expect. We had another farm, years ago.... where the soil wasn't good. It was just eighteen miles from where we live now. It was a folly farm!" Claude laughed.

"What's a folly farm? Mr. Rains." Miss Elfenbin asked.

"Well it's a farm where you just plow in the money and nothing happens. This farm we have now.... it's a good one. I manage it. I have my books to work on and it proves it's a good one!" He said proudly.

"Do you have any regrets about playing hooky? Mr. Rain s." Rains thought for a second, then said, "No.... no I have no regrets."

After the interview Jennifer made her way to the pool area, with her father, while Francis went back to her room, to get a few more winks of sleep. Claude loved to watch his daughter swim like a fish. Then in the afternoon they all went for a bike ride in the country side, shopping in the little country stores along the roadside.

A representative of the Blue Bonnet Butter, had read the interview with the Rains'.

Carmella Felice

    A few weeks later a letter arrived at the farm, asking Mrs. Rains, if she would like to represent the butter company as the "Blue Bonnet Butter Lady?" Francis agreed to do the publicity campaign with her husband's blessing. It was the first time in a long time that she earned a living, and she enjoyed the freedom of meeting new people. Francis had finally grown up, which soon would be bad news for the older actor.

CHAPTER 15

BACK TO THE STAGE.. YOU SAY!

Kingsley had first approached Edward G. Robinson for the lead. But Edward turned down the role, because he was having troubles of his own with the "House Committee On UnAmerican Activities". The government was looking down Edward G. Robinson's throat with some contribution he had made to some organization, they thought was Communist. Eddie told Kingsley. "I don't have anything to hide, but the implications might hurt your play."

By this time Rains was a friend of the government having many friends in the Army.

He had just promoted the new Vice President's flag, which was made in Pennsylvania.

Kingsley thought Rains would be good in the role, and after doing two strenuous films in Hollywood, Claude was ready for a play, which turned out to be more telling on his health. After eight weeks of rehearsing, his voice was very tired. Edmond O' Brien even had a heart attack, from all the rehearsals and had to pull out of the play, leaving his understudy Jack Palance in his role. Palance turned flips on the stage when he was told he was going to star with Claude. Claude would watch as Palance would excercise, between breaks and wished he had that energy again.

The sets were kept simple, just a couple of walls to represent the prison cell. Palance's office and his girlfriend's bedroom. The inquistor's office was simple too, a desk, two chairs, a metal file cabinet and a lamp. His cell contained a wooden bunk bed, a chair and a stool. Kim Hunter played his girlfriend and Claude in his dreams, would move from set to set in the dark. With his eyesight, he had to be very careful, as he went from scene to scene in the dark. Robashov lives in two worlds, his prison cell and the love he had in his youth.

For weeks Kingsley pushed his cast to their limits at rehearsals. He moved around the actors like they were chess pieces. Sidney had made life strenuous for all his players.

Francis became very angry at her husband allowing Sidney to talk to him in such foul language towards him and the rest of the cast. "He yells at you all as though, you were laborers, not artists." Francis was at almost all the rehearsals at her husbands request.

Sidney had slowly turned his directing into torment for everyone. Kingsley was conditioned by Broadway, to sleep during the morning hours then stay up most of the night, with his theatre friends. In the morning hours when Claude was at his best, Sidney wasn't at rehearsals. When Sidney came to the theatre at two in the afternoon, he wanted rehearsals to be repeated for another two times. The play was suppose to open in Philadelphia on the 26th of December. In late November the strain started to show on everyone's face. One day day at about five, Kingsley was nervous cursing out the actors during rehearsals. Off stage Francis was making faces at her husband, not to take the bad language, that Sidney was handing out. The director had run through the play three times, without a good response from his boss. Everyone was exhausted, when Sidney let out with another bunch of curse words. Claude rose to his feet and threw the script' onto the stage floor, as if he was a sword-fighter, slapping his opponent to the face.

"Sidney! You are going to make us all sick, before we can open this play in Philadelphia."

"Yah.... Why don't you call it quits for the day?" Palance chimed in. Sidney shook his head, and sat down on the piano stool, holding his head. "What you all don't understand is, I have all my money invested in this play."

"We understand it means a lot to you, but if you don't easy up, we are all going to wind up like Edmond!" Claude exclaimed.

"Yes I know you're right, and I don't want to see anyone sick."

"Then we are in agreement. We know you have a difficult job to do. But we all have our reputations to up hold. We want to suceed too! Dear boy."

"I know you're right. I'll try to control my passion and my mouth." Sidney laughed as the cast looked on.

But the damage was already done to Claude's voice, by the time opening night came in Philadelphia. The night of the performance, Claude's voice was so hoarse, that the critics reported the next day the following. "Mr. Rains's voice could hardly be heard in the back of the theatre. His years of making movies in Hollywood has spoiled his voice for the theatre."

Sidney closed the play the next day, because Rains had become ill. Francis drove him back to the farm, and his doctor attended to him. He had to spray his throat three times a day and not speak for a few days. Sidney telephoned a few days later to see how the actor was and asked if he might drop by the house. Francis invited him that afternoon and she told her husband. "If he lets you out of your contract.... take the offer!" When he showed up at "Stock Grange", Francis showed him into the library, where Claude was standing smoking his pipe. Claude told Sidney if he wanted to drop him from the play, he wouldn't make a fuss. But Sidney said "No.. you're the only man that can play that character. I just came to tell you, we are going straight to Broadway, in a week. Rains was really happy, that the director-producer, didn't remove him from the play.

Jennifer stayed close to her father while he was ill, bringing him hot tea with honey and lemon for his sore throat. The doctor came to the house for the next few days until Claude was ready to use his voice again.

While Claude was performing in the play, the Rains ' took up residence at the Plaza Hotel. While her husband rehearsed at the theatre Francis visited with family and friends.

Claude thought his wife needed a new outfit, for the theatre, so he took her shopping at Madame Pola, a dressmaker of reknown. Madame Pola has designed the clothes for President Truman 's inaugural Ball. Mrs. Truman and her daughter always came to her, when they were in town. Living on the farm was easy to dress for. Francis would wear a pair of blue jeans and a blouse. But in New York City, she had to dress the part of a famous star's wife. Her "Phelps Deep Country", Clothes wouldn't do going to the theatre and to dinner afterwards.

Claude liked to go shopping with his wife some times he insisted on it. He especially liked beautiful French Brocade dresses, which he had bought for her a couple of seasons ago. Sometimes their tastes conflicted but Claude always got his way, because Francis knew her husband had good taste. She valued his opinion in almost anything she tried. She would say "Claude takes an interest in my clothes and he likes it that way!" Some would say he dominated her..... Maybe it was because of his fear of losing his wife, but most of the time it put a great strain on their relationship. The dress he picked out at Madame Pola, was a "Traina-Norell" design, with full shirt, faced in taffetta for extra swirl. Then he picked out a pink lilac and green leafed hat to go with it. Claude liked Madame Pola because she made up outfits that could be interchangable, to make two or three outfits from just a few pieces of clothing. It was winter time, so he bought her black, brown and gray woolens shirts with silk blouses.

These were for day time use to the theatre. Francis later wore them on a trip to Paris, where a designer asked where she had bought her outfit, Francis always wondered if the designer really liked her dress or was making fun of it!

Claude still had to spray his throat twice a day, as opening night neared. He hoped that the Laryngitis wouldn't come back on Broadway. Then on opening night he watched as hundreds of people poured into the theatre. He took his place on the stage and waited for the curtain to go up. The curtain lifted, as the lights slowly came up.

When the audence saw him on the stage, the audience rose to their feet and started cheering and clapping. Rains was overwhelmed by their love and affection for him.

He took a low bow, and took his place again. You could hear a pin drop when the play started. As he played the last scene he knew he had the audience in the palm of his hand. As he is lead away to his death, you could hear people crying in the audience. When he took his curtain bow, he could see some of the faces in the crowd cheering for him. Francis and Jennifer were in a box seat waving to him. It had been the biggest night in his career, as a thrilled crowd cheered for five minutes. He even saw his best friend Bette Davis and her family in the audience.

Later, backstage everyone wanted to kiss Claude as he moved to his dressing room. As Francis closed the door behind them, he said. "I was paralyzed with fear!"

"You didn't seem that way on stage, Honey."

"Oh thank God! I was sweating when the audience gave that cheer. This heavy night robe is very warm. I thought to myself as they cheered. Now I have to give my all to these wonderful people."

"The crowd did seem to go a little crazy, before the play even got started." Francis said helping her husband off with his robe. Then he sat down at his makeup table and opened up a jar of cold cream, to clean his face with. Sidney knocked on his door, and Francis opened it, to an esthetic producer.

"We have a winner, Claude! Did you hear that crowd?"

"Yes, Sidney, Claude said smeering more cold cream on his face, to remove the heavy make-up. It really came together for me tonight! All that rehearsing sure paid off didn't it Sidney?"

"Yes it did. Will we see you at the party tonight?"

"For a little while, but I do have a show to do tomorrow." Rains smiled. As Sidney opened the door to leave, a cheer went up from the crowd mulling around in front of Claude's door. Claude couldn't believe the attention he was getting from his peers. As Sidney closed her door, Claude said. "I made a mistake with my first line...... did you hear it, Francis?"

"No what was it?"

"Instead of saying.... I've been dragged from my sick bed." My mind was on the "S" sound. So it came out... I've been snatched from my sick bed! Didn't you notice the difference?"

"No.... and I don't think any one else did, honey."

"My hands were so clammy as I did the death scene. I thought I was going to pass out.

"When that curtain dropped I was drained of all emotions! he said taking Francis's hand and kissing it.

"Come on.... take a shower and change and I'll meet you outside with Jennifer ".

Flowers, telegrams and gifts started to pour into the theatre for Claude. It was an outpouring of his fans' affections. Sidney couldn't believe how good the reviews were.

One newspaper wrote: "The Royale Theatre has a winner with "Darkness at Noon". Rains's performance is magnificent!"

After one hundred and ten performances, Rains was near exhaustion, trying to keep the flame alive every night, in his portrayal of "Rubashov". When Sidney asked Claude to go on tour with the play, after he had performed for nearly four months. Claude refused. Telling the director.."I'm just too burnt out, to carry on with the play. Please find someone else to do it in "Summer Stock".

The cheapest ticket price to see the play was $4.80. Rains had the theatre packed every night for sixteen weeks. 1,035 fans flocked each performance earning from $27,000 to 30,000 a week. That was big money for Sidney to give up. Without Rains, he needed another big star to keep the play alive.

Sidney decided to give Edward G. Robinson another call, to see if he had changed his mind. Back in Hollywood, Robinson couldn't find work, because of the bad publicity he was getting from the "Committee". Edward decided to see what Sidney had to offer and he got on a plane to New York. On the flight over, Rains was being nominated for the Critics' Award. Then in February of 1951, he was nominated for the Tony Award for "Best Actor in a Dramatic Play". His family was excited that they all told him, he was going to win! But after losing four Oscar Nominations, he didn't have much hope of winning the Tony.

At the meeting between Sidney and Edward, the actor told him that the Committee had dropped all the charges of being a Communist. But Robinson wouldn't be cleared completely till April 30th, 1952. On that day Mr. Walter, chairman of the Committee, would make this comment, about the actor. "Mr. Robinson". This Commitee has never had any real evidence presented to it, to indicate, that you were anything more than a very choice sucker! I think you are number one, on the sucker's list, in the country." That completed the investigation on Edward G. Robinson, but it didn't help him regain his reputation in Hollywood.

After talking to Sidney about talking to Claude about the role. He came by one afternoon to talk to Rains. The Rains's were in his dressing room when a knock came at the star's door. "Come," Claude said in his stage voice, as Francis opened the door to see Edward standing in the doorway, hat in hand.

"Mr. Robinson, it's so good to see you again." Edward walked into the room to a smiling Rains. "Eddie.... good to see you.... how long has it been?"

"About five years.... I think it was on the Warner Brothers' lot."

"Yes.... sit please.... I tell you.... you came at the right moment."

"Claude is very tired, Mr. Robinson." Francis said relieved that her husband could finally take it easy.

"I hear your're up for the Tony, after winning the Critics' Award!"

"I'm not holding my breath waiting for it. I had enough disappointments, when I lost the Oscars." Claude smiled as he greeted Robinson.

"Well, usually when you win the Critics' Award, the Tony isn't far behind. I saw the play last night.... and.... I'll tell you.... that audience was stuck to their seats. Especially when Gletkin motions you to walk slowly out of your cell and cocks his pistol. I could hear sighs from the audience, hoping he wouldn't pull the trigger!"

"Oh yes, when the iron gates close behind me and the audience hears the gun shot.

There's that moment of complete silence."

"Has Mrs. Robinson come with you?" Francis asked.

"No, she has been sick and under a doctor's care. This investigation with the government has taken the life out of her. It has left her a shell of what she was.

We had to sell a couple of her favorite paintings, to pay for our lawyers. I couldn't find work until Sidney called me to take over from Claude, in summer stock." Eddie sighed heavily. Taking a last puff from his pipe, Claude put it out on his ashtray as he said, "Jules is having the same problem. I told him to take on a play for a while, to get away from those hot shot producers in Hollywood."

"Your friend Paul Henreid is also in the same boat. He shouldn't have tried to fight the government. I understand he's directing now to make a living!" Edward informed Rains.

"Yes.... Bette told me.... it's a real shame."

"I'm lucky Sidney took me on. I told him I couldn't play the role like you have. Being a Rumanian Jew, I might bring another aspect to the character." Edward smiled.

"You'll be fine. I've seen you on the stage, when I first came to America. I thought you were great then and you'll do fine in this role." Rains smiled.

"You're very kind.... but your fans threw flowers at you last night. They might throw stones at me tomorrow!" Edward laughed.

"May I ask how.... you found yourself in this trouble?" Francis asked as her husband gave her a cold look as if she had asked the wrong question. "Just like some of my fellow actors, I recieved letters from organizations, asking for money to help "Jews" who had suffered in the war! I thought they were honest clubs so I didn't check on them. A year later, the government charged me of being a Communist, because the money had gone to them and not the people for whom it was slated."

"My husband recieved letters like that too. But he threw them away." Francis injected, while Claude looked on, eyeing his wife coldly.

"He's cheap! That's the only reason, he stayed out of trouble." Francis said dryly lighting a cigarette. Claude snapped back saying. "And.... it's a good thing I did!.... my girl! Or we would be in the same boat as the others." Claude huffed.

"He's right Mrs. Rains. I should have thought about my family first, as I'm sure your husband did."

Claude agreed. "My wife is being sarcastic. I know I am frugal, but I can't help it. I've been this way as a child, who didn't have anything!" Claude said sharply, "I hope the worst has passed for you Edward as you begin this play."

"I think so." Edward said as Francis brought over a heavy robe, that Claude uses in his first scene. "Here you go Honey. Francis said as Claude rose from his chair to put on his costume.

"Sidney has been promising to get me a light weight robe. Make sure he gets you one, that is lighter for the summer time, or you will sweat out ten pounds the first week." Claude laughed.

After weeks of rehearsing, Robinson took over the play from Rains, who went back to his farm to rest.

A month later Rains won the Academy 's Merit Medal for Drama" at a joint annual ceremonial Dinner of the Academy and National Institute of Arts and Letters. Then he won the "Donaldson Award" for best performance by an actor in a play. But when he won the "Tony" award or his live performance as best actor. That was the cream on his cake! Restless on the farm, he did some radio shows. During the war years he had done a lot of radio, making a lot of friends in the medium, like Jack Benny and Fred Allen. On one Fred Allen show Fred Allen kidded him about his farm. Fred would ask him about his farm, when he visited his show.

Rains: "Yes, I have a hundred and fifty acre place in the east."

Allen: "Do you have any cows on this farm of yours?"

Rains: "Yeah, I have a large herd."

Allen: "Then could I get a pound of butter from you?"

Rains: "I came here thinking I could get a pound from you, Fred."

He liked doing these radio shows. He didn't have to tax his brain any with the lines written for him to read right in front of him. But he missed the stage especially his friend Alexander Scourby, who had played "Ivanoff" in the play. They had talked every afternoon before taking to the stage, about other plays on Broadway. Like Frederick March's production of "Enemy of the People", where March plays, Dr. Stockmann. Then his friends Ben Hecht and Charles MacArthur had produced a play with Gloria Swanson and Jose ' Ferrer called. "Twentieth Century at the Anta Playhouse. While Peter Lorre was in a German production of "Spring Awakening". Rains told Alexander about all the pranks Peter played on the cast of "Casablanca". Peter had told him once that he had gone to medical school in Germany to become a brain surgeon, but left when he saw things go badly for his government. Lorre was a nice person who just liked to see things pop out of boxes to see how he could scare his friends out of their wits. But he never played any pranks on Claude, maybe it was that he respected him too much. When Peter couldn't work out a line to his liking, Claude would sort it out with him.

He had helped many of the Warner Brothers actors, when he worked at the studio.

He thought about that as he made his rounds on his large farm. He would inspect his farm on a daily basis playing the Gentleman

Farmer. One morning he met up with his foreman as he was watching his cows.

"Good morning Mr. Rains!" smiled his foreman.

"Yes it is... and the cows like it too!" The actor said taking a puff from his half lit pipe.

"That they do.... have you seen the new calves? Mr. Rains."

"Yes.... good size too."

"It's that English bull you bought a couple of years ago. He's had a field day with our stock."

"There was a time there.... I didn't think.... he would." Claude quipped.

"Oh he's a real trouper. I was so happy to hear about all your awards."

"Yes.... it was a total surprise to me."

"My wife enjoyed the play.... she cried at the end, when you get killed!"

"She did? Well tell her I'm just fine now. Bullets just go right through me every night!" Claude laughed.

"Would you like to see the hogs? Sir."

"Yes let's push off and see the little ones".

"They are not small any more. They sure can eat." his foreman laughed.

"Well I see, I have to go back too work, just to feed the pigs."

"Maybe you can do another one of those "Angel On My Shoulder" type films."

"You liked that one?"

"Oh yes.... the wife loved it too! That set looked so real when you're in Hell!"

"That was my directors's brain storm. Archie Mayo was very perplexed on how to build the "Hell" set. Then he read an article in "Times Magazine", showing pictures of a volcano island, which had suddenly appeared in the waters of the Pacific Ocean." Claude informed the farmer.

"Oh.... yeah.... I remember that story."

As they continued to walk up the hill toward the red barn, Claude continued the story. "Well.... upon seeing these fabulous pictures, he rushed to his telephone to call the art director, Bernard Herz. "Get over to my house quick. I want you to see some photos."

When Bernard arrived at Mayo's home, the director showed him what he wanted as far as a set for his film. I want all that steam with furnaces on Fire! I want it to look hot and steamy, can you do that?"

"So long as I know the conception of what you want.... I can do it!" Bernard bragged.

The day I set foot on the set, I couldn't believe it. I felt like I was in hell! Steam was pouring out of every pore of that furnace. I felt like I was back in the Great War, being gassed again. It was very hard on my sinuses. I must have gone through six hankerchiefs a day. It was the damnest thing to work in."

"Oh, my.... I didn't realize, what went on behind the scenes, in that film."

"Oh, it was ghastly... I had to change costumes every few hours, because the devil was properly dressed in a black suit." laughed Claude.

"Your lucky to have a place like this to come back to". said the foreman.

"Oh yes.... Here I only have to worry about the size of my hogs!" Claude quipped.

"Are you sticking around the farm today?" asked the farmer.

"No I have to press on to a county-fair, Mrs Rains wants to go to. She wants to enter a pie contest and Jennifer is meeting some friends there. Maybe I can check out some cattle!" Claude said as they finally reached the barn.

"School should be out in a week's time. Are you going on vacation?"

"Jennifer wants to go to camp with her friends at school. We haven't decided if we want her to go."

"It's good for children to go off by themselves for a while. It makes them stronger I think, Mr. Rains."

"Yes.... that's what my wife has been saying. And I know the Quaker school she goes to, has the camp well in order."

"I don't know too much about Quakers?" wondered the foreman.

"Well.... they believe in the freedom to worship god, like any other religion. But in old England, the Quakers were given a church tax to pay. England was good at taxing every thing a person did or bought. The Quakers being frugal people, didn't want to pay the taxes. Which caused ill feelings between them and the King. They were absolutely honest people, in business and have great self-discipline. I came in contact with a few Quakers, during the first world war. You see they were only allowed to be in the Ambulance service, because they won't kill a human being. When I was gased, a Quaker, picked me up and carried me onto his ambulance. I was half-dead as he put me on a boat back to England. I only wished I could have found that Quaker, but records weren't kept in detail about who rescued me that day!" Claude said as he passed through the doors of his barn. "Look how big these babies have gotten. my word." the actor said walking around the pigs' pen.

"They have that sir.... so do you think that Quaker made it through the war?"

"I hope so.. The English government never really gave them credit. In 1915 they were called "Tithes" by the men, because they wouldn't carry a gun. A lot of them came to America after the war to find the freedom, they wanted.. just like me!" Claude smiled".

"Now the Quaker Church doesn't pay taxes here!" his foreman laughed.

"Well I did tell you, they were frugal." Claude said dryly.

Mr. Rains."

That afternoon, Claude drove his family to the county fair, ten miles down the road.

Francis had six pies she wanted to enter in to a contest. As she packed them very carefully in the trunk of the car, Jennifer jumped into the back seat of his ford. It looked like rain and Francis told her family to put on their raincoats. At first, he was going dressed in his jeans. But his wife talked him out of it quickly. "What if a reporter sees us dress in our jeans.... no.... put on a suit!" she ordered.

"What if they did... it would be a novelty, dear! Claude said raising one eyebrow.

But he gave in to his wife's request. When he came down from redressing, his daughter said.

"Pop.... you look real cool..... a dude!

"Dude" '....dude' ....I spent so much money on your education and that's the only word you can come up with for my outfit!" Jennifer thought for a while, then said. "You are handsome, daddy."

"That's a little better, my girl!"

"She is buttering you up for something." Francis told her husband.

"The child doesn't lie, Francis! Do you Jennifer?" Claude eyed his daughter.

"Of course not daddy.... but can I have a cotten candy when I get there?"

"See I told you!" smiled his wife.

"I don't see why she couldn't have it Francis!" Claude said getting in the driver's seat.

"Well you're paying for her dental bill. She gets enough cavities, chewing on the bubble gum. When I was a kid I didn't have half of what she gets.." Francis said, a little jealous.

"Oh my goodness you are not going to start that again!" he said starting the engine.

"Adieu little house, adieu!" Jennifer called out to her house.

"Well at least that school is teaching her a little French!" Claude said taking off down the roadway.

Most of the town folk knew that Rains lived at the big farmhouse. Sometimes they would see him shopping in the town with his wife or going to the bank. But as their most prominent citizen, they treated him as such. Rains wanted his privacy which the town people gave him, unless he talked to them. Claude was friendly.... but not overly sociable. The Rains's had a few close friends in the town, which came to the house for dinner. Like his doctor and his wife and his banker and his family.

It was a short ride to the open fair grounds by a near by lake. Jennifer could see the large ferris wheel a mile away, as it turned in the blue sky. As they approached the fair, they could see all the concessions, lined up in a row. Jennifer's friends were waiting for her as they entered the grounds. Their parents, said hello to the children as they ran around the grounds. Francis was left at the stand with all the pies while Claude went to look at the pig pen. The smell of animals filled every corner of the fair, but the Rains' were use to it and hardly noticed the difference. He saw a couple of nice horses, chewing on some oats that he liked, but

Carmella Felice

he didn't buy any animals that day. Walking back to the stand where his wife was hoping to win a prize, he stood watching the judges taste each pie. Frances was all smiles as the judges took a bite of her pies. They smiled and walked on. Claude giggled as one of the judges made a face at the next contestant's pie. Frances didn't win that day, but one judge told her that her pies were very tasty. Jennifer was given her allowance to buy a few things, including cotton candy. The drive home was quiet, till Claude said " I'm sorry about the apple pies."

"Ya Ma, there's always next year."

"Yes that's right my girl. And Jennifer why do I spend so much money on your education , when you keep saying ....Ya Ma."

"Sorry Mother... I love your apple pies."

Jennifer's discipline was left mostly to her mother, as the parent she spent most of her with. Her father hated to yell at his daughter, when she did something wrong, because he thought of as perfect.

When Jennifer finally found out her father was a big movie star, she couldn't believe it. She would go to the movies to see the films her parents allowed. Her friends were the ones who finally told her about her father. She told her father she would like to see him in a comedy. Jennifer only knew her father as a soft-spoken man who listened to her problems. As she grew older, she thought of being an actress like her father. She was given piano lessons to complete her education. Claude wanted her to grow up into a re-fined woman, who could be anything she wanted to be. He gave her chances to accomplish her wishes in life.

CHAPTER 16

LONESOME AGAIN

On May 20th, 1952, John (Jules) Garfield became ill, while staying at a friends apartment. The Garfields had been separated again, and Jules took up residence in New York City. Actress Iris Whitney found Jules the next morning dead in his bed. The hotel doctor was called in, but he was pronounced dead. The police were called in and the body taken to the Medical Examiner's office, where he was declared dead from "Coronary Thrombosis."

Rains was riding down the road in his Ford, when he heard the news come over the radio. He stopped the car, to mourn the death of his youngest friend. When he reached home he asked Francis if she had heard the news? But it was a shock to her too. She tried to reach Robbie by telephone at the hotel and finally tracked her down at another hotel. They asked if they could do anything for the family? But Robbie had her family with her, who were helping out. They felt very badly for the widow of their friend who's kind heart had finally given out. Francis was upset to find out about Jule's involvement with Iris Whitney, but Claude told her not to be so naive. "That's why Robbie left him in the first place!" Claude also thought the government investigation had closed the lid on his coffin. Garfield had suffered for eight years, with his heart, involving three mild heart attacks!

Claude knew his friend's suffering, because he had known the same pain. When Jenniifer was born, he was a nervous wreck to make good, and to keep his family safe.

After the Lindberg kidnapping, he built Jennifer's room in the attic, to hide her away from harm. He kept rifles and guns in the house in case an intruder got any ideas to force their way into his house. Jules had felt the same way about his children, especially after losing one child to sickness. Now Jules was gone and he thought about the last time he had seen his friend.

Meanwhile his agent had found another vehicle for his talents, in the European market.

The film was going to be called, "The Man who Watched The Trains Go By". After the Rains's read the script, his wife told him she didn't like the storyline. But Claude told her it was a paycheck, and a trip to France. At first she didn't want to go, because he had started drinking again, but he promised to stop. The death of Garfield had hit him harder than he realized, because he felt his own life was slipping away. When they reached the studio, he sat down with the producers, to see if they would change a few pages for him. They worked out pliable lines for him to speak, which satisfied the actor.

His co-stars were mostly Europeans. Manta Toren a French actress played "Michelle", while Herbert Lom's role was that of "Julius Dekoster". Lom was an Englishman with a sharp wit, which matched Claude's. Herbert had a wonderful speaking voice too, which was a bit of a competition, to the older actor. The distinguished actor, Marios had settled for second billing to accomodate Rains. "Inspector Lucas Maigret", was Goring's character and he did a little scene stealing too. His role of the inspector, had the ability to get inside a criminal's psyche. Today we would call him a "Profiler".

Claude plays the chiefbookeeper, "Popinger". When the Inspector comes to town looking for a French "black-market" gang, who have been leaking Dutch money into the French open market. Dekoster (Herbert Lom) has been stealing from his own business for years, because he is in love with one of the gang members. When the Inspector confronts both men, "Popinger", knows he's not the crook, so it must be his boss. Dekoste packs up all the remaining money in a suitcase, and buys a ticket to Paris. Popinger on his nightly walk, sees his boss near the waterfront heading for the train station. Popinger confronts his boss and a fight ensues and Dekoster loses, by falling into the river to his death. Popinger takes the suitcase, leaves his family, and takes the train instead of his boss. Inspector Maigret is on the train thinking he is going to trap Dekoster, but finds Popinger on the train instead. In Paris he locates Michelle, and the gang. He falls in love with Michelle, fights her boyfriend for the money, and loses his life in the process.

When the film was released in the United States, Jennifer and her mother went to see the film and didn't care for it. The reviews felt the same way. The critics felt the character was too physical for Rains, to be believable.

In 1953, he started the year off with a television appearance on January 25th, on a show called. "The Bentons at Home". He was one of the guest stars, along with Susan Redd, a folk singer. Claude recited a long comic poem by Carl Sandbury.

On March 28th, he performed on N.B.C.'s "Our Hidden Wealth". Sticking close to home because his stomach problems, he starred in N.B.C's "Living Declaration" with his old buddy, Nelson Eddy.

On October 12th, he made a recording of his favorite poetry and short stories, to the music of Johannes Brahm's!

On October 3rd, The "Archer Case" was shown on Medallion Theatre. For the holidays, he couldn't resist doing a show for the Philadelphia Orchestra. The studio was only thirty minutes away from his home. The day of the performance, the whole family went to the studio to see the show.

Jennifer watched as her father put on his glasses, and approached the microphone.

Claude gave him family a smile, as the music began to play. It gave Claude the "Willies", as he called the nerves in his stomach. Then the prompter gave him his signal to begin.

"At that time Emperor Augustus sent out an order for all citizens of the "Empire" to register themselves for the census. When the first census took place, Ouirinius was the Governor of Syria. Everyone, then went to register himself, each to his own town. Joseph went from the town of Nazareth in Galilee to Judia, to the town named Bethehem, where King David was born, Joseph went there because he was a descendant of David". Rains continued the story from verses 1-20 from chapter 2, of St Luke's gospel as the orchestra played Handell's Pastoral. His voice was clear, as he pronounced each word with deep feeling. His voice seemed to bounce off the walls, as they gave a chill up everyone's back.

The new year brought a new script to his mail box called "The Confidential Clerk". His role was that of Claude Muhhammer, a successful English financier. He had always dreamt about being "Knighted". But after becoming an American Citizen, that dream passed from his cup. But his fellow actors called him Sir Claude, while he was on stage.

Even Jennifer got caught up in calling her father, 'Sir '.

On February 11th, 1954. His old friend at the New York Times wrote: "The curtain rises on the spacious clerk's office in the London town house of Sir Claude, He and Eggerson, his old confidential clerk are discussing his successor, young Colby Simkins.

It turns out that Colby is really Claude's illegitimate son, though not one but these three are in on the secret. Sir Claude is anxious to have his fiesty wife, Lady Elizabeth take to Colby. If she does like him, Sir Claude will tell her about his son, so he can adopt him legally. But what Sir Claude doesn't know is that his wife had an affair a long time ago and she starts to look upon Colby as her own lost son. The complications set in as the plot thickens with Sir Claude's daughter who is illegitamate, starts to fall in love with Colby, not knowing he could be her brother.

In the last act, Sir Claude finds out that Colby is not his son after all. Colby's father long dead was a second rate organist and Colby's aunt is his real mother, who practiced a deception on Sir Claude, in order for him to bring up her child as his own."

His co-stars were Ina Claire and Jean Greenwood, a pair of accomplished stage actresses, who loved working with Rains. The play was fun for the actor, but it wasn't a "Tony" winner. The play ran on Broadway for ten months and many of Claude's close friends made it backstage, to wish him well.

In 1954, also brought the death of another of his good friends Sidney Greenstreet, who was seventy five years old. Francis had loved living in New York City while Claude was doing the play. Big advertisers would take her to lunch, as they tried to talk her into doing commercials, for their products. After the play was finished, the Rains's marriage became estranged. Jennifer was about to finish high school. Francis feared her life was over, because her daughter was growing up so fast. She wanted more out of life, then retreating to the farm as her prison.

The Fonda's had bought a home in New York City, and Francis thought it was time to sell most of their holdings, including the farm and take up residence, in a big city. But Claude didn't like that idea. He was willing to sell their home in Brentwood, for it didn't serve a purpose any more, but he wanted the farm to escape to. Claude was losing weight because of his ulcer, but he refused to give up drinking for pleasure.

One night after his performance of Sir Claude, an old friend showed up at his dressing room door. Alfred Hitchcock had seen the play and he had come back stage to say hello. As the chubby director knocked on Rains' door, he heard the mellow voice of Rains say, "come in".

Rains was taking off his make-up, as he turned to see "Hitchcock".

"Good God, Hitch! It's so good to see you!" the actor said standing to shake hands with the director. "Please come in... take a seat.... do you want a bit of tea?" asked the nervous actor.

"No.... thank You.. Sir Claude.. are you trying to tell the Queen something?"

"No.... no.. that dream is dead. How about you?"

"Too heavy to be a Knight! Hitchcock laughed.

"So how is the Hollywood scene, these days?" Rains asked taking off the rest of his make-up.

"Not so good, except when I write my own stories.... you know!"

"Television?.. I've done a few shows myself.... the money's good."

"Yes.... so I see! It's a mystery series, with some fair scripts."

"That's great Hitchcock.... lots of luck with it!"

"I've talked to Bette and Peter Lorre, about doing my stories. Now I'm asking you.

"Sounds wonderful.... just send me your best script, and I will do it!" quipped Rains.

"Of course..... I wouldn't have it any other way! smiled the director then continued. We old timers have to stick together, with all these pretty faces taking the big screen away from good actors. The deal will take a few months to finalize, but I do want the best for my shows!" Hitchcock added.

It will be lovely working with you again, Hitchcock. You're the only director that didn't let me overact! Claude said dryly.

I only direct... those players, that know what they are doing. Hitch smiled. I talked to Bette and Peter and signed them up for a show. How about you?

What do you have in mind for me?

A play called "And So Died Riabouchinslea" Next season maybe you can do a couple of more shows. Hitch added.

Claude accepted and the next day in Hitch's office, while the director served tea, the contract was signed.

Rains didn't want to be overexposed on T.V., but he loved Radio. So he accepted a Radio Series for a few months, where he portrayed "Thomas Jefferson."

In the mid 1955's, the problem with his drinking, was finally getting on his wife's nerve's. Suddenly he was at ther crossroads of his life. The woman he had loved for twenty-five years was dissatisfied with their life together.

He felt life slipping away away from him.The only thing that gave him happiness was his daughter and work!

So when Ray Milland called him to be in his new production..... Claude jumped at the chance to put some space between Francis and himself.

Ray would direct him in The part of "Aristedes Mavros", a suave crime lord.

Claude would taunt Ray, "Oh you want me to play myself!

His costar would be the lovely redhead, "Maureen O'Hara" (Sylvia Merrill) and "Yvonne Furneaux" (Maria Magdalena). The young actresses were the romantic interests for both men. Milland was pulling triple duty on this film, actor, director and producer.

Rain's trip to Lisbon was paid for by the production company, along with a bright and sunny hotel room, over looking the sea. Milland, a Welsh-born actor, had always wanted to be in a film with Claude, even if it was a "B" picture! Claude would have taken the part just to see the coastline of the Iberian Peninsula.

He darted around the sets, looking over everyone's shoulder, trying to be of assistance.

He knew Ray had a lot on his plate, and he was only trying to be helpful. He felt guilty taking a paycheck, for having so much fun. He wrote his long time friend, Norman MacKermott, a former producer from the Everyman Theatre, ...How wonderful the landscapes were! And how he enjoyed working with two such lovely creatures as Maureen and Yvonne.

Ray thought Claude was great in every scene, as he played his scoundrel with class.

He always kept a twinkle in his eye! There is one scene that is wonderfully played by Rains. He is awaken by his butler, to a bright shinny day, with birds singing by his window. Claude gets out of bed.... takes a little bird seed and places it on the window sill. When the little bird goes to eat, Claude kills the little thing. In his close-up, he gives the camera the biggest sneer.

When Rains finally finishes the film and returns home, he finds a note from his wife, that she has left him. A few days later his lawyer, is contacted, that Mrs. Rains, has taken up residency in Cullman County, Alabama, for a year. She claimed Claude had deserted her, but in reality she was the one that had left the marriage. Her lawyer, Jack Martin Bains kept in communication with Claude's lawyer. She asked that her husband not contest the divorce, because she couldn't live with his drinking problem anymore.

Rains roamed around the eleven room house, or took his rifle out to shoot some ducks, waiting to see if she would return to him. But Francis was serious this time. She felt her daughter was grown up enough to understand her predicament. Jennifer was now at college, but her talks with her parents about getting together again went unheard. Claude figured there was another man, probably a younger man, who could satisfy her needs.

Rains stuck close to the farm, most of 1955. He was sick about the divorce and he was losing weight, because he would not eat properly. Within a years time, he went from a proud man, to a shadow of himself. His life became uncertain, as he wandered his farm, from daylight to sunset.

One day while picking up his mail by the roadside, a neighbor passed by asking about his wife. He told her she was away for a while. Then she went on about hearing him on the radio, on May 26th, on N.B.C. called Builders of America. Claude and Walter Huston did poetry readings, about Washington and Lincoln, for the Memorial day celebration. She asked if he would go to Waco, Texas?

"What's in Waco.... Texas?" he asked.

"My mother, Mrs. Armstrong. she runs a little theatre group in her town, and she would love for you to come do one of your recitels!"

Sounds interesting. I'm working on one now, that I did in 1953. I'm calling it "Music and Words." I was thinking about taking it on cross country tour. Maybe if I do it.... I will contact your mother in.....???"

"Waco Texas!" his neighbor smiled.

Claude put a show together called "Words and Music", later that year. He went on tour with it and in early winter of 1956, reached Waco Texas. Mrs. Armstrong was overjoyed that her favorite actor was coming to her town. She took care of everything for the actor, the theatre, selling the tickets, and the advertisement. Claude had hired his own pianist to accompany his words. Mrs. Armstrong was a very rich lady and she sent a limousine to the airport to pick up the two men. Her husband had been very charitable in his life time, building hospitals for the people of Waco, Mrs. Armstrong helped her husband with all his work and he built her the Waco Theatre, to carry on charitable works, to raise money to keep these institutions running. She told Claude that the tickets were already sold out, and there was only standing room only that was left.

"Well, I hope you sell those too!" Claude said dryly.

"Believe me Mr. Rains I will fill up the theatre with ease." Rains felt in capable hands, as she arranged a tea for a reporter's conference, at her large country estate. After a day's rest, Mrs. Armstrong showed Claude the Waco Theatre, and he just loved it.

He started rehearsals, that day and the next. Mrs. Armstrong was having her tea, she sent her limosene to his hotel to pick him up, and take him to her home, which reminded him a lot of his own home. He was shown to the back yard, where Mrs. Armstrong was fussing with waiters about the food.

It was hot in Waco, even though it was winter time in the rest of the country. He wore a light weight suit and no tie. Mrs. Armstrong greeted him in a flowing dress, and a large brim hat. She showed Claude around her gardens, just before the first reporter arrived.

Claude took a seat at the head table where Mrs. Armstrong poured him some tea. A few minutes later the garden was filled with reporters, from every newspaper in town. After having something to eat, the reporters took their seats to begin the interview. Mrs. Armstrong stood up to welcome her guests to her home, in an old southern fashion. Then the interview began with the first question. "Mr. Rains. Mr. Rains.... went up a shout from the crowd. "How do you like Waco?"

"Quite well.... but it's a little warm for this time of the year for me." he quipped. Then Gynter Quill of the Waco Times Herald asked. "Which of your stage roles did you enjoy the most?" Softly Claude smiled saying. "I have never enjoyed any of them.... I suffer every time I'm on stage" he concluded.

"Then what role has given you the most satisfaction?" Miss Quill asked.

"Darkness at Noon"! came a quick answer.... that was a once in a life time role.... but I'm looking forward to another like it."

"How does Waco strike you compared to Hollywood? asked another reporter.

"A very dry piece of land!" Rains said dryly. The crowd laughed at his remark, as another question was asked. "Some of your fellow actors have been talking about going into politics.... like George Murphy. What do you think of actors as candidates?

"Mr. Murphy is a very fine gentleman.... very witty. But I'm a Pennsylvanian. I don't vote in California. We have our own troubles where I live.... like ticks!"

"Are you going to make another film?"

"I have been reading a few scripts, but nothing has hit my fancy!"

"Do you like making films?" came another question.

"I love it!.... Hollywood has been very good to me."

"We understand your father made films in England.... is that true? Mr. Rains."

Claude cleared his throat and said. "Yes.. yes. he did... in silent films, ...in the twenties. He directed a few too. I guess you can call him a pioneer in the world of films, ...in Britain."

"Is he still alive.... Mr. Rains?" Miss Quill asked.

"No.... Claude sighed.... He died shortly after I made Caesar and Cleopatra in 1944, he was eighty-two, at that time."

"You went to England during the war?....wasn't that dangerous?"

"Oh quite.... I had to get permission from the United States, Canada and Great Britain.

Carmella Felice

I took a train to Canada.... then flew to New Foundland, which is a British colony.

Then a British bomber, flew me to England. It was quite a long trip, over ice and the like! But I met some wonderful Canadian soldiers who were going to England with me."

"How long did it take to make the movie?"

"Too long! came a quick answer.... nearly six months."

The interview went on for a few minutes more, then Mrs. Armstrong called a halt to the questioning. Mr. Rains has graciously given his time and now he has to go to rehearsals, at the Waco Theatre. You will find free tickets to the show, at the door.

Please enjoy the performances.

A few nights later, the show opened to a full house. When the Rains took to the stage, a large roar went up from the crowd. He was dressed in his tuxedo, as was his pianist, and they couldn't begin the show until the crowd calmed down. Claude took his seat on a high stool, in front of a podiuum. He waved to the crowd, as the lights were lowered to begin. "It's our pleasure for us to be in Waco Texas!" Claude smiled, and cheers went up again. His pianist started to play, which calmeddown the audience. Softly Claude spoke."I will now read a poem called, Enoch Arden, by Alfred Lord Tennyson!" As the pianist played the Ballad in DS minor by Johannes Brahms, the Texan's settled down to listen. For two hours the audience was transfixed on Claude's voice, which filled the theatre with precision of his delivery. At the end of the night, the crowd cheered for a good ten minutes, as they stood up in awe, in the magic of his voice.

CHAPTER 17

A NEW LIFE

A year later, Rains was driving back from his lawyer's office after signing his divorce papers from Francis. His lawyer had given him a drink at his office. Then he went to a nearby bar and drank some more. Except for the farm, his wife was given half of his fortune. Money that he sweated for, and almost given his life for was gone.

By the time he got into his Bentley, he was feeling no pain. Ten miles from his farm, he started to swerve the car, back and forth on the road. Suddenly, the car hit a pot hole, and the car took two roll-overs. On the third roll, he was thrown from the Bentley, onto the dirt road. The cars on the road swerved to get away from the body in the roadway, and the flaming car. A nearby farmer in the fields ran to his house to call the police, the fire department, and an ambulance. People were taking care of the actor, as his car was burning out of control. When the police arrived on the scene they recognized the actor, and took him quickly by ambulance to a hospital, where his cuts and bruises were treated.

After spending a few hours in the hospital, where his doctor was called to scene. His doctor gave him a big argument about drinking. "Stop the drinking now, if you want to live to see your grandchildren. Your stomach is like a piece of raw meat!" Returning to the farm, he knew his doctor was right. He knew he wasn't finished, and he set out to prove it. The Kaiser Aluminum Hour, had asked him to look over a script called. "Antigone". The role he was to play was "King Creon", but in modern dress. The new version looked interesting, so he took the job, as he started to build up his fortune again. He had recovered enough to work, and knew his limitations, as far as drinking was concerned. Now he had to think of Jennifer, and her future. The day after the show was aired on television, Jack Gould wrote this in his column, on September 12, 1956.

> "Claude Rains is the star, but the play disappoints. A potentially provocative experiment in drama, a modern dress version of "Antigone", done against impressionistic settings flounded most disappointly last night on the "Kaiser Aluminum hour", on Channel 4.
>
> Claude Rains in the part of Creon strived earnestly and sometimes very tellingly to impart meaning and emotion to the tragedy, the scenery of Rouben Ter Arthunian was uniformly striking in it's composition. And Lewis Galantiere's adaption for television of the Jean Anouilh play contained the moving passages for a fine hour.
>
> But "Antigone" needs an Antigone, and the Aluminum Hour unfortunately succumbed to the Hollywood star system. For the part of the regal figure who put human dignity above materialistic happiness the producer selected Marisa Pavan, The beautiful child was simply out of her depth".
>
> On the screen especially in color, Miss Pavan had the chiseled features that understandably could have recommended her for the Greek tragedy. But in the exacting role, which puts a premium on deeply felt emotions and principles, she was capable only of a recitation. The part that called for the power and feeling of a woman dedicated to principle emerged only as a querulous school girl's railing against authority.
>
> In these difficult circumstances Mr. Rains met the test. Playing tragedy by one's self is not the easiest of acting chores, in the absence of any response from Antigone, it was remarkable that he made Creon come even partly alive. Single-handedly he could not be expected to make the duel of minds consistently credible and gripping.

As the chorus, Alexander Scourby contributed assurance and style, his explanation of the death scene in the tomb was much exciting then anything that had happened on stage. The supporting cast was visibly self-conscious.

Franklin Schaffner's direction was rather static and not too impressive. With a cast in modern dress, timeless settings and a Greek tragedy he seemed undecided as to which style he was going to use. The aimlessness of his direction did not help propel the tragedy towards it's climax.

Experimentation in T.V drama is certainly to be encouraged, however it is wise not to forget that a title role generally needs acting before glamour. Inexperience at the top handicaps everyone all the way down the line!"

Claude wasn't to thrilled with the review, but agreed on a lot of the things, Jack Gould had stated in his review. Some actors just weren't ready, for a Greek tragedy. He quickly was picked up to do a new play called, "The Night of the Auk." His co-stars in this production were all fine actors, like Wendell Corey (Colonel Tom Russell), Dick York, (Lt. Mac Hartman) and Martin Brooks as Lt. Jan Kephart. The play had a good director Sidney Lumet, but the auidience didn't like the story line. Rains had gone from one extreme to another, but he didn't care, so long as those pay checks were coming in.

Claude played a knowledgeable scientist. His clear mellow voice sounded across the theatre like his performance in "Darkness" Christopher Plummer to was a Shakespearian actor. His voice was wonderful to listen to, and his acting was perfect. But the audiences weren't ready for a space play. Arch Oboler's play opened in December 3rd, at the New York's Playhouse Theatre. But closed eight performances later for lack of interest. He was very upset in having two failures in a row. Without Francis' input, he felt lost, as he picked each new project.

Claude's old friend critic Brooks Atkinson was still around to cheer his favorite actor on, in his review of the play. Claude couldn't understand why it had closed so fast, after two months of working so hard. When they had played out of town inWashington D. C. at the Sam Shubert Theatre, critic Richard L. Coe, had praised all the actor's performances.

Carmella Felice

Early in February, Hitchcock gave Claude a call, to see if he would do "The Cream of the Jest". Rains agreed to play a drunken actor Charles Gresham. It seemed to Claude that Hitchcock was writing about his life, because he had heard about the car accident. Claude handled the script with all his smoothness of fifty years of experience.

In the summer time his daughter came for a visit, then she went to see her mother who had bought a house in Philadelphia. Her grades were very good! Which made Claude very proud! Jennifer told her father that she wanted to be an actor too! Her father tried to talk his daughter out of it, but finally gave in to his daughter's wishes. For a time Jennifer tried to get her parents to make-up their differences, but it was to late for a reconcilliation. Francis especially didn't want to go back to Claude, with a new life staring her in the face.

Claude had just returned from England, where he went to do a recording, "The Song of Songs" and the Letters of "Heloise and Abelard." with Claire Bloom and Nancy Wichwire. While in England he visited with family and friends, not knowing if he would ever see them again. Depressed he told his old pal Norman, he didn't have anything to live for anymore. "There's always somethinng over the rainbow Claude. Your fans love you! Jennifer loves you! So don't give up just yet!" Believing his friend's words, he came back to the United States, feeling like a new man.

His agent had a new project for him when he returned home from England. The story, "On Borrowed Time", seemed an appropriate vehicle for him to do. But the next scrpt a musical, "The Pied Piper of Hamelin", wasn't his type of role. His agent told him to think it over. Claude decided to do both.

In, "On Borrowed Time!" he played Mr. Brink, the angel of death. Who comes for Gramps played by Ed Wynn. Gramps tries to out smart Mr. Brink, but in the long run death wins out, when Mr. Brink wants to take a small child who had befriended Gramps.

Gramps trades his own life for the sick child's life. Claude had a lot of fun making the Television show with Ed Wynn, who kept him laughing all the time. In a review in Variety on November 20th, 1957, had this to say about the program.

> "Rains recreating his old role as Mr. Brink suffered ocassional troubles with his lines. But overall his performance

was a fine contribution in perfect counter balance to Ed Wynn's contrasting calm, wisdom and inevitability, with impatiency abruptness and contrariness."

The "Pied Piper of Hamelin has him paired off against Van Johnson in the lead. When he arrived in Hollywood he wasn't to happy with the role. In an interview about his role, he had this to say about Mayor Hamelin, "After the producers sent me the script, they phoned from Hollywood and asked, if I sang? Of course, I answered No! Once I got there, they suggested, they just play the music for me.... just so I could hear it. Well.... as you know, it was based on Peer Gynt Suite and the melodies are very tenacious. I found myself humming along with the piano and within a week, I was bawling the music as loudly as any of them!"

Rains was very proud of himself for trying a new forum for his art. While in Hollywood, he cleaned up all of his holdings, thinking he would never return to California again. On the ride back to the east coast, he thought of what he wanted to do next.

He hated to go back to the farm, without Francis or Jennifer there. So he decided to sell Stock Grange, his beloved farm. It was becoming too much for him to handle anyway and a Mr. Harrison Wetherill, one of the farmers in the area, had always wanted the extra land. Wetherill was wealthy enough to afford it and he knew he would keep all the animals and his farm crew intact. His land-agent had found Claude a large house on the outskirts of a town called, "Hawthorne House". It was in a rich neighborhood of the country and had plenty of land, and trees about it. High on a hill, the house stood for generations.

He carefully packed all his antiques and shipped them over to "Hawthorne House". Francis haven't wanted any of the antiques they had bought together, now she was into modern and more up to date furniture.

A month later, he and his cook moved to his new place on the hill. He would wander the rooms at night, moving from room to room, in his loneliness. When Jennifer came to the house on Holidays and during the summer time, It was a complete joy for him.

She would tell him about her school in Vermont, and how she was doing in her studies to become an actress. He would ask her to read to him and sometimes told her where she made her mistakes.

When Jennifer first told him about becoming an actress, he didn't like the idea. She wanted to do it on her own without her father's friends helping out, so when she finally did graduate and took to summer stock, she changed her first name to Jessica. Most of his friends knew Jennifer as a child, but when she went out on her own, she didn't want her father's reputation to cloud their thinking.

After a few months of roaming the eleven rooms, he thought it was time for him to go back to work.

Early in February, Hitchcock arranged for Rains to go lunch with him, to discuss a T.V. play. Hitchcock talked about those old days on the English stage, and all the old timers, that had passed away in their generation.

After performing in a T.V. play for Alfred Hitchcock, Claude decided he wanted to do a show all by himself.

So he put all of his favorite poems and stories together, along with his favorite music, on paper.

Now he needs a medium to try out his show. Bryn Mar College was the closest school to where he lived, so he decided that was where he would put on his Theatrical Extravanganza.

After consolidating some of the shows, he had done for radio, Rains called his new show, "Words and Music". He then wrote to the Dean of Bryn Mar College, to see if he wanted him to put on a show for the college. He sat on boards of a few colleges and he figured it was a good way to give back to the community. The Dean wrote back that he would be happy to help. They set up an appointment and Rains was introduced to Madame Agi Jambor, the college's music professor. She also had been a concert pianist in Germany before the war. Her career over, because of the war years, she came to America to teach at the college. Rains showed her what music he wanted to go along with his poems and she did very well setting up a musical program.

The fifty year old Agi had dark brown hair, that was shoulder length her dark eyes set off her oval face. She stood about five foot seven-inches just a little shorter then Rains.

They worked on the show for two weeks, as the school sold tickets to make money for the college. Claude loved the way she played the piano, and they became good friends over the course of setting up the show. He took her out to dinner almost every night, to talk about the program. Slowly their friendship grew into a love affair.

Agi was fascinated by the attention that Claude was showing her. She had been married before, which had ended badly. But Claude seemed to be a gentleman, so she was taken in by his smooth moves. Claude had heard from his daughter that her mother was going to be married soon to a man named Henry Fader, so his friendship grew stronger with Agi.

After having such a good year in 1958, by making "This Earth is Mine" with Rock Hudson and a film in Italy called "Battle of the Worlds". The news of his ex-wife's marriage hit him hard. So when he asked Agi to marry him in late fall of 1959, it might have been spite work on his part. Agi agreed and they were married in his home on November 5th, 1959. Jennifer greed to attend the services along with two other guests.

Justice of the peace George Bonsall performed the ceremony with friends Adolph Vogel of Meron and Edward Lener of West Chester. A light lunch was served after the wedding ceremony.

The next morning at breakfast, Claude sat down too drink his orange juice, and read the daily paper. Suddenly he rose in a huff, throwing the paper to the floor. Agi jumped almost out of her skin, as he went into a temper.

"What's the matter?" she asked.

"This reporter has made a mockery of our wedding!" Claude ranted, then rushed into the living room in a huff. Agi followed saying. "I read the article and didn't see anything wrong with it!" Agi said calmly. Angry at Agi's remark, he picked up a small lamp on one of the end-tables and threw it at the wall. As it smashed into pieces, he ran up the staircase to his room, closing the door hard behind him, leaving Agi with her mouth open, not knowing what to do or say.

Rains felt belittled by the reporter implying he had only two good friends in the world.

When in fact, he had thousands of friends through out the world. But he couldn't invite everyone to his wedding, so he kept it to three people.

A few weeks later, unhappy in his marriage, he started drinking again. Agi couldn't handle his mood-swings so she decided he should go back to work. He was offered a Christmas show at Carniegie Hall on December 7, Rains was to be the narrator for "Christmas Oratorio". The vocal music was sung by the Collegiate Chorale, along with the stars from the Metropolitan Opera. The show was called, "For the Time Being".

Agi insisted on going to opening night to meet the opera stars, but it seemed to upset Claude, because it reminded him of when Francis would accompany him everywhere.

He thought he was over Francis, but the memories still held on. Then Jennifer decided to marry and asked her father to walk her down the the aisle. Claude pulled himself together, when he saw his ex-wife. Francis, walking down the aisle on her new husband's arm. Claude liked his new son-inlaw, Edward Brash, a Philadelphian, but was confused at the reception, when all he saw around him was Francis's family!

After a few months of marriage, Agi couldn't take Claude's mood-swings anymore.

She filed for a divorce after being with him for five month's. She told the court that her husband had a bad temper, and he drank a lot. In the few months thay had been married, Claude had given her nine dollars and fifty cents, for groceries. On July 30th 1960, a degree was awarded by the Chester County Court to Mrs. Agi Rains on the grounds of indignities. Rains' lawyer settled out of court, as Agi went back to teaching.

One has to wonder if he knew he had made a mistake by marrying Agi, and put on a lunatic performance, so that she would get a divorce. If he did fake Agi out with his acting experience, it worked out perfectly. Vowing not to marry again, he decided to write his autobiography. Needing a ghostwriter, he asked his doctor if he knew of anyone in the town, that could write? The doctor recommended a woman by the name of Rosemary Clark. Finding out where she lived, he wrote to Mrs. Clark about his book.

They agreed to meet for dinner, and talk about the assignment. Claude picked up the slightly overweight woman at her home, where he met one of her children, a young woman named "Angel". Rosemary was twice married and had always been a fan of the actor with the beautiful voice. For her it was love at first sight. From that very first date, Rosemary knew she wanted to marry the star. After a few meetings, Claude felt the same way about Rosemary. He felt this time he had found a soul-mate again, so he married the writer after the divorce Agi.

Rosemary was loving, and didn't ask anything from him but his love. Her three children enjoyed the fact that their mother was going to marry a big movie star, especially Angel, who would become like a sister to Jennifer.

Many of his friends couldn't believe he was getting married so quickly after his divorce, but Claude was like that. When he called Bette Davis to ask her to the wedding, she was upset that he hadn't asked her. "We would tear each other apart!" he kidded his old friend. "Where are you having this next wedding.... in your wine cellar?" she asked.

"That's not a bad idea, Bette!" he laughed. This wedding he had more guests, because he wasn't going to be annoyed by critics on his wedding day. Besides, Rosemary wanted a large wedding. She had three children, plus family who wanted to come see her get married to Claude Rains. Jennifer attended with her husband but didn't seem happy, as she kissed her father good luck. Claude thought it was because he had married so quickly after Agi, but Jennifer was having marital problems of her own.

While married to Rosemary, he stopped drinking, except at family gatherings.

The house was always filled with family, and he didn't mind that, because he liked her children.

While married to Rosemary he performed in "To Walk In Silence" a Naked City" episode on September 11th for A.B.C. titled "To Walk in Silence". Then "Shangri La" for the Hallmark Hall of Fame on October 24th on N.B.C., where Rains played the "high lama". On March 14th, he appeared in another Alfred Hitchcock presentation, "The Horseplayer", in this his role is that of a priest. In Paris, his old friend David Lean had married again to Leila Matkar, on July 4th, 1960. David was about to start a new film, "Lawrence of Arabia", and he wanted his friend to play "Dryden", a British diplomat in the film.

Claude thought it would make a wonderful honeymoon trip for his wife, so he took the role. They would be shooting Claude's scenes in Spain, where some of the buildings resemble moorish architecture. David told Claude shooting would start in Seville on December 18th

Carmella Felice

1961, but first he had to come to England to be fitted for a "time costume".

The Rain's enjoyed their stay in England then were transported to Seville in a four engine plane, which Claude wasn't so happy to be riding in. Neither was Anthony Quinn, and he made every one know about it.

Seville was warm even though it was winter in England. Some of the crew had forgotten to get iron shots, which was required by the studio to work in Spain. The producer sent a few cast members to get their shots, including Peter O' Toole. The local doctor who injected Peter, plus twenty other crew members gave them "Hepatitis" with his dirty needles. Peter developed a boil on his back side, which made camel riding out of the question.

Spanish hospitals weren't known for their cleanliness, so most of the sick were flown back to England to be treated, which held up shooting for a couple of days. The Rains's took it easy in the hotel's bar talking to Jack Hawkins, who was glad Senator McCarthy had died that year. Jack had liked the writings of Dalton Trumbo, who finally went back to work for a major studio. Claude agreed with Jack that the whole thing was a disgrace, because he had lost some good friends to 'MacCarthism'.

The Rains' took in the sights of Seville, with it's wonderful architecture. Rosemary loved the trip as she took photos of everything to show her family. New Year's Eve was spent in Seville with the production company, in the hotel's ballroom. Rosemary met most of the cast, including quiet Alex Guinness, charming Jack Hawkins and handsome Peter O'Toole.

When they returned home, her daughter Angel was the first to see Rosemary's collection of photos. In the meanwhile, the "Lawrence" production company had moved to another country to film the desert scenes. It would take almost a year later for the picture to be shown in London. The Royal premier of "Lawrence of Arabia" was held on Monday, December 10th, 1962, but Claude couldn't make the London showing because he was ill. When the picture was shown in New York City on December 16th, "Lawrence" recieved a standing ovation for it's stars. But when Claude read his friend 's column in the New York Times, he called David Lean at his hotel. "I just read Bosley Crowther's review of the picture, and he hated it." Lean assured him that Crowther was probably upset, because there was talk in New York of a newspaper strike. A few days later the picture opened in Hollywood to good reviews. David Lean told all the reporters that he wanted to thank his crew.

"Everyone talks about the wonderful acting, directing and writing. But the crew is a major reason for success with this kind of movie.

The actors were not in the front line. They could shoot a few hours and get out of the sun. They would have time off, when they weren't working. So I want to thank my crew, for a job well done!"

Claude's family went to see the film and Jennifer called to tell her father how much she had enjoyed his performance.

By 1962, Claude had lost three more close friends, Charles Laughton, Errol Flynn and Humphey Bogart. Alfred Hitchcock still had his show and he asked Claude, to do another "Hitchcock Presents". Packing again, they went to do a television show with Billy Mumy, as his co-star. Claude's movement was slow and deliberate on this show and you could tell he was ill.

But he continued his television work with C.B.S., the "Rawhide Show" with Clint Eastwood. Rains played a drunken western judge in "Incident of Judgement" on February 21st. Then he went on to do a "Wagon Train" episode called, "The Daniel Clay Story". After a short vacation, he came back to the Brooklyn Studios, to make "The Outpost", for a Dupont show of the week. It marked Claude's thirtieth anniversary with N.B.C. During taping he was interviewed by the press stating "Broadcasting is a real miracle of entertainment. The theatre hasn't substantially changed in four hundred years.

Movies have progressed from silent to talking pictures, to wide screen epics. But against this broadcasting has in less than four decades grown from local broadcasts to network television.. and now Telstar".

N.B.C. asked him to do another show called, "Sam Benedict" on September 29th, with his friend Edmond O' Brien. Rosemary was at his side while filming this program, to give her husband moral support.

In the summer of 1963, Claude and Rosemary decided to move to Sandwich, New Hamphire. They bought the "Weed House", in Lower Corner of Sandwich. The new house looked much like his house in West Chester, but had more land around it. The family helped the couple move into their new home. Angel especially was a great help to them.

The name of the house came from William Weed, who made major additions in 1850, including the handsome portico, to an earlier house. His decendants had lived in the town for generations. They lived in the house, until Claude bought it in 1963.

The town was very small numbering one thousand two hundred when the Rains's moved in. Claude had spent many vacations in Sandwich, with his doctor's family. Claude didn't change anything in the house, because he honored the integrity of the historic house.

The stately building, with its square columns across the front and a red brick walk leading to the entrance, blended in with the two large willow trees in front, shading the great house. Jennifer's old summer camp still was around as Claude made the rounds, with his good friend Doctor Charles Uhie. When Jennifer visited her father, she would drive over to the camp, just to take a look. The Rains' were happy living at Weed House. They would spend their time with friends, as well as time spent at Squam Lake.

The former resident of Weed House was eighty-four year old Dorothy Weed, who didn't have the money to take care of the large house. Claude made only a few alterations. The kitchen was updated. A porch which had been potting shed was enclosed as a small room. An icehouse once attached to the barn was converted into an art studio for Mrs. Rains.

The library, near a back corner of the house was painted in dark green, just like the one in the "Hawthorne House". All his books and scripts lined every shelf of his library.

Which covered one wall of this room, from floor to the ceiling.

While Claude maintained his privacy, Rosemary was quite friendly with the town folk.

She was a very witty person and a pleasure to be with the towns people said. They were often invited to local dinner parties, which made Claude a little nervous, so most of the time, Rosemary attended the functions by herself. She enjoyed the social gatherings very much, because it reminded her of the olden days of the Revolutionary days. Claude was content to stay home and read a good book.

CHAPTER 18

ALL THINGS ONCE ARE THINGS FOREVER

On the outskirts of town lived an old man who collected junk, along the road sides of the town. One weekend Rosemary had ordered a king size mattress, to be delivered from a local furniture store in town. The owner of the store drove it out to "Weed House" and unloaded it by the road side, because there wasn't a road going up to the house. As he walked up to the door to tell the Rains of the delivery, the junkman came down the road. He stopped by the mattress and thinking someone had left it for collection, he placed it in the back of his truck. When Claude and the family came out to collect it, they saw the junkman, heading up the hill, very slowly. Angel and the rest of the family ran after the truck, to tell the man he had made a mistake. Claude watched as the truck slowly drove backwards down the hill to rest in front of him. Laughing, he watched as his stepchildren took the mattress into the house, as Rosemary gave a long look of displeasure to the junk collector. That's how they learned not to leave anything by the roadside, except things they didn't want!

The town's people soon learned of their famous movie star in their community. They thought he was a real character, when he would take his two mile walk into town to do business at the bank. He would wear a long black cape and a broad rimmed hat and dark glasses. He told Rosemary he dressed that way as not to bring attention to himself. But she knew it was just the opposite. While they respected his privacy, they enjoyed his company when he came to town. After banking he would

Carmella Felice

stop and have tea, or a cold drink, before heading back to the house. He found the beauty of the landscape breath taking as it had not really changed in two hundred years.

In the early spring of 1963, Claude went back to work on a new film for M.G.M. Rosemary went with her husband to keep him company on location. Claude had worked with Richard Chamberlain on his popular television series. "Doctor Kildare". Now he was to do a motion picture, with the young actor called "Twilight of Honor". The Rains' packed up to go on location to do the film, when David Lean called him up. "How would you like to play "Herod the Great"?" Claude responded, "I'll do it for nothing!" So after Rains concluded his filming, he went to pick up the script from David to play Herod. Rains loved the lines that George Stevens and James Lee Barrett wrote for him and he did the scenes for "no pay". Claude played the evil Herod to the hilt, as he says to the three wisemen. "If you find this child, bring me word that I too, might worship him! After he has the three wise men followed he says. "Good.... mmm! Where is god?.... or the child of God, except in man's most dangerous imagination! The child of imagination is the child.... I fear!"

It would be almost two years later that United Artists would release the "Greatest Story on Earth". It had hundreds of movie stars in it including old friends like Jose Ferrer, and Angela Landsbury, Lean thought Claude played Herod marvelously.

When the picture was finally released in 1965, Rains was named in several reviews, Variety February 17th, 1965 stated that he was "outstanding!" With Herod behind him, he headed back to his home in Sandwich. He knew he was tired and couldn't make any more of those taxing films.

But Rosemary fell sick and when the reports came in she had cancer of the pancreas.

Her family came to Weed House to help out Rosemary, but the cancer took over quickly and she died at the age of forty-eight, on New Year's Eve 1965.

Claude was devastated, that his young wife should die so quickly and painfully.

After her death, he would sit on a small couch in her bedroom and stare out the window for hours. He was sick himself, as he underwent several major operations on his bleeding ulcer. Jennifer and the stepchildren came to visit him on a daily basis, until he returned home. Jennifer was near the end of her marriage, and that made him feel extra sorry for her.

In 1965, he had tried to reactivate his career, hoping it would help him cope with the depression he felt over losing Rosemary. All he looked forward to was the company of his housekeeper, who served his meals and took care of his needs. He had lost almost forty pounds when he was asked to do a television play called "Cops and Robbers".

One could hardly recognize him or his voice, because he looked so frail. He played "Valentino", a retired man living in an old Italian hotel. When Casare played by Bert Lahr comes to live with him they decide to hold up a bank, just for the fun of it. It was fun for him to get together with old buddies again, but everyone could see he was not up to it.

In early summer, he was approached to do a play called, "So much of Earth, So much of Heaven". On August 23rd, he opened at the John Drew Theatre. Jennifer was worried about her father. She pleaded for him to quit show business, but he wouldn't hear of it. The critics tore up the play, in the Westport paper. "The play is talky, tedious, tiresome and trite.... The boredom builds up act by act. By the time the audience gets to the few moments of real tension in act three they are so embarrased and benumbed that they are hardly in a condition to appreciate it. Competent professionals like Claude Rains, Leueen MacGrath and Larry Gates showed themselves baffled by a pompous and pretentious script. Direction was at a snail's pace" September 2nd, 1965.

Jennifer was worried about her father as they came into the last stop for the tour. Bucks County Playhouse. She knew Bette Davis was coming to see the play and asked her to tell her father, he had to stop before something happened to him. After the play Bette came back stage and greeted him with a kiss saying, "What are you doing.... you old war-dog?"

"Living!" Claude responded. That night he forgot his lines and made up new ones as he went along. He loved the applause of the audience and wanted it never to stop. But within a few hours after the play, he was rushed to a hospital and diagnosed with severe internal bleeding.

During the six weeks he was hospitalized, Claude wrote to all of his friends, in various fields, thanking them for putting up with him, when he worked with them. He also told his friends that he missed Rosemary very much, because she had loved him completely.

He hoped there was an after life as he wanted to join her after he passed from this earth.

He ended each letter with, "I miss my house and garden and soon I hope to be walking up a brick path again."

While assisting her father in his last play, Jennifer met a tall good looking actor named Rick Lenz. He had straight dark brown hair and brown eyes and he reminded Jennifer a lot of her father, in many ways. Rick was called "Igor", by his friends and Claude used to laugh when his daughter, called Rick by that name. He recieved that name because he was an admitted "pool shark". He would play actors, agents or stage managers to make a few extra bucks. He asked Claude to play a few times, but Claude told him, "I don't want you to look bad, in front of the cast!"

Lenz was an actor with vast experience in stock and regional theatres. He had played ten leads in summer stock. A graduate of the University of Michigan, he served as resident director-teacher of the Jackson Civic Players for two years. He had studied with Phillip Burton at the American Musical and Dramatic Academy and the Herbert Berhof Studios. He had made a few television commercials, which brought in a few bucks every month, which he used to play pool. In his way, Rick had the same background that Claude did, so they became fast friends. It was not a wonder that Jennifer came to fall in love with Rick. Her first marriage had ended in dispair, with no hope of a reconciliation.

Two months later, Claude was walking up his brick walk way on the arm of his daughter. When Jennifer couldn't be with him, his housekeeper was his only company, with a weekly visit from his doctor. Jennifer had followed Rick to Broadway and Claude felt quite alone in his large house. His doctor wanted him to take walk around his home, to exercise his weakened legs. On one of these trips to the mail box, he found a letter from Rick, which stated:

Feb. 9th, 1967
Dear Mr. Rains;

The Life and Times of Claude Rains

Just a note to say I hope your illness is a short one and you feel well again. I know being alone and ill as you have been is a disheartening thing and I wish you high spirits to see you back to health.

I have spent a pleasant winter largely because of Jennifer's company. I have to confess that steady work has also affected my happiness. My play, though not too good, is at least successful, and I'm happy to be working while waiting for something else.

I am presently taking a course in Shakespeare and poetry reading from Phillip Burton and enjoying it. It also makes me remember with pleasure the reading you did when I was your guest in October. Please have a speedy recovery.
My warmest regards.
Rick Lenz

The ill actor knew his daughter had fallen in love with "Igor" and he hoped his daughter had finally found happiness. He promised his daughter that he would listen to the doctor, while she was away, but he longed for company. At major holidays, Rosemary's children would drive up for a short visit to see how Claude was doing. Rick was getting good at storytelling himself and entertained Jennifer's family, as he looked over at Claude to see if he was doing it right. Claude would stand at the fireplace as the Patriarch of the family, smiling at all, as he was king of his domain.

Most of his days were spent seated on his balcony, watching the scenery and remembering old times. He remembered Rosemary and how it was when he was young. He would walk to the little summer house where Rosemary liked to paint, and looked at her paintings one by one. He would also listen to his records, especially the one he made with Glenn Gould. He laughed to himself remembering how his wife had gotten mad at Glenn, for keeping Claude waiting at the recording session, while he soaked his hands in ice-water for an hour. Glenn was a great pianist, but he had a weird personality. He was afraid of germs, and insisted that a screen be placed between Claude and himself to protect him from germs. Claude had thought it was a big joke, but it wasn't for his wife, who had felt insulted. Glenn's behavior was strange, but Claude didn't care, if the end product was of high quality. Mrs.

Rains watched from her enclosed booth, as her husband sat on a stool in front of the microphone and Glenn sat at his piano behind the screen. He was dressed in a light sweater and scarf, even though the studio had air conditioning. After the first take, the artist listened to the play back as Glenn moved on his side of the screen to the music. Waving his hands in the air, as he tried to feel the mood of the take. Claude worked with Glenn, but never could sustain a conversation with Glenn Gould.

In November of 1966, Rains had been made Honarary Fellow of the Boston University Libraries, for his work in the theatre, movies and television. He was very proud of that degree, because except for the army, he didn't have a formal education. He was self-taught and proud of that! But the Degree had validated all that he had taught himself.

In early spring of 1967, his health deteriorated and he became housebound again. He watched from his bedroom window at the early morning sun blasting through his windows. The trees around his house had started to spread their new foliage and he could smell the summer coming. His grass was freshly cut and he could smell that sweet scent in the air. He collasped that afternoon and his doctor had him admitted to Lakes Region General Hospital. His family was called to his side, and the next morning Mr. Rains died on May 30th 1967 at the age of seventy-five. He wished that his funeral be private, with only his family present.

After services, a small procession of cars, went to a small cemetery near the village of the Center Harbor. There the great actor was laid to rest next to Rosemary.

Jennifer completed his wishes by buying a black polished marble tombstone, which was erected next to his wife's tombstone. He had chosen the following words to be set in the stone.

> "All things once are things forever.
> Soul once living, lives forever!

We his fans have seen a whole new set of stars rise to the movie screen, but none the caliber of Mr. William Claude Rains. An army of mourners, seems to grow with each year of his death. They collect his works like fine wines.

In his will, he left gifts to Rosemary's children, plus twenty five thousand dollars to the Actor's Fund of America. But the bulk of his fortune was left to his daughrter in a trust fund.

Jennifer married Rick Lenz and started her own family. She also started "Stock Grange Productions", to protect her father's name and interests.

In 1999, his film Casablanca was chosen the second best picture of the twentieth century. We his fans salute a fine actor's body of work, as he disappers into the fog, we say.... Thank You Mr. Rains, it has been a wonderful friendship!

SOME ARTICLES WRITTEN ABOUT CLAUDE RAINS

April 27th 1914	Providence Opera House on Fanny's first play, by G.B. Shaw.
January 21st 1927	The Constant Nymph., D.W.B.
December 1933	Movie Classic "The Star Nobody Knows" by Whitney Williams.
February 16th 1935	"Why I Left Hollywood" by Beatrice Moore.
February 22nd 1935	Film Weekly "Bad Boys" by Claude Rains.
August 9th 1935	Claude Rains, "As I Know Him" by Fay Wray.
August 8th 1936	Movie Herald "Hearts Divided".
April 2nd 1938	Film Weekly, "He Hates Humbug" by Wilt Mooring.
1938	Four Daughters, Exhibitor promo.
October 1939	Colliers. "The Plow and the Star".
March 24th 1939	Close-Up of Claude Rains by Phil Lonergan.

All New York Times' Play and Movie reviews by critic Brooks Atkinson.

March 9th 1940	Picturegoer "Doesn't He Have Fun
December 3rd 1940	Family Circle "Lady With The Red Hair"
April 2nd 1941	The Evening Bulletin Philadelphia "Actor's Haven" by Monley Cassidy.
January 16th 1942	Family Circle "The Wolf Man".
October 9th 1942	The Family Circle "Now Voyager".

Carmella Felice

January 23rd 1943	Picturegoer "Casablanca".
January 29th 1943	Family Circle "Casablanca".
March 4th 1944	Picturegoer "He's never Himself" by M. Chadbourne.
May 10th 1944	"Rains is still Enjoying Himself" by Gladys Hall.
June 24th 1944	Picturegoer Mr. Skeffington.
1946	Press book Bette Davis and Claude Rains.
November 1946	Screen Romance "Deception".
June 11th 1946	Picture Show "The Life Story of Claude Rains".
October 20th 1946	Los Angeles Times. Claude Rains Career Just Luck" by Phillip Leschecer.
April 1947	Movie Play "The King Rains".
December 1947	Silver Screen "Claude Rains is Frightened.
March 7th 1948	Picturegoer "Claude Rains" by Brenda Cross.
July 21st 1944	Picturegoer "Acting is My Job" E. J. Smithson.
All New York Times' review by Brooks Atkinson for the 1940's.	
June 6th 1950	Los Angeles Times "Farmer Rains" by Edwin Schallert.
March 31st 1951	Cue "Claude Rains, cops a Tony" by M. Cassidy.
April 2nd 1951	New York Times "Reds Threaten Claude Rains". by Howard Rushmore.
January 12th 1954	Boston Post "The Confidential Clerk".
November 21st 1960	Patriot Ledger. Quincey Mass.
November 11th 1963	Films Vol XIX No 9. Confidential Clerk by Jean Stein.
June 1972	Flashback Take 2.
June 9th 1979	The Sun "Film Buff Turns History" by Kim Brown.

February 1982	In Praise of Claude Rains, Film and Filming by Richard Jeffrey.
1998	The Sandwich Historical Society's booklet.
1998	Vignettes of Sandwich "Mr. Rains and the Weed House". by Toby Irene Cohen. Copywright 1995.

AGATE, JAMES.	ALL OF JAMES AGATES'S PLAY REVIEWS.
ARLISS, GEORGE.	MY TEN YEARS IN THE STUDIOS, LITTLE BROWN AND COMPANY BOSTON 1927
ARLISS, GEORGE	UP THE YEARS FROM BLOOMSBURY LITTLE BROWN AND COMPANY BOSTON
BEAVER, JAMES N. JR.	JOHN GARFIELD HIS LIFE AND TIMES. A.S. BARNES AND COMPANY 1978
BEHLMER, RUDY	INSIDE WARNER BOTHERS, BIKING NEW YORK, 1985
BEHLMER, RUDY. THOMAS, TONY. MACARTY, CLIFFORD.	THE FILMS OF ERROL FLYNN, CITADEL PRESS, SECAUCAS, N.J 1969
BLANKE, HENRY. RAINE, AEILLY NORMAN. KEIGHLEY, WILLIAM.	ROBIN HOOD SHOOTING, SEPT. 26, 1937 TO JANUARY 4TH 1938.

MILLER, I. SETON. BOGART, STEPHEN HUMPHREY.	BOGART IN SEARCH OF MY FATHER, PLUME N.Y 1996 WITH GARY PROVOST
BRANDRETH, GYLES.	JOHN GIELGUD PAVILLION BOOKS, UNLIMITED 1985.
BROWNLOW, KEVIN.	DAVID LEAN A BIOGRAPHY, RICHARD COHENS BOOKS, LONDON, 1996.
DAVIS, BETTE.	THE LONELY LIFE AN AUTOBIOGRAPHY G.P PUTNAM'S AND SON 1962.
DEAN, MARJORIE, PASCAL, GABRIEL.	PASCAL'S CAESAR AND CLEOPATRA, MCDONALD PRESS.
DESHNER, DONALD.	THE FILMS OF CARY GRANT, CITADEL PRESS SECAUCAS N. J. 1973
DUKORE, BERNARD. F.	THE COLLECTED SCREEN PLAYS OF GEORGE BERNARD SHAW. UNIVERSITY OF GEORGIA, ATHENS GREECE, 1980.
FREDERICH, OTTO.	GLENN GOULD A LIFE AND VARIATIONS. LIFETIME LONDON 1998.
GIELGUD, JOHN.	DISTINGUISHED COMPANY, DOUBLE DAY AND COMPANY INC. GARDEN CITY, NEW YORK 1973.
GIELGUD, JOHN.	EARLY STAGES. 1921-1926. TOPLINGER PUBLISHING COMPANY N.Y. 1926.

HARRES, ROBERT AND SLASKY, MICHAEL.	THE FILMS OF ALFRED HITCHCOCK. CITADEL PRESS, SECAUCAS N. J. 1976.
HYMAN, B.D.	MY MOTHER'S KEEPER. WILLIAM MORROW AND COMPANY N.Y.
LEAMING, BARBARA.	BETTE DAVIS A BIOGRAPHY. SIMON AND SHUSTER N.Y.
MCBRIDE, JOSEPH.	FRANK CAPRA, THE CATASTROPHE, SIMON AND SHUSTER N.Y
MACQUEEN, W. POPE.	HAYMARKET THEATRE OF PERFECTION
QUIRK, LAWRENCE.	FASTEN YOUR SEAT BELTS. THE PASSIONATE LIFE OF BETTE DAVIS W. MORROW N.Y 1991
RAINSBERGER, TODD.	JAMES WONG HOWE CINEMATOGRAPHER. A.S. BARNES AND COMPANY SAN DIEGO CALIF. 1988.
RILEY, PHILLIP.	THE WOLFMAN 1941. MAGIC IMAGE FILMS BOOKS
SINGER, KURT.	THE LAUGHTON STORY. THE JOHN C. WINSTON COMPANY. PHILADELPHIA 1954
SAINT JOHN, CHRISTOPHER GRAY, EDITH.	THE ELLEN TERRY'S MEMOIRS. LONDON

SHAW, BERNARD GEORGE.	TO A YOUNG ACTRESS. CLARKSON POTTER INC. 1949
STINE, WHITNEY.	I'D LONE TO KISS YOU. POCKET BOOKS.
STINE, WHITNEY.	MOTHER GODDAM. THE STORY OF THE CAREER OF BETTE DAVIS HAWTHORNE BOOKS
THOMAS, TONY BEHLMER, RUDY. MCCARTY, CLIFFORD.	THE FILMS OF ERROL FLYNN. CITADEL SECAUCAS N. J. 1969
TODD, ANN.	THE EIGHT VEIL. G.P. PUTNAM'S SONS N.Y. 1988
WALLIS, HAL AND HIGHAM, CHARLES.	STARMAKER THE AUTOBIOGRAPHY OF HAL WALLIS.
TREE, BEERBOHN, HERBERT.	THE PRIVATE PAPERS OF SIR HERBERT AND LADY TREE.
TREE, BEERBOHN HERBERT,	SOME MEMORIES OF HIM AND HIS ART. MAX. 1920.
TREE, BEERBOHN HERBERT.	THOUGHTS AND AFTERTHOUGHTS LONDON.
WINDELER, ROBERT,	BURT LANCASTER. ST. MARTIN'SPRESS N.Y.
HENSHAW, LAURIE	FILM ILLUSTRATED MONTHLY VOL #3 No. 1 THE INVISIBLE MAN.

HIBBERT, H.G.	KATE TERRY GIELGUD A PLAYGOER'S MEMORIES. LONDON.
HIRSCHORN, CLIVE.	THE WARNER BROTHERS. CROWN PUBLISHERS INC. N.Y. 1979.
FOUR BOOKS OF HOLROYD, MICHAEL AND BERNARD SHAW,	THE LAST LAUGH AND EPILOGUE. RANDOM HOUSE. N.Y. 1979.
PERRY, GEORGE.	THE COMPLETE PHANTOM OF THE OPERA, HENRY HOLT AND COMPANY. 115 WEST 12TH STREET. NEW YORK. 10011 1988

RADIO SHOWS

Claude Rains loved to perform on the radio, because it was easy work, with a good pay check. He would be sent a script to look over, then have a couple of rehearsals, to keep within the commercial time slots. With the script in front of him, the strain of his stage and movie work was not there.

Here is a list of his known radio shows. Most of these tapes I found with the following company. Radio yesterday Box C. Sandy Hook Connecticut 06482. Just ask for a list of the Claude Rains collection.

DATE	PRODUCTION	STUDIO	ROLES AND GUESTS.
09 13 32	The Good Earth	N.B.C.	Rains (Wang Lung)
02 02 33	A Bill of Divorcement	N.B.C.	Rains co-star Starred with Janet Beecher.
03 17 34	The Feischmann Hour	N.B.C.	Co-starred with Rudy Vallee
01 06 35	The Green Goddess Lux Radio Theatre	N.B.C.	Rains (Rajah of Rahh)
04 04 35	The Tell Tale Heart The Feischmann Hour	N.B.C.	Co-starred with Rudy Vallee
07 27 36	Anthony Adverse At the Hollywood Hotel	C.B.S.	Co-starred with Olivia De Havilland

Carmella Felice

07 24 36	The Lux Radio Theatre	C.B.S.	Rains (Napolean)
04 29 37	The Game of Chess Royal Gelatin Hour	N.B.C.	Co-starred with Rudy Vallee
06 26 37	Julius Caesar Shakespeare Festival	C.B.S.	Rains (Cassius) Co-starred Walter Abel
07 01 37	The Gifts of the Gods The Royal Gelantin Hour	N.B.C.	Co-starred Rudy Vallee and "Bojangles" Robinson
08 12 37	The Kraft Music Hall	N.B.C.	
01 02 38	Episode of Park Avenue	C.B.S.	
06 09 39	The Kraft Music Hall	N.B.C.	
11 03 38	Julius Caesar	N.B.C.	
11 21 38	Confessions The Lux Radio Theatre	C.B.S.	Co-Starred Miriam Hopkins and Richard Green Hosted by Cecil B. Demille
01 05 39	There's always Joe Winters The Royal Gelatin Hour	N.B.C.	Co-starred Rudy Vallee and Boris Karloff
10 11 39	With Ken Murray	N.B.C.	With Kenny Baker
04 02 40	The Story of Benedict Arnold Calvalcade of America	N.B.C	Rains (General Arnold)

Date	Title	Network	Notes
10 11 39	Kind Lady Texaco Star Theatre	C.B.S.	Co-starred John Barrymore
01 14 39	The Littlest Rebel	C.B.S	Shirley Temple's first Radio Show.
01 15 41	As a Man Thinketh Calvacade of America	N.B.C	Co-starred Jeanette Nolan, Agnes Moorehead and John McIntire
02 22 41	Lincoln Highway	N.B.C.	
07 02 41	Calling America	N.B.C	
07 12 41	Lincoln Highway	N.B.C.	
07 25 41	Calling America	N.B.C.	Co-Starred Everette Stone
08 01 41	Blind Alley	N.B.C.	
09 26 41	A Man to Remember	C.B.S.	
09 28 41	The Haunting Face Inner Santum Mysteries	N.B.C.	
10 14 41	Millions for Defense	N.B.C.	
12 27 41	The Cavalcade of America	N.B.C.	Rains (John Paul Jones)
01 26 42	Here Comes Mr. Jordan The Lux Radio Theatre	C.B.S.	Rains (Mr. Jordan) with James Gleason and Evelyn Keyes
02 02 42	Keep'em Rolling	C.B.S.	Co-Starred James Stewart

03 20 42	Criminal Code Phillip Morris Playhouse	C.B.S.	Co-Starred John Garfield
04 07 42	In This Crisis Cavalcade of America	N.B.C	Rains (Thomas Paine)
07 07 42	Back Where You Came From Plays For America	N.B.C.	Co-starred Bette Davis and James Stewart
09 07 42	Soldier Of The Free Press The Story of Richard Harding fiirst war correspondent	N.B.C.	
09 18 42	Underground Phillip Morris Playhouse	C.B.S.	
09 27 42	The Man Who Played With Death Inner Sanctum Mysteries	N.B.C.	
10 25 42	The Missioonary and The Gangster Reader's Digest	C.B.S.	
11 08 42	The Laughing Murderer Inner Sanctum Mysteries	A.B.C.	
01 24 43	The French Underground Radio Reader's Digest	C.B.S.	Hosted by Conrad Nagel
02 07 43	The Texaco Star Theatre	C.B.S.	Co-starred Fred Allen

03 18 45	Philco Radio Hall of Fame	N.B.C.	Co-starred Chico Marx
03 20 45	Theatre of Romance The Citade Colgate Tooth Power and Halo Shampoo	C.B.S.	
05 15 45	President Franklin D. Roosevelt's death and funeral, a special tribute to the late President.		
06 06 45	Dr. Christian Diagnosis of Death	C.B.S.	
06 13 45	Jere To Bieb	C.B.S.	
06 20 45	The Lady and The Wolf	C.B.S.	
11 07 46	The Radio Reader's Digest Hallmark Cards Presents. "Murder in The Big Bowl"	C.B.S.	
12 08 46	The Fred Allen Show	N.B.C.	
03 20 47	Wax Work Suspence Theatre	C.B.S.	Co-starred William Conrad and Herbert Marshall.
05 29 47	The Kraft Music Hall "Many Moons"	N.B.C.	
07 16 47	Freedom Pledge broadcasted from Freedom Rally in Philadelphia, Pennsylvania. Five thousand children attended.		
10 30 47	A Piece of String. The Radio Reader's Digest	C.B.S.	Co-starred Tom Shirley.
07 06 48	Topaze-Studio One	C.B.S.	

Carmella Felice

11 14 48	Valley Forge U.S Steel Hour	A.B.C.	
12 02 48	The Hands of Mr. Ohormole Suspence Theatre.	C.B.S.	Co-starred Vincent Price.
01 02 49	The Game of Love and Death Theatre Guild on the Air.	A.B.C.	Co-starred Katherine Hepburn and Paul Henreid
02 27 49	Jack Benny Program	C.B.S.	
	Claude tries to get out of his contract with Benny, to perform in the "Horn Blows at Midnight" for C.B.S.		
03 04 49	The Horn Blows At Midnight	C.B.S.	Co-starred Jack Benny.
04 04 49	The Goal is Freedom	C.B.S.	Appears with Lyndon Johnson.
05 08 49	Experiment in Terror Broadcasted via the Armed Forces Radio Network.		
05 20 49	Crime Without Passion The Ford Theatre.	C.B.S.	
10 08 49	Madame Bovary	C.B.S.	Co-starred Marlene Dietrech and Van Heflin.
11 29 49	W.C.O. Radio began broadcasting at 1000 watts from Downtown West. Chester Pennsylvania. Rains performed a dramatic reading for no pay, for his fellow town's people.		
01 06 50	Mr. Peale and the Dinosaur Calvacade of America.	N.B.C.	Co-starred Agnes Moorehead.

01 06 52	Midnight Blue	N.B.C.	Co-starred Tullulah Bankhead.
02 10 52	The Catbird Seat	N.B.C.	The Big Show.
02 19 52	Three Words Cavalcade of America.	N.B.C.	
03 01 52	Rains signed to do 12 shows for N.B.C. called "The Jeffersonian Heritage". It was a program to educate the people of America to what Thomas Jefferson stood for.		
03 28 53	Our Hidden Wealth Medicine U.S.A.	N.B.C.	Rains (Mr. Wheelock)

MOTION PICTURES

1920   BUILD THY HOUSE.... England. directed by Fred Goodwins.

1933   THE INVISIBLE MAN United States. 71 minutes ***1/2. Directed by James Whale. Co-stars Gloria Stuart, Una O'Connor, William Harrigan, E.E. Clive, Dudley Diggs and Dwight Frye. Story by H.G. Wells.

1934   CRIME WITHOUT PASSION. *** 72 minutes Directed by Ben Hecht and Charles MacArthur. Co-stars, Helen Hayes (Mrs. Charles MacArthur) and Fanny Brice. Story by Ben Hecht.

1934   THE MAN WHO RECLAIMED HIS HEAD. *** Co-stars, D. Edward Ludwig, Lionel Atwioll, Joan Bennett, Baby Jane, Henry O'Neill and Wallace Ford. From a play written by Jean Bart.

1935   THE MYSTERY OF EDWIN DROOD. **1/2 87 minutes Co-stars Robert Powell, Michelle Evans, Jonathan Phillips, Rupert Rainsford, Finty Williams, Peter Pacey, Nanette Newman, Freddie Jones, Gemma Craven, Rosemary Leach, Story by Charles Dickens.

1935   THE CLAIRVOYANT. England **1/2 80 minutes. Co-stars, Fay Wray, Jane Baxter, Mary Clare, Athole Stewart, Felix Aylmer, Donald Calhrop. Also known by the title "The Evil Mind".

1935   THE LAST OUTPOST. 70 minutes. Co-stars, Cary Grant, Louis Gasnier, Charles Barton, Gertrude Michael, Kathleen Burke and Colin Tapley.

1936   ANTHONY ADVERSE. ***1/2 141 minutes Co-stars, Frederic March, Olivia deHavilland, Donald Woods, Anita Louise, Edmund Gwenn, Louis Hayward, Gale Sondergaard, Akim Tamiro, Billy Mauch, Sondergaard won an "Oscar" for Best Supporting Actress. Directed by Mervyn LeRoy.

Carmella Felice

1936 HEARTS DIVIDED. 87 minutes Co-stars, Marion Davies, Dick Powell, Charlie Ruggles, Edward Everette Horton and Arthur Treacher. Directed by Frank Borzage.

1936 STOLEN HOLIDAY.

1937 THE PRINCE AND THE PAUPER ***1/2 120 minutes Co-stars, Errol Flynn, Billy and Bobby Mauch, Alan Halke, Montague Love, Henry Stephenson and Barton Maclaner. Directed by William Keighley.

1937 THEY WON'T FORGET. 95 minutes. Co-stars. Gloria Dickson, Otto Kruger, allyn Joslyn, Elisha Cook Jr. Edward Norris. directed by Mervyn LeRoy. From the book "Death in the Deep South" by Ward Greene.

1938 GOLD IS WHERE YOU FIND IT. **1/2 90 minutes Co-stars, George Brent, Olivia deHavilland, Margaret Lindsay, John Litel, Barton Marlane. Directed by Michael Curtiz.

1938 ADVENTURES OF ROBIN HOOD. 101 minutes. Co-stars. Errol Flynn, Olivia de Havilland, Basil Rathbone, Patrick Knowles, Eugene Pallette, Alan Hale, Herbert Mundin, Una O'Connor, Melville Cooper, Ian Hunter, Montague Love. Directed by Michael Curtiz Scripted by Norman Reilly and Seton I. Miller.

1939 THEY MADE ME A CRIMINAL. **1/2 92 minutes. Co-stars, John Garfield, Gloria Jackson, May Robson, Billy Halop, Huntz Hall, Leo Gorcey, Bobby Jordon, Gabriel Dell, Barbara Pepper, Ward Bond, Ann Sheridan. Directed by Busby Berkeley.

1939 JUAREZ. *** 132 minutes. Co-stars. Paul Muni, Bette Davis, Brian Aherne, John Garfield, Gale Sondergaard, Donald Crisp, Gilbert Roland, Louis Calhern, Grant Mitchell. Directed by William Dieterle.

1939 MR. SMITH GOES TO WASHINGTON. *** 124 minutes. Co-stars, James Stewart, Ian Arthur, Edward Arnold, Guy Kibbee, Thomas Mitchell, Eugene Pallette, Beulah Andi, Harry Carey, H.B. Warner, Charles Lane, Porter Hall, Jack Carson. Directed by Frank Capra. Script by Sidney Buchman.

1939 FOUR WIVES. **1/2 110 minutes. Co-stars, Eddie Albert, Priscilla Lane, Rosemary Lane, Lola Lane, Gale Page, John

Garfield, May Robson, Frank McHugh, Jeffrey Lynn, Directed by Michael Curtiz.

1939 DAUGHTER'S COURAGEOUS. *** Co-stars, John Garfield, Fay Bainter, Priscilla Lane, Rosemary Lane, Lola Lane, Gale Page, May Robson, Donald Crisp, Frank McHugh. Directed by Michael Curtiz.

1940 SATURDAY'S CHILDREN. **1/2 101 minutes Co-stars, John Garfield, Ann Shirley, Lee Patrick, George Tobias, Roscoe Karns, Dennis Moore, Elizabeth Risdon, Directed by Vinent Sherman. Based on a play by Maxwell Anderson.

1940 LADY WITH THE RED HAIR. **1/2 81 minutes, Co-stars, Miriam Hopkins, Richard Ainley, Laura Hope Crews, Helen Westley, John Litel, Victor Jory. Directed by Curtis Bernhardt.

1941 FOUR MOTHERS. **1/2 86 minutes. Co-stars, Priscilla Lane, Rosemary Lane, Lola Lane, Gale Page, Jeffrey Lynn, May Robson, Eddie Albert, Frank McHugh. Directed by William Keighley.

1941 HERE COMES MR. JORDON. **** 93 minutes. Co-stars, Robert Montgomery, Evelyn Keyes, Rita Johnson, Edward E. Horton, James Gleason, John Emery, Directed by Alexander Hall. Screenplay won an Oscar, by Harry Segall.

1941 THE WOLFMAN. ***1/2 70 minutes. C o-stars, Lon Chaney Jr. Evelyn Ankers, Maria Ouspenskaya, Ralph Bellamy, Patric Knowles, Warren William. Bela Lugosi, Fay Helm. Directed by George Wagner. Written by Curt Siodmak.

1942 KINGS ROW. ***1/2 127 minutes. Co-stars. Robert Cummings, Ronald Reagan, Betty Ford, Charles Coburn and Judith Anderson. Directed by Sam Wood. Screenplay by Casey Robinson, from the best selling book by Henry Bellamann.

1942 MOONTIDE. **1/2 92 minutes. Co-star, Jean Gabin, Ida Lupino, Thomas Mitchell, Jerome Cowan, Helene Reynolds, Ralph Byrd, Sen Yung, Tully Marshall. Directed by Archie Mayo.

1942 NOW VOYAGER. ***1/2 117 minutes. Co-stars, Bette Davis, Paul Henreid, Gladys Cooper, Bonita Grandville, John Loder, Ilka Chase, Lee Patrick, Mary Wickes, Janis Wilson, Olive Higgins Prouty's best seller was adapted by Casey Robinson. Directed by Irving Rapper.

Carmella Felice

1942   CASABLANCA. **** 102 minutes. Co-stars, Humphey Bogart, Ingrid Bergman, Paul Henreid, Conrad Veidt, Peter Lorre, Sydney Greenstreet, Dooley Wilson, Marcel Dellio, S.Z. Sakall, Joy Page, (Jack Warner's adopted daughter). Directed by Michael Curtiz.

1943   FOREVER AND A DAY. *** 104 minutes. The English community pooled their talents and money together to film this story. The proceeds would go to help the war efforts in England. Co-stars Edmund Goulding, Cedric Hardwicke, Frank Lloyd, Victor Saville, Robert Cummings, Ida Lupino, Charles Laughton, Herbert Marshall, Ray Milland, Anna Neagle, Merle Oberon, Victor Mclaglen, Herbert Day, Buster Keaton, Jessie Matthews, Roland Young, C. Audrey Smith, Edward Everette Horton. Elsa Lanchester, Edmond Gwenn. Eighty stars donated their time and money to this picture. It was a once in a life time cast and made three million dollars for the war effort. Directed by Rene' Clair.

1943   PHANTOM OF THE OPERA. *** 92 minutes. Co-stars, Susanna Foster, Nelson Eddy, Edgar Barrier, Jane Farrar, Miles Mander, J. Edward Gromberg, Hume Cronyn, Fritz Leiber, Leo Carrillo, Steven Geray, Fritz Feld. Directed by Arthur Lubin.

1944   PASSAGE TO MARSEILLE. **1/2 110 minutes. Co-stars Humphey Bogart, Michele Morgan, Phillip Dorn, Sydney Greenstreet, Peter Lorre, George Tobias, Helmut Dantine, John Loder, Victor Francen, Vladimir Sokoloff, Edward Cianelli, Hans Conreid. Directed by Michael Curtiz.

1944   MR. SKEFFINGTON. *** 102 minutes. Co-stars Bette Davis, Walter Abel, Richard Waring, Jerome Cowan, Charles Drake, Gigi Perreau. Directed by Vincent Sherman.

1945   THIS LOVE IS OURS. **1/2 Co-stars, Merle Oberon, Charles Korvin, Carl Esmond, Sue England, Jess Barker, Harry Davenport, Ralph Morgan. Directed by William Dieterle.

1946   CAESAR AND CLEOPATRA. London England. ** 134 minutes. Co-stars, Vivien Leigh, Stewart Granger, Flora Robson, Francis l. Sullivan, Cecil Parker. Directed by Gabriel Pascal. Play by George Bernard Shaw.

1946   ANGEL ON MY SHOULDER. *** 101 minutes. Co-stars, Paul Muni, Anne Baxter, Onslow Stevens. Directed by Archie Mayo.

1946   DECEPTION. ***1/2 Co-stars, Bette Davis, Paul Henreid, John Abbott, Benson Fong. Directed by Irving Rapper.

1946   NOTORIUS. ***1/2 101 minutes. Co-stars, Cary Grant, Ingrid Bergman, Louis Calhern, Leopoldine Konstantin, Reinhold Schunzel. Directed by Alfred Hitchcock. Written by Ben Hecht.

1946   ROPE OF SAND. *** 104 minutes. Co-stars, Burt Lancaster, Paul Henreid Corrine Calvert, Peter Lorre, Sam Jaffe, John Bromfield, Mike Mazurki. Directed by William Dieterle.

1947   THE UNSUSPECTED. **1/2 Co-star, Joan Caulfield, Audrey Totter, Constance Bennett, Hurd Hatfield. Directed by Michael Curtiz.

1942   STRANGE HOLIDAY. ** 62 minutes. Co-stars, Bobbie Stebbins, Barbara Bates, Paul Hilton, Tommy Cook, Martin Kosleck. Directed by Arch Oboler. This picture was originally sponsored by General Motors and intended to be shown only to its employees.

1949   PASSIONATE FRIENDS. (British) **1/2 95 minutes. Co-stars, Ann Todd, Trevor Howard, Betty Ann Davies, Isabel Dean, Wilfred Hyde-White. Directed by David Lean. Book by H.G. Wells.

1949   SONG OF SURRENDER. ** 93 minutes. Co-stars, Wanda Hendrix, Macdonald Carey, Andrea King, Henry O ' Neill, Elizabeth Patterson, Eva Gabor. Directed by Mitchell Leisen.

1950   WHITE TOWER. ** 1/2 98 minutes. Co-stars, Glenn Ford, Oscar Homalka, Cedric Hardwicke, Lloyd Bridges. Directed by Ted Telzlaff. Filmed in the French Alps. Scripted by Paul Jarrico from James Ramsey Ullman's best seller.

1950   WHERE DANGER LIVES. ** 84 minutes. co-stars, Robert Mitchum, Faith Domergue, Mareen O' Sullivan. Directed by John Farrow.

1951   SEALED CARGO ** 90 minutes. Co-stars, Dana Andrews, Adele Mara, Adrian Booth, Chill Wills. Directed by Alfred L. Werker.

1953   PARIS EXPRESS OR THE MAN WHO WATCHED THE TRAINS GO BY. (British) 80 minutes. Co-stars, Marta Toren,

Carmella Felice

Marius Goring, Anouk, Herbert Lom, Lucie Manheim, Felix Aylmer, Freddy Mayne, Eric Portmann. Directed by Harold French.

1956   LISBON. **1/2 90 minutes. Co-stars, Ray Milland, Maureen O'Hara, Yvonne Furmeaux, Francis Lederer, Percy Marmount, Jay Novello. Directed by Ray Milland.

1959   THIS EARTH IS MINE. **1/2 125 minutes. Co-stars, Rock Hudson, Jean Simmons, Dorothy McGuire, Kent Smith, Anna Lee, Ken Scott. Directed by Henry King.

1960   LOST WORLD. ** 98 minutes co-stars, Michael Rennie, Jill St John Fernando Lamas, Richard Hayden. Directed by Irwin Allen.

1961   BATTLE OF THE WORLDS, * 1/2 Co-stars, Maya Brent, Bill Carter Umberto Orsini, Jacqueline Derval. Directed by Anthony Dawson.

1962   LAWRENCE OF ARABIA **** (BRITISH). 216 minutes. Co-stars, Peter O 'Toole, Alec Guiness, Anthony Quinn, Jack Hawkins, Anthony Quayle, Arthur Kennedy, Omar Sharif, Jose Ferrer. Directed by David Lean. Screen Play by Robert Bolt and Michael Wilson.

1963   TWILIGHT OF HONOR. **1/2 1 20 minutes. Co-stars, Richard Chamberlain, Nick Adams, Joan Blackman, Joey Heatherton, James Gregory, Pat Buttrum, Jeanette Nolan. Directed by Boris Sagal.

1965   THE GREATEST STORY EVER TOLD. **1/2 141 minutes. Co-stars, Max Von Sydow, Charltoin Heston, Carroll Baker, Angela Lansbury, Sidney Poiter, Shelly Winters, John Wayne, Ed Wynn, Jose Ferrer, Van Heflin, Telly Savalas and a cast of hundreds. Directed by David Lean. Both Lean and Rains did the film for "FREE".

TELEVISION PLAYS

In the early fifties, television plays were performed live, and recorded in Kinescope at the same time. Many of these recordings haven't survived time which was a great shame. Broadway and Hollywood stars were used mostly to carry a live performance, so there was little chance for mistakes.

His first endeavor for television was for C.B.S on April 8th 1951, with the show "The Toast of the Town". It was hosted by Broadway columnist Ed Sullivan. Some of the show was turned over to John Chapman, President of the New York Drama Critic's Circle, who gave out the Circle's awards to the winning plays of 1951. Mr. Rains enacted a short scene from, "Darkness at Noon" before his director, Sidney Kingsley was awarded the Trophy, for best drama-play. Rains was thrilled to see his friend's work, being recognized by the Circle.

It took almost two years before Rains took on television again. On January 25th, 1953, he was a great on the "Bentons at Home" (Omnibus). The T.V audience was taken to visit a family of artists.

Thomas Benton's guest were Rains, and folk-singer Susan Reed. They discussed folklore, legal issues and one of Claude's favorited topics, architecture. Variety noted on January 28th, the following: "It didn't fully come off due to an obviously "set-up" atmosphere. Rains however was excellent in his recitation of a long comic poem by Carl Sandburg". At the time Rains couldn't believe he was getting paid for something he did when company came to his home.

On August 1st, 1953, he appeared again for C.B.S.'s Medallion Theatre, in the live drama of "The Man Who Liked Dickens". It was one of Claude's favorite stories and he thought the public would enjoy it. Rains play a recluse who had left him all his books, which he read to his son. Never teaching the boy how to read, the old man relied on

Carmella Felice

people who could read, to tell him the stories in his books, even it it mean't keeping them in the jungle for the rest of their lives.

On Medallion Theatre, he portrayed Sir Edward Carson, in the Archer Ace", for C.B.S. it was aired on October 3rd, and Claude played a lawyer, representing a small boy, who takes on the British Empire, to gain his individual rights.

On December 17th, he was on a Philadephia Station WFILO-TV. Claude appeared with the Metropolitan Opera, as he reads verses 1-20 Chapter 2, of St Luke's Gospel.

February 4th, 1954 he again went to work for C.B.S. on Omnibus, appearing on a segment from his play "The Confidential Clerk".

Then old friend Alfred Hitchcock invited Claude to his office for tea, and offered him he part of "Fabian", a vetriloquist in love with his girl dummy.

The Kraft Television Theatre, was next on his list, as he narrated "A Night to Remember", the story of the sinking of the Titanic!

In the "President, (The Alcoa Hour), Rains plays Paul Westman, a retired Supreme Court Justice, looking for a man to nominate for president for his party.

Variety gave this praise to the production, which was written on May 16th, 1956

> "Claude Rains persusively drawn portrait corrected any tendency of the script to fall into generalization about the conflict of ambition and idealism. Rains made the obstractions come alive." After this showing, Bette Davis called Claude up and told him, that he had her vote!"

On the Kaiser Aluminum Hour, airing on September 11th, 1956 on N.B.C. he enjoyed the role of King Creon, in a modern version of "Sophocles" classic drama. His good friend Alexander Scourby joined him in this production. Rains' performance was thought "excellent" by Variety September 19th, 1956.

Another tea party was set up at Hitchcock's studio, to get Claude to play Mr. Brink, the angel of death, along with Ed Wynn, who would play Gramps. Mr. Brink comes to take Gramps to heaven, but the old man doesn't want to go. But when Mr. Brinks wants to take a small young boy who is Gramps' friend, he talks Brinks into taking him instead, which was Brink's plan all along.

When he was asked to take the role of the Mayor of Hamelin, in the play The Pied Piper of Hamelin, he turned it down at first, because the producers wanted him to sing. After hearing the music played for him on the piano. He found himself singing along to the Peer Gynt Suite".

On December 2nd, 1957 Rains appeared as Dr. Manette in "A Tale of two Cities" on the Dupont Show of the month. Hitchcock called upon Rains to play, Andrew Thurgood in the "Diamond Necklace". Just before Thurgood is to retire from Maynard's Jewelry store, it is robbed of $100, 00, diamond necklace. The young woman who robs it is Thurgood's daughter. On February 22nd, 1959 it was shown on C.B.S. and two days later, Variety came out with this review, This Sarett Rudley yarn is good fun and Rains and Betty Von Forterberg have themselves a ball enacting it. Rains goes through all the fake misery and repentance in the book with a relish! All the Alfred Hitchcock Presents stories, can be obtained on videos.

In demand for his services was A.B.C. in the "Naked City", in a story called "To Walk in Silence". His character is John Weston a financial expert, and horseplayer, who accidentally gets shot in a bookie joint. Afraid of jeopardizing his position, he refuses to allow police to extract the bullet and testify against the culprit.

Shown 11/9/60 Shangri La, was his next enterprise, for the Hallmark Hall of Fame on October 24th, 1960 for N.B.C. He plays "The High Lama" in this version of "Lost Horizon". Richard Basehart, who played Conway was in awe of the acting giant, in his presence.

Basehart like Rains played "Nut-Cases", in the movies, so they talked a lot about being pigeon-holed into playing the same type of character.

Back to a tea party in Hitchcock's office, Rains was offered the role of Father Amion, in the "Horseplayer". As the story goes, Charley Sheridan (Ed Gardner) has good fortune praying to God, to make his horses win. While Father Amion needs fifteen thousand dollars to fix the roof of the church. When Charley starts to win at the track, he gives a donation to the church, in hope for more winners. Charley tells the priest what God has done for him and the priest decides to pull his savings from the bank and bet it on the next horse that Charley bets on. After Father Amion gives his money to Charley, he has a change of heart. He prays that the horse loses and when Charley returns, from the track, he says, "Sorry Fathner, the horse didn't come in first! The priest looks to heaven, as Charley hands him $15, 000. "I thought the horse lost?" He did, but I wouldn't bet your money to win, Father. I put your money for "Place".

He didn't return for another tea party, until January of 1962, when Alfred handed him the script to "The Door Without A Key". Rains played Leonard Eldridge, an amnesiac, who finds himself lost. Finding a police station, he tells the officer he doesn't know who he is. Billy Mumy is Mickey, who hasn't a family and is waiting to be taken to Child's Care. After a while Eldridge remembers who he is and wants to adopt Mickey, to take the place of his dead son.

At the "Rawhide" studios, Rains is Alexander Langfold, in "Incident of Judgement Day", for C.B.S. Clint Eastwood (Rowdy Yates) was a big fan of the older actor, as Claude played a drunken judge in this show.

Not to be topped, "Wagon Train", hires Rains to be Daniel Clay", on February 21st, with old friend John McIntire.

A few pounds heavier, he took on the role of the Commandant of the Desert Outpost in, "Dupont Show of the Week". "The Outpost", marked Rains' 30th anniversary year as a performer at N.B.C. The proram was taped in the Brooklyn Studios and his co-stars were Richard Conte (The Captain) Neville Brand (The Sergeant) and Everett Stone (The Private). When Claude was interviewed for his anniversary he said this: "Broadcasting is the real miracle of entertainment. The Theatre hasn't substanially changed in 400 years. Movies have progressed from silents to talkies, to wide screen epics. But against this, broadcasting has in the last four decades grown from local radio broadcasts to network television and now.. Telstar!"

On February 27th, he appeared on a Dr. Kildare Show, "Why Won't Any Body Listen?" He is Edward Fredericks, a Man who has lost a love in the hospital as the doctors in the hallways laugh about other things. Frederick thinks no one cares about the death in his family. Thinking Dr. Gillespie (Raymond Massey) doesn't care, he builds a bomb to blow up the hospital. Planting the bomb in Dr. Gillespie's office, he has a change of mind, and takes the bomb to an empty park across from the hospital, and it blows up killing Claude's character.

Crossing over to C.B.S., he performed in the Reporter, in an episode called, "A Time to be Silent". Rains was surrounded by heavy hitters in this episode, with co-stars, Harry Guardino, Gary Merill, Eddie Albert, Sidney Blackmer, Lee Phillips and Pippa Scott.

In his last project for N.B.C. he was very weak, after losing almost fifty pounds. In his role of Valentino, one cannot recognize him. But the program, "Cops and Robbers", was alot of fun for him. Old timers like Bert Lahr (Casare) and Billy DeWolfe, as the inspector, gave character to the show. The scene takes place in an old Italian Villa where a few retired gentlemen live together. There's excitement in the air as new blood is injected into the group, with the arrival of a safe-cracker, named Casare. After hearing about Casare's life, the old men decide to rob a bank at night. After the robbery, they find out the towns people have lost everything, so they break back into the bank to return the money. This will be Claude's last job on N.B.C. and Television.

ABOUT THE AUTHOR

Carmella Felice was born in Harlem, to poor immigrant parents, Jennie and Joseph Felice. She attended "Our Lady Queen of Angels" while in New York City.

At the age of twelve her mother moved to Brooklyn with her two children. She worked while going to "Manuel Training High School". After which she went to art school for two years. Miss Felice had a dream to be a cartoonist at the Walt Disney Studios. But that profession was never realized.

Instead at the age of twenty-two she took a City test for "Parking Enforcement Agent!". She worked for the "Department of Traffic for "thirty-five years, until she retired in 1995, with the title of Lieutenant!

This is her first attempt at writing a book, after years of composing Traffic reports, Evaluations and ways to control Traffic patterns in Brooklyn.

Miss Felice could have written about her many adventures with the Traffic department. But fate stepped in and she researched The Life of Claude Rains for nine years.

The author hopes she has done justice to the life of her favorite film star and his family.